Socrates and the Political Community

An Ancient Debate

Mary P. Nichols

State University of New York Press

Published by
State University of New York Press, Albany

© 1987   State University of New York

For information, address State University of New York
Press, State University Plaza, Albany, N.Y., 12246

Library of Congress Cataloging in Publication Data

Nichols, Mary P.
    Socrates and the political community.

    (SUNY series in political theory. Contemporary
issues)
    Includes index.
    1. Socrates—Contributions in political science.
2. Political science—Greece—History.   I. Title.
II. Series.
JC71.S62N53   1987   320'.01   86-14421
ISBN 0-88706-395-0
ISBN 0-88706-396-9 (pbk.)

10 9 8 7 6 5 4 3 2 1

Contents

Acknowledgments

Professor Joseph Cropsey first taught me the meaning of political philosophy and made me aware of its charms. My study under him at the University of Chicago raised for me the questions that animate this book: in what ways can philosophy guide politics, do the thinkers of antiquity offer a perspective that can help us understand political life, and, finally, should we accept Socrates as a model for political theory? Although Professor Cropsey's answers to these questions may differ from my own, he has been for me a model and a guide. To his penetrating thought, his breadth of vision, and his gentle humor, I shall always be indebted.

Susan Benfield, Paul Lowdenslager, and Arlene W. Saxonhouse read earlier versions of this manuscript. Their comments and criticisms led me to make many improvements in the final draft, as have my discussions over the years with Ann Charney, Chris Colmo, and Pam Jensen. The readers for SUNY Press made many suggestions that were helpful to me in revising.

I am grateful to my students at Catholic University, both graduate and undergraduate, who permitted me to test my ideas in class and to share with them my sometimes tentative explorations. I could not have found a better audience—receptive, critical, and enthusiastic.

To Estrella Dizon, Office Manager of the Department of Politics at Catholic University, and her assistant Edelin Fields, I am grateful for assistance in preparing this manuscript for publication, and especially for their help and encouragement throughout my years teaching at Catholic.

After the only copy of my manuscript was stolen from my car in 1983, the police department of the District of Columbia undertook an extensive search of an unsavory Washington neighborhood. I shall always be grateful to the diligent officer who recovered my manuscript from the garbage can of a fifth floor apartment building. The incident provided me a forceful lesson in the power of chance in human affairs.

My book owes most to my husband David. He helped me refine my thesis by eliminating false starts and pursuing slow ones. He often showed me the implications and connections of my ideas. The vision of the whole formed by the sides of this debate on Socrates is as much his as my own. Without David, I would not have understood so well the goodness of life, a fundamental principle that must guide thought. Only by comprehending this relation between life and thought can one recognize the truth in Aristotle's response to Aristophanes and Plato.

Introduction

Socrates is one of our heroes—an undaunted inquirer into the truth who sacrificed his life for philosophy. Maintaining to the end that "the unexamined life is not worth living" (*Apol.*, 38a),[1] he was executed by his community for questioning even its most sacred beliefs. We derive our image of Socrates primarily from Plato's dialogues, in which Socrates' conversations with others reveal the character of his philosophizing and his way of life. Greek literature, however, presents us not only with Plato's immortalization of Socrates but also with criticisms of him. One of his most influential attackers, Socrates claims in the *Apology*, was the comic poet Aristophanes, who portrayed him as a ridiculous yet dangerous figure, a subverter of justice and the laws of the community (*Apol.*, 19c). Attacks on Socrates, moreover, come from philosophy as well. Aristotle himself argues that Socrates' ideas are destructive of political communities (*Pol.*, 1261a ff.).[2] The question at issue between Socrates' accusers and his defenders is the effect of philosophy on the political community, or, more generally, of theory on practice.[3] Can ideas have a beneficial effect on politics, guiding political action and giving it direction and cohesion? Or do theoreticians lead practical men astray with subtleties that separate them from political realities and enervate political life? Should our admiration of Socrates be unqualified? If not, what should our reservations be? By examining this ancient debate on Socrates, we can explore the relation between theory and practice, between ideas and political life.

My examination of Socrates will take the form of an analysis of three works from Greek political thought, Aristophanes' *Clouds*, Plato's *Republic*, and Book II of Aristotle's *Politics*. My analysis of these

1

works assumes that each of them is the result of its author's reflection on the conflict between philosophy and politics[4] and that the details of these works, however minor, have an important bearing on the work as a whole. My discussion of the *Republic*, in particular, demonstrates the relevance of the drama of the dialogue to the philosophic and political issues raised.[5] I shall be concerned, moreover, not merely with providing an interpretation of each of these works considered individually but also with showing the ways in which they constitute a debate on the proper relation between philosophy and politics. I have chosen, in the first place, Aristophanes' *Clouds* because no other work presents such a classic criticism of the philosopher, such a clear attack on Socrates and what he represents. Its influence is acknowledged in the *Apology* by Socrates himself (19c). While many of Plato's dialogues may be read as defenses of Socrates against Aristophanes' charges,[6] these charges provide a background or a context for the *Republic*, in particular, because its primary theme is justice. The triumph of justice that Socrates orchestrates in the *Republic* reverses the triumph of injustice that he permits in the *Clouds*.[7] In this way, the *Republic* constitutes an answer to Aristophanes' play. Finally, in Book II of the *Politics*, Aristotle, in turn, explicitly criticizes Socrates' proposals in the *Republic*. His criticism, moreover, is reminiscent of Aristophanes' attack on Socrates in the *Clouds*. Both, for example, although in different ways, maintain that Socrates undermines the political community.[8] These three representatives of Greek thought therefore can be viewed as engaging in a dialogue on Socrates and on the relation of philosophy to the political community. Their disagreements shed light on the tension between thought and politics, revealing the difficulty in achieving an alliance between the two that is beneficial to both.

Aristophanes is critical of Socratic philosophy and dramatizes the harm to political communities and family life that Socrates causes. According to Aristophanes, philosophy leads to abstractions that detach men from their concrete lives, to universalities that remove them from the relationships they form in families and political communities. From Aristophanes' point of view, Socrates denies the fundamental truth about human beings, namely, that their lives develop and mature only in limited and particular settings. Socrates' search for universals therefore leads to a dehumanization of men. More specifically, Aristophanes' Socrates does not take the beliefs and the authority of the city seriously. He denies both the existence of the city's gods and the sacredness of familial bonds as a result of his investigation of natural phenomena. He leads his disciples to look at the world as scientists rather than citizens. Free from society's restraints, they disdain as merely conventional the piety and justice that support families and cities. Socrates therefore undermines these associations in which Aristophanes thought men could best find happiness. Aristophanes, as a comic poet, attempts to mock the pretensions of philosophy and thereby curb its pernicious influence on men.

Plato defends philosophy against Aristophanes' charge by showing that Socrates is a *political* philosopher. He portrays Socrates as talking to men in the marketplace about what most concerns them, while Aristophanes shows Socrates isolated in a "thinkery," where he investigates natural phenomena.[9] Because Plato's Socrates investigates men's actions and associations, such as families and political communities, he does not lose himself in abstractions that have no relevance to human life. By offering men an understanding of their situation which helps them to accept and temper the tensions and conflicts which arise in their families and political communities, Socratic political philosophy counteracts the attempt to escape from human life that Aristophanes depicts in the *Clouds*. Moreover, that temptation arises not primarily from philosophy, as Aristophanes claims, but from politics itself, as we see when the political community insists on an absolute solution to its problems.

The city Socrates founds in the *Republic*, I shall argue, is meant to illustrate this extreme to which politics can be brought. In its communistic institutions, it detaches men from particular relationships and asks them to identify with the city as a whole. Plato thus replies to Aristophanes that it is politics rather than Socratic philosophy, especially a politics motivated by a desire for a perfect justice, that leads men to lose themselves in empty abstractions. He even suggests that politics is able to corrupt philosophy. The communistic city requires philosophic rulers in order to come into being. These philosophers, unlike Socrates, pursue mathematical studies with perfectly homogeneous objects. Their studies prepare them to institute communism in the city, which imitates the homogeneity of their mathematics.[10]

Plato implicitly contrasts the philosophers required and educated by the city with Socrates. Socrates' philosophy, far from imposing homogeneity, explores the differences among men and the conflicts that stem from those differences. Socrates reveals the diversity that makes the city in speech impossible, especially when he describes its degeneration. Moreover, Socratic philosophy not only examines the differences among men that stand in the way of a homogeneous community, it involves Socrates in a heterogeneous community with his interlocutors, one which recognizes the integrity of men, or their irreducible differences. The community constituted by the characters in a Platonic dialogue is an alternative to the city in speech. At the core of political philosophy for Socrates and Plato, then, is not a search for *the* good, of which the various goods that men seek are pale reflections. The desire for such unity or perfection, the *Republic* teaches, underlies the city in speech and its mathematically oriented philosophers. Political philosophy, in contrast, is an exploration of the complexity of human life. Socrates reveals the different things that are good for men and that are nonetheless good although they lie in tension with other goods.[11]

Because through Socratic political philosophy man exercises his capacity to reflect on the world and his place in it, it is, according to Plato, the best way of life. It is not clear, however, that Aristophanes would find Plato's defense of philosophy satisfactory. Although Socratic philosophy recognizes the necessity of the families and political communities Aristophanes defended, it nevertheless does not resolve the conflict between them and philosophy. Although Socrates devotes himself to understanding the value of these communities and his own relation to them, the best way of life still lies in thought, rather than in the activities of family and political life. Aristophanes would not be likely to accept Plato's defense of philosophy because it denigrates politics in favor of thought. The guidance philosophy provides for politics is only negative: philosophy tries to moderate the city's excesses by turning the most ambitious men away from politics to a philosophic understanding of the city's limitations.[12]

Aristotle addresses the questions at issue between Aristophanes and Plato when, in Book II of the *Politics*, he criticizes the city that Socrates founds in the *Republic* and offers an understanding of the relation between philosophy and politics different from either Aristophanes' or Plato's. Aristotle argues against the political proposals of men, especially Socrates, who lack practical experience of politics (*Pol.*, 1273b28–30). He claims, in effect, that their proposals are the result of abstract thought divorced from the concrete realities of political life. In particular, Aristotle criticizes the excessive unity at which the *Republic*'s city aims and the abolition of the family which that unity necessitates. Political communities, he claims, are not homogeneous. They are composed of diverse human beings and groups, with different characters and interests. Aristotle therefore defends the particular associations that Aristophanes thought so important. In his criticism of a philosophy that overrides these associations in the interest of abstract truth, Aristotle comes close to Aristophanes' position. Moreover, by showing that political life does not necessarily lead to the homogeneity of the city in speech, Aristotle defends politics against Plato's criticism in the *Republic*.

In Book II, however, Aristotle also criticizes the most highly reputed cities that exist in his time or that existed in the past. He claims that their laws and institutions are defective because they are too much the product of chance, rather than the intentions of lawgivers or statesmen. In later books of the *Politics*, Aristotle shows how to preserve and even improve the different regimes in which men live. His political science therefore provides more positive direction for politics than the political philosophy of Socrates and Plato. It demonstrates that philosophy, or thought, can and should guide political development. Just as Aristotle defends politics against Plato's critique, he defends philosophy against Aristophanes' critique. Aristotle's political science offers an alternative not only to the *Republic*'s homogeneous city but to the abstract life of philosophy portrayed by Aristophanes.

Part I

Aristophanes' Laughter (The *Clouds*)

Introduction

Aristophanes' *Clouds* presents a classic criticism of the "intellec-tual" or philosopher. Aristophanes portrays the philosopher as living in the clouds and being unaware of what is going on in the world. Socrates lives in a "thinkery" with a group of students and spends his time suspended in a basket contemplating the heavens. Aristophanes shows how ludicrous such "abstraction" or "drawing away" from the world is. He makes us laugh at such follies, and, because we laugh at them, we are less likely to commit them ourselves. His comedy is conservative, protecting the community by mocking what diverges from it.[1] Aristophanes, however, does not merely defend the com-munity by laughing at Socrates; he also shows us how the ordinary life of a common man generates the tensions and the desires that lead to the Socratic way of life. Aristophanes is therefore much more sympathetic to Socrates than he is usually taken to be, for while he criticizes Socrates' ethereality he also understands why it exists.[2] If men are drawn to the Socratic way of life because political communities inevitably fail to satisfy their desires, Aristophanes' defense of the community is qualified. Man must live within the community and not "up in the air" with the philosophers, but he should not expect complete happiness. Aristophanes is a conservative who sees the limitations of what he is trying to conserve.

Strepsiades' Problem

The *Clouds* begins with Strepsiades' scream of lament (1).[3] Strepsiades is distressed because he cannot pay the debts which his son has incurred through horse racing. The action of the play revolves around his attempt to escape this indebtedness. The Greek word for debt (*chreos*) would remind a Greek audience of the word for necessity (*chreon*). Not only do the words sound alike, they are etymologically related. A debt is what one is bound to pay, just as necessity is inescapable. Necessity refers to what binds a man and, consequently, limits his freedom. In portraying a man trying to escape his debts, Aristophanes parodies man's tragic attempt to escape from necessity. Like a tragic hero, Strepsiades, blind to the implications and consequences of his deeds, pursues a hubristic course of action and meets disaster.[4]

The passage of time troubles Strepsiades. Aware that the day on which his debts must be paid is approaching, he cannot sleep. The night seems to him "endless." He longs for day (2–3). Although the night is passing too slowly for a sleepless man, the days are passing too quickly for a man in debt. Strepsiades calls for his slave to bring him a light so that he can read how much he owes. Light, which permits him to see the extent of his indebtedness, only confirms his misery. He wishes he had blinded himself before he incurred such debts (24).[5]

Meanwhile Strepsiades' son, Phidippides, the cause of Strepsiades' debts, is snoring loudly and dreaming of the race. His sound and dreamy sleep shows his lack of concern with the debts his father must pay. Strepsiades soon reveals that the origin of his problem with his son is his own marriage. A match was made between himself, a rustic of simple tastes, and a sophisticated city woman of an aristocratic line. Strepsiades is concerned with life's necessities, while his wife is aware of its niceties. The marriage of two such different human beings is not harmonious. Strepsiades mentions his having had to reproach his wife for her extravagance (53–55). Moreover, they quarrel over the naming of their son. Strepsiades wanted to name him Phidonnides, a name meaning "sparing" or "frugal." His wife wanted to give him a name like Callippides, which contains the suffix "horse" (*hippos*) and is therefore suggestive of an aristocratic way of life. They compromise over his name: Phidippides is a combination of "frugal" and "horse." However, husband and wife continue to compete for their son. Both want to reproduce themselves in Phidippides. Strepsiades tells his son that when he grows up he will be like his father, driving goats and wearing a simple leather jacket. But his mother gives him an image of himself as a brightly robed charioteer taking part in the city's festivities. Phidippides, taking after his extravagant mother, spends lavishly on race horses. He rejects the limited life his father represents. A desire for freedom underlies his extravagance. Owning race horses is possible only for a man who does not have to use his money to buy the necessities, and racing is possible only for a man who has leisure. Phidippides' love of horses reveals his desire for freedom.[6] Horses are known for their spiritedness—for their resistance to bondage or restraint. The same man who can forget about his debts in order to sleep, and even to dream, is also the man who refuses to obey his father. And yet, his desire for freedom leads him to accept the extravagant tastes of his mother—to whom he is even more closely connected physically than to his father. His freedom will be only illusory.

Strepsiades asks his son to be instructed in rhetoric. He has heard that there are "wise souls" who can teach a man to conquer in speech, regardless of whether he speaks justly or unjustly (94–99). If Phidippides learns this "unjust speech," Strepsiades "will not have to pay back a penny of the debts" he now owes on account of his son (116–18). Strepsiades is looking for a rhetoric that makes the weaker argument the stronger, in order to escape paying his debts. He imagines that rhetoric will bring him freedom, since it seems to confer on its user a power to persuade others of whatever he desires. If a man possessed the absolute power rhetoric promises, what he says would depend only on his desires. He would be free of any need to speak the truth, or to make his speech reflect the world. Rather than be restrained by the external world, his speech could portray that world to his own liking and make others see it that way. Such a freedom is implied in a rhetoric that makes the weaker argument the stronger and serves to tempt men who resent the constraints under which they live.

Strepsiades asks Phidippides to learn the unjust rhetoric out of love for his father (86). Phidippides, however, will not obey. He will not risk losing his manly tan by associating with people who spend their time talking indoors (119–20). The "pale" Socratics are like shades (103);[7] they seem to deny life, which Phidippides loves. After his son's insubordination, Strepsiades refuses to feed him any longer and orders him out of the house (121–23). Phidippides claims that he will go to his maternal uncle, who will not allow him to go horseless (124–25). He dismisses not only his need for food but also the particular ties that bind him to his father.

Because his son will not obey, Strepsiades decides that he himself will attend Socrates' school, which Aristophanes calls the "thinkery." But he knows that he is an unlikely student of Socratic rhetoric, for he is aware of his age, his poor memory, and his sluggish mind (129–30). He is aware of his own limits. He is an ordinary man with no delusions that he is capable of any exalted freedom. And yet, he is driven by his situation to seek the extraordinary freedom that Socrates is reputed to offer. It is a desire for such freedom that leads a man to the tragic denial of necessity. By showing us that even a man of such limited pretensions as Strepsiades will go to Socrates, Aristophanes reveals how great the tensions of ordinary life are and how widespread tragedy might become.

Strepsiades' Introduction to the Thinkery

At the thinkery, a student introduces Strepsiades to the ways of the school. Socrates' recent achievement, the student tells him, is measuring how many of its own feet a flea jumped, when it jumped from the eyebrow of one of Socrates' associates to the head of Socrates himself. Socrates' cleverness in handling this problem consisted in melting wax around the flea's foot, removing the "slipper" formed by the hardened wax, and using it as the measure to compute the distance between Chaerophon's eyebrow and his own head (148–52). In taking this measurement, Socrates, of course, is trying to do the impossible, for the distance between himself and Chaerophon constantly changes as they move. His endeavor presupposes that they are both fixed points. Moreover, Socrates' science explores the relation between himself and his disciple as a relation of bodies, understood in mathematical terms, rather than as a relationship of friendship or love. Through the absurdities of Socrates' undertaking, Aristophanes suggests that the Socratics believe that they are more permanent than they are,[8] at the same time that they view their relationships in terms of body. Other Socratic activities reveal a similar paradox: the denial of body accompanies a full-scale immersion into body. Although Socrates suspends himself in the air, he is occupied primarily, as we shall see, by most earthy matters.

Socrates is asked whether the gnat sings out of its mouth or its behind. Having looked within its body and seen the shape of its insides, Socrates knows that it must sing out of its behind, for its behind is close to a narrow intestine, in which sound echoes as air is forced through it (156–64). Strepsiades calls Socrates fortunate in what is well translated as "inner-sightedness" (166). Socrates' insight is insight into bodies. The music that interests Socrates is the humming of gnats, and he seeks to discover the causes that precede it and account for it. But while Socrates concerns himself with the behinds of gnats, he does not see them for the low things that they are. Confusing farting and singing, he supposes that behinds produce music.[9] By means of the next story that the student tells, an account of a lizard crapping on Socrates as he gapes up at the revolutions of the moon (171–73), Aristophanes reminds Socrates of what behinds are really for.

Socratic misunderstanding of the low things becomes even more obvious in the case of the students who are "investigating the things below the earth" (188). They bend down and look to the ground in order to pursue their studies. They resemble "beasts" (184). Man loses his dignity as an upright being, Aristophanes is saying, when he limits his view of the world to material nature. Strepsiades notices that when the students bend down to examine the earth, their "behind[s] look up to heaven" (193). The low things about men now see the light of day. The study of the earth, or of matter, brings into prominence what men share with beasts. But the Socratics fail to see the low character of the low, for the student claims that the behind, which looks up to heaven, is "engaging in astronomy" (194). The behind and the head are indistinguishable; both exercise intelligence, at least of a sort. The Socratics see only the movements of bodies but deny that the corporeal character of the world places any limitations on men.[10]

When Socrates first appears on stage, he is suspended in a basket because, he maintains, he must elevate his mind in order to think high thoughts; he must mix his rarefied mind with the rarefied air. Moreover, high thoughts would be impossible for him, he explains, as long as he is close to the earth, "for the earth forcibly drags to itself the moisture of thought" (232–33).[11] The watercress, Socrates acknowledges in passing, suffers the same thing (234). Socrates' mind, if it is affected by the pull of matter, is material. It is for this reason that Socrates must suspend himself in the air in order to think high thoughts. His materiality underlies his ethereality. Suffering the same thing as the watercress, Socrates' mind is in the same class of things as unintelligent nature, yet Socrates sits aloft, looking down on the "ephemeral" Strepsiades (223).

The rustic Strepsiades cannot follow Socrates' sophisticated explanation of the earth's effect on thought. "What are you saying?" he asks. "Does thought drag moisture to the watercress?" (235–36). Although he hears only nonsense in Socrates' explanation, he does, in his common sense way, continue to see thought as active. He imagines that thought is in control, rather than that it is controlled by the earth's pull. In Strepsiades' understanding of Socrates' description of thought, Aristophanes lets us see the Socratics' own lack of self-understanding: their "suspension" suggests their mind's independence of matter, while their study of the world reduces mind to matter.

The Socratics desire to be free, and, in their desire for freedom, they forget about their human limitations. When Strepsiades says that his memory is good in remembering what others owe him but poor in remembering what he owes to others (484–85),[12] his statement is more true of the Socratics than of himself. It is Strepsiades who remembers his debts and the Socratics who forget theirs. Aristophanes shows us that their forgetfulness extends to physical needs, families, and politics.

We see that the Socratics forget their bodies when a student tells Strepsiades that they had nothing to eat for supper. In order to remedy the inconvenience, the student recounts, Socrates "sprinkled fine ashes on the table, bent a little spit, took a compass, and stole a cloak from the palaestra" (177–79). Socrates' "geometry," however, fails to provide the much needed food. Having first forgotten about supper, Socrates then provides only what is inedible for his students to eat.[13] The incident indicates both that Socrates acts as if he were free of his bodily needs and that he is not as independent of his body as he would like to be. Philosophy cannot free men from the demands of their bodies. When Strepsiades hears that students are "investigating" or "searching out" things under the earth, he believes that they are looking for onions and offers to show them where onions can be found (188–90). Again, Strepsiades' misunderstanding reveals a truth: the Socratics do not know how to find food. Strepsiades' practical knowledge is in fact needed at the thinkery.[14]

Just as Socrates tries to silence the claims of the body, whether by suspending himself in the air or by substituting geometry for food, so also does he neglect family connections. Neither he nor his disciples appear to have any relatives. Aristophanes indicates Socrates' una-wareness of family ties when Socrates gives Strepsiades a scientific or "natural" account of the cause of thunder and rain. Not Zeus, but Whirlwind, compels water-filled Clouds to hit each other, break, and clatter, Socrates claims (376–78). As usual, Strepsiades misunder-stands. The misunderstanding turns on the similarity between the Greek word for whirlwind, *dinos*, and the Greek word for "the son of Zeus." Strepsiades interprets Socrates to mean that Zeus's son has replaced Zeus as the cause of thunder and rain (380–81).[15] But Socrates fails to understand Strepsiades' misconception (383–84). He is obli-vious to the patronymic, which indicates the close connection between a son and his father and even suggests that a man's identity is conferred by his father. Strepsiades, who immediately understands Dinos as Zeus's patronymic, introduced himself at the thinkery as "Strepsiades, son of Pheidon, from Cicynna" (134), whereas neither Socrates nor any of his students identify themselves or one another by reference to their fathers.

The Socratics have as few political connections as they do family connections.[16] Aristophanes contrasts Socrates' student, whose vision is strictly cosmopolitan, with Strepsiades, who understands what the student tells him only in political terms. When the student explains the utility of geometry for making maps, Strepsiades thinks that the geometricians are measuring land for the sake of dividing it among the people (203–05). And then he refuses to admit that Athens is on the map, since he does not see the jury in session (207–08). He also looks for his nearest neighbors, the men of his deme, on the map (210). He is shocked at how close Sparta is and asks the student to move it farther away (215–16). The student, in contrast, does not seem aware that Athens is at war.[17] He looks at the whole world as its spectator without any personal interests, whereas Strepsiades reacts as an Athenian. The latter constantly reminds us that man is not simply a spectator of life but that he is an actor limited by his particular time and place.

The universality of Socrates is most apparent in his denying the traditional gods and in his worshipping the Clouds. The Clouds have no shape or forms.[18] They are not limited or bound by anything; as Socrates tells Strepsiades "they become all things, whatever they please" (348). Socrates prays to the Clouds "to arise, to appear in the air" (266). The Greek word translated "in the air" also means "raised up" or "suspended." In suspending himself in the air, Socrates takes the Clouds as his models. Although the ethereal Clouds appear on stage as women, they can shake off their mortal forms as they rise in the air (288–90).[19] Socrates says that the Clouds are divinities to "idle men," for "they supply us with thought, dialectic, intelligence, marvels, circumlocution, cheating, and comprehension" (316–18). "Idle," in Greek, is literally "without deeds." The Clouds, formless abstractions, nourish men so that they can live in a world of abstractions. By conversing with the Clouds and learning the truth about celestial matters, Socrates claims, Strepsiades will become the clever speaker he wants to be (250–61). The formlessness of the Clouds is the visible manifestation of the formlessness of the rhetoric that Strepsiades seeks. The rhetorician will be able to argue any side of an issue, just as the Clouds take on any form that they wish. Their formlessness symbolizes the chaos of a world that lacks distinct elements which limit a man's power. It is not surprising that Socrates claims to believe in no god but Chaos, the Clouds, and the Tongue (424). The Clouds reveal the Chaos which makes possible the freedom belonging to a rhetoric that can make the weaker argument the stronger.[20]

Although the Clouds seem to be free in their formlessness, they ar part of a mechanical nature.[21] When Strepsiades supposes that Dinos rules in the place of Zeus, he thinks of the world as ruled by wills rather than by material necessity. But, according to Socrates, the Clouds are "compelled" to move along by a Whirlwind; their crashing into one another is their thunder; their breaking apart accounts for the rain (376–79). Socrates illustrates the principle of their movement by the clatter in Strepsiades' stomach when it is overfull (385–91). Socrates' divinities have no more freedom than Strepsiades' stomach.[22] Socrates recurs to mechanical necessity to explain even the thunderbolt—an element that was thought to be an instrument of Zeus's justice (395–411).

The freedom of the Clouds is as illusory as Socrates' transcendence of the earth by suspending himself in a basket. Man's desire to be free from his particular time and place through knowledge of what is universally true eventually blurs his vision of what is distinctively human. He forgets that his humanity develops through his controlling and adjusting himself to the accidents of a particular time and place. Man's self-forgetting, his attempt to be formless and free, is revealed in the activity of the Clouds. Because of their very formlessness, they can imitate the natures of men, but the shapes of men they reveal are nonhuman—wolves, deers, and centaurs (346–55). Man's reaching for absolute freedom, his worship of the Clouds, obscures his human shape. Even the Clouds admit that Socrates is somewhat misshapen, for he "swaggers in the streets" and "rolls his eyes to the side of his head" (362). By showing us Strepsiades' frustration in trying to follow Socrates' path, Aristophanes demonstrates how that path leads to a destruction of man's humanity.

The Clouds promise Strepsiades that they will make him a clever speaker if he can endure hard work and shivering from cold, fast without difficulty, refrain from wine, and not tire when standing or walking (412–19). They ask him, in effect, to triumph over his body in order to acquire the power of speech. The hardy Strepsiades, who is not used to comforts anyway, accepts their challenge (420–22). He soon lists the ways in which he yields his body to his teachers—to be beaten, to be starved, to be flayed, for example—in order to become a clever cheat (439ff). He also lists different characterizations of the clever cheat he intends to become. Many of them are not only non-human but also lifeless. They include, for example, a law tablet, a rattle, a fox, a drill, and a leather strap (448–49). He finally offers himself up to be eaten "as sausage by the deep thinkers" (455–56). We glimpse Strepsiades' ruin.

Strepsiades' list of the clever cheat's characteristics is the traditional *pnigos*—several lines of verse delivered by the actor in one breath. The man delivering a *pnigos* pretends to be so powerful a speaker that he does not have to stop "speaking" in order to breathe. The physical demands of delivering a *pnigos* constitute a triumph over body. However, *pnigos* literally means something that "chokes" or "suffocates." This triumph over body that comes, as the name suggests, at the cost of choking or suffocation is a fitting way for Strepsiades to enroll himself in the thinkery.

The **Parabasis**: *The Clouds' Address to the Audience*

While Strepsiades begins his education within, the Clouds perform the traditional *parabasis*, in which they speak directly to the audience and break the dramatic illusion. The chorus does not merely speak to the audience about the play in which it is performing, as it does in other comedies of Aristophanes, however. In the *Clouds*, Aristophanes himself speaks to the audience through the chorus. The

Clouds are evidently amorphous enough that the poet can give his own words, and in that sense his own form, to what the Socratics worship as the symbol of chaos. Perhaps Aristophanes intrudes himself into the *Clouds* more than he does in his other plays in order to contrast himself with Socrates, who seems to forget himself as he contemplates material nature. Aristophanes soon refers to his comedy as his offspring (530–32), reminding us that the self-forgetting Socrates generates nothing of his own.[23]

Aristophanes' offspring, the "wisest" of his comedies, has come, he claims, in search of wise spectators.[24] It is looking for its like (520–24; 534–35). Socrates, in contrast, seeks his like, not among human beings but in the rarefied air that is akin to his ethereal mind. By writing plays, which are performed before his fellow citizens and judged by them, Aristophanes differs from Socrates, who separates himself from others. But, because Aristophanes searches for wise spectators, he does not entirely control whether he will find the like he desires. He tells us that an earlier version of the *Clouds* was rejected by the citizens (524–25). The union that Socrates seeks, in contrast—between his mind and the air that is akin to it—is without such limitations, subject to neither the caprices of human affairs nor the imperfections of men.

Aristophanes speaks through the chorus in order to encourage the judges to vote for the *Clouds*. His comedy deserves to win, he argues, because of its moderation. He claims that its moderation consists in its refusing to resort to low devices, such as wearing a leather phallus, performing obscene dances, or engaging in such slapstick measures as rowdy beatings (537–43). As is generally acknowledged, however, Aristophanes' comedy is guilty of all these offenses against moderation that he lists.[25] But could Aristophanes' wisdom lie in his employing these low devices for the sake of moderation? The low devices do not simply encourage enjoyment of physical pleasures, they call attention to that aspect of humanity which the Socratics ignore— not merely the body, but also the passions that delight in obscene dances and those that generate beatings, good-natured or otherwise. By ignoring the body and the passions, the Socratics are able to indulge their conceit that they are ethereal and timeless beings, a conceit that deprives them, Aristophanes believes, of that happiness which men are capable of achieving in their limited mortal lives. From Aristophanes' standpoint, Socrates' misguided desire for freedom, not man's indulgence of his physical desires, may be the greatest example of immoderation. Aristophanes' comic devices, by reminding men of what makes that freedom impossible, then, may support moderation against Socrates' immoderate abstraction from life.

Aristophanes claims merit also for attacking Cleon at the height of his power, rather than after his fall (549–50). Moreover, although Aristophanes attacks Hyperbolus as he did Cleon, he does not stoop to the practice of other comic poets, who ridiculed Hyperbolus' mother as well.[26] To generalize, Aristophanes praises himself for his citizenship—his defense of Athens by mocking corrupt politicians. However, he acknowledges that there are limits to his mockery, since he will not trample on a man's mother. For Aristophanes, there do remain some things that are sacred.

When Aristophanes allows the chorus to speak as Clouds again, they acknowledge the gods of the city, for they call upon the traditional gods to join their chorus (563–74; 595–606). They then reproach the Athenians for not honoring them, although they protect Athenian politics, raining and thundering when Athens undertakes imprudent expeditions or appoints Cleon general (575–86). The Clouds have become both pious and politically responsible. When they reproach the Athenians for not honoring them, they remind us of Aristophanes' reproach of the Athenians for not rewarding his comedy. Aristophanes seems to have left his imprint upon the Clouds.

The Clouds conclude their *parabasis* with a message from the Moon, who is angry at the Athenians. Although she benefits them by giving light at night, the Athenians confuse the days of the month by trying to reform the calendar. They do not realize that "it is nec-essary to spend the days of life according to the Moon" (626). The Athenians' attempt to control time by imposing an unnatural order upon it leads to chaos and impiety (615–16). They do not sacrifice to the gods at the regular times, for example (617–20). And, as a result of the changes in the calendar, when "the gods are observing a fast, or mourning Memnon or Sarpedon, [the Athenians] are pouring libations and laughing" (621–23). The Clouds' rebuke of the Ath-enians reveals that the Athenians resemble Socrates in believing they are more free than they are. The Athenians suppose that they can control time when they revise the calendar or that nature provides no limits to their choice of conventions. In their conceit about their power over time, they finally forget about death, laughing when they should be mourning. Although the Clouds now condemn Athenians for celebrating at times when even gods fast and mourn, they earlier were delighted by the Athenians' "festivities in all seasons" (309–10). Under the influence of Aristophanes, the once free and joyful Clouds now remind men of their limits, just as the comic poet himself reminds men of the reasons for sadness.

Socrates' Instruction of Strepsiades

After the *parabasis*, we see Socrates' frustration in teaching Strepsiades. Socrates first tries to teach him about poetry—measures and rhythms. Socrates asks about "the most beautiful" measures, but Strepsiades thinks only about food (636–44). Nor can the impatient Strepsiades learn about rhythm, for he cannot see how it contributes to providing the necessities of life (648).[27] When Strepsiades makes an obscene reference to body, Socrates turns away to an abstract discussion of language. The names of some animals refer to both male and female of the species. Socrates demands the creation of new words, so that there is one designating the male and another designating the female (658–66). Socrates' second reform involves a peculiarity of the Greek language—there are masculine nouns with feminine noun endings. Socrates proposes to give masculine noun endings to all masculine nouns.[28] In each case, Socrates tries to purify language of its ambiguities—the peculiarities which have evolved and which are not strictly rational but which have become acceped as custom. Names will then reveal the world's rationality: each thing is simple, either male or female, and therefore easily classified and comprehended. Socrates is still searching for the "most beautiful" measure. Strepsiades does not yet see, however, how such rationality will free him of his debts.

Strepsiades' impatience finally impels Socrates to turn to the issue of his debts. He is delighted with Strepsiades' suggestion that a witch could be paid to draw the moon into a box, thus stopping the passage of time (749–56). The day on which the debts are due will never come. Strepsiades then suggests a second means of escaping his debts. He will direct the sun's heat through a magnifying glass to the wax tablets on which his debts are recorded. He will use his knowledge of nature to melt the record of his debts. Socrates is again delighted with Strepsiades' device.

These two proposals that Strepsiades makes aim at overcoming all restraints—not only the restraints of nature indicated by the inevitable passage of time but also the conventional restraints men impose on themselves so that they act justly toward one another. When a man agrees to undertake future actions, such as paying his debts, his life gains continuity and permanence. This comes through accepting the restraints that Strepsiades finds so burdensome. To eliminate the need to act within the confines of time, as Strepsiades wants to do, is to uproot life from its necessary context. It is analogous to death and reproduces tragedy. It is not surprising, then, that Strepsiades' final proposal for freeing himself from his debts is his own death.

If he is about to be sued, and if he has no witnesses to help him, Strepsiades will run away and hang himself (779–780). For "no one," he asserts, "will bring suit against me when I am dead" (782). In order to escape necessity, he yields to necessity, for death pays all debts. In order to be free, he will destroy himself. He had indeed become like Socrates, who, in order to escape the ephemerality of life in a particular community, reduces man to universal body, making him completely ephemeral. Strepsiades has stated clearly the situation in which the man who longs for absolute freedom entangles himself. Socrates is no longer delighted. He refuses to acknowledge the dead end to which his own activities lead. He drives Strepsiades from the thinkery, railing against the old man's stupidity (781, 783, 789–90).

The Contest Presented Before Phidippides

Expelled from school, Strepsiades again tries to persuade his son to learn rhetoric. This time he appeals not to Phidippides' love for him (86), but to his sense of justice: formerly, when Phidippides was a child, Strepsiades obeyed him, and now Phidippides should obey him in turn (861–64). Strepsiades reveals that he never had the proper authority over his son, since he was accustomed to obeying his son rather than demanding the obedience due to a parent. Since Strep-siades has spoiled Phidippides, it is not surprising that Phidippides ignored his father's request that he study rhetoric. Now, however, Phidippides concedes. Perhaps he is attracted by an argument that assumes an equality between himself and his father: as Strepsiades treated him, so he should treat Strepsiades. The argument applies with the same force to any two individuals and bypasses any obligations that a son has to his father.

At the thinkery, Phidippides witnesses an agon, or contest between the Just Speech and the Unjust Speech, who compete for the privilege of educating him. The Just Speech defends the old ways and the gods of the city. Above all, he praises moderation and restraint. In the old days, the youth were silent, respectful of their elders, behaved decently in the presence of their lovers, and became manly and courageous through gymnastic pursuits. The Just Speech blames the new ways encouraged by the Unjust Speech for the current corruption and license of the youth, who respect neither the authority of their parents nor the laws of the city (961–1023). The Just Speech lists for Phidippides the physical characteristics that come from the practice of moderation, as well as those that come from a life of vice (1010–23). The two lists constitute another *pnigos*. It is appropriate that the Just Speech deliver this physical feat in a contest with the Unjust Speech, for his vaunted moderation necessitates a conquest of his body. By the end of the contest, however, he will be "choked" into silence.

The Unjust Speech tells Phidippides about the pleasures which moderation will deny him—boy lovers, women, gaming, delicacies, drinking, and merrymaking. But what is life worth, he asks, without these? (1071–74). He asks Phidippides to consider "the necessities of nature." His desires may lead him into adultery, and he may be discovered. He will be ruined if he is unable to defend himself through rhetoric. But, if he acquires the Unjust Speech, he may "indulge his nature," for he will be able to talk his way out of punishment (1075–82).[29] Speech will permit him to act without suffering the consequences of his actions. His crimes will not result in punishment. Clever speech will prevent Phidippides' past from affecting his future, just as Strepsiades hopes it will free him from his debts.

After the Unjust Speech addresses Phidippides by appealing to his desire to be free, he argues against the Just Speech by revealing the contradictions inherent in traditional beliefs and attitudes. He juxtaposes the Just Speech's moral teaching with that implied in certain stories about heroes—stories that the Just Speech, as the representative of tradition, must accept. For example, warm baths, deplored by the Just Speech as effeminate, are called Heraclean baths, but the tradition honors Heracles as heroic and brave (1043–52). Furthermore, while the Just Speech blames the youth for disputation and chatter, the revered Homer represents the heroic Nestor as a rhetorician (1055–57). Finally, although tradition teaches that Peleus was married to Thetis as a result of his moderation, it also teaches that Thetis left Peleus because he was not "lustful" or "pleasant to spend the night with in bed" (1067–69). In other words, tradition praises tough labors (Heracles), but is also desires comforts (warm baths); it holds that nobility resides in action (criticizing chatter), but it also values speech (Nestor); it praises moderation (Peleus), but is also wants pleasure (Thetis). Indeed, as the story of Peleus reveals, traditional opinion likes to think that the pleasure which the moderate man denies himself comes as a reward for moderation. As has often been pointed out, the Just Speech himself dwells at unnecessary length on the erotic parts of boys' bodies.[30] He too loves certain pleasures. The opinion which supports a decent society tries to comprehend all the good things or to unite opposites, much as the matchmaker tried to wed the rustic Strepsiades to an aristocratic lady. The Unjust Speech shows that the position of the Just Speech is inconsistent and argues that its official or public side should reflect its seamy underside.

The Unjust Speech defeats the Just Speech, finally, by pointing to the audience—all the leading men, the lawyers, the rhetoricians, and the poets—who are nothing more than "buggers" (1087–1104). The Just Speech has tried to find justice in the authoritative beliefs of the Athenian city, but the Unjust Speech shows him that even the authorities of the city do not live according to those beliefs. In the deeds of the men in the city, the seamy underside of tradition has already openly replaced official morality. In defending tradition, the Just Speech defends what no longer exists. He concedes his defeat.

The Just Speech's final act of concession to the Unjust Speech is stripping off his cloak, throwing it to the spectators, and joining the audience of buggers (1102–04). He throws off his body's covering—the opinions and customs of society that indicate that man is not merely a physical being pursuing bodily pleasures. Socrates himself has been implicated as one who steals cloaks. Socrates, by his students' direct admission, stole a cloak with one of his geometrical instruments (179), and Strepsiades has lost his cloak in the thinkery (499; 856). Socrates removes cloaks or reveals man as body. But he practices the asceticism professed by the Just Speech, for he seems to have no concern for the physical pleasures his rhetoric would permit him to enjoy. Socrates has escaped from traditional opinion only to hold a position plagued with another contradiction. While, in practice, the city's authorities aim at pleasure, their theory urges restraint. And although Socrates' theory permits license, his practice is ascetic. Neither traditional opinion nor Socrates go so far as to accept the simple bestiality of man, as the Unjust Speech does so shamelessly. The Unjust Speech, however, is not a man, only a personification of an abstraction. Phidippides, who acquires the Unjust Speech, will not be willing to follow him in accepting this utterly degrading view of man.

Its Aftermath

The victory of the Unjust Speech affects everything that follows. The Clouds now deliver a second *parabasis*. They claim that the *Clouds* should win the contest, not because of the merits of the play, as they had in the major *parabasis*, but because of the rewards they offer the judges and the punishments they will otherwise inflict (1115–30). They promise the physical pleasures of food and wine, and they threaten the use of force if they do not get their way. They imitate the Unjust Speech in appealing to man's desire for pleasure and his fear of pain. Yet, in the major *parabasis*, under the influence of Aristophanes, they pointed out the good they could do for the city and the evil they could help it avoid. The amorphous Clouds have now adopted another shape.

Meanwhile, Socrates returns Phidippides to his father. Socrates promises that as a result of Phidippides' education Strepsiades will win whatever suit confronts him. (1151).[31] We sample Phidippides' rhetoric when he tells his father that his debts cannot be collected on the due day, designated by law as "the Old and the New." It is the last day of the lunar month, when one can see both the last of the old moon and the beginning of the new moon. Phidippides argues that there can be no such day, because something can be both old and new no more than the same woman can be both old and young (or new) (1181–84). Since the Old and the New Day cannot exist, one needs a new interpretation of the law to purify it of its inconsistencies (1185–86). In taking this position, Phidippides follows his mentors: Socrates, who removed the inconsistencies in language, and the Unjust Speech, who criticized the inconsistencies in tradition. In each case, inconsistent human conventions are brought into line with nature. Socrates revised language so that it captures natural distinctions between male and female, and the Unjust Speech sought to remove the artificial restraints upon men's natural desires. And now Phidippides insists that conventional designations correspond to what nature reveals of growth and decay. The same thing cannot be both old and young at the same time.

Old and young, however, are not absolute terms: they designate relationships. A woman is old in relation to some women, but young in relation to others. So too is the day of the old and new moon old in relation to the past month and new in relation to the coming one. This appears to be the reasoning behind the legal description of the due day. Moreover, when is a woman no longer to be considered young, and when must she be called old? Phidippides' argument assumes that a woman is either young or old and that she is not subject to the process of change. Phidippides thus follows Socrates and the Unjust Speech not only in trying to make conventions consistent with nature but also in the view of nature that he adopts. Something that cannot be both old and new is simple rather than complex. It cannot be characterized by its relations with others, and it does not change. Phidippides views nature as composed of absolutes, unrelated to other things in nature, and uninfluenced by time. Strepsiades rejoices because his son's clever argument removes his debts. Since no one day can be both old and new, the creditors who claim their money on this day need never be satisfied.

In the next scene, Strepsiades meets his creditors and dismisses them with arrogance. He believes that Phidippides' rhetoric will free him from his debts to them. However, he acts as if his knowledge of nature has already made him free. To swear by Zeus is ridiculous, he boasts, "to those who know" (1241). He claims he would not pay even a penny to someone who puts the customary masculine ending on feminine nouns (1250–51). Men with knowledge cannot possibly be in debt to men who lack knowledge, he assumes. He asks one of his creditors, "how is it just that you recover your money, if you know nothing of meteorological matters?" (1283–84). Strepsiades then argues that interest cannot be owed on borrowed money: no more can money increase from day to day than the sea can increase its size from the influx of rivers (1286–95). He here implies that human affairs cannot be controlled by men's agreements or conventions; they must conform to the laws that govern nonhuman nature. In assimilating man to the rest of nature, Strepsiades is unknowingly proclaiming the principle of his own downfall.

We next see Strepsiades running from the house, followed by Phidippides who is beating him. The quarrel began, Strepsiades tells the Clouds, when Phidippides rejected the traditional poets, Simon-ides and Aeschylus. And the situation worsened when Phidippides recited a passage from Euripides about incest between a brother and sister. When Strepsiades reproached his son, Phidippides began to beat him (1353–76). The father is appalled by his son's newly acquired tastes, for they do not show families the proper reverence or respect. Although Strepsiades has learned to deny many authoritative opinions through his association with Socrates, he still believes in the sacredness of the family. After all, he has debts which are now due only because he accepts responsibility for his son.

Phidippides claims that he can persuade his father of the justice of father-beating. His argument is based on reciprocity: as the father beat the child out of good will when the child needed a beating, so too should the child beat the father when he is in error. As did Strepsiades' argument about reciprocal obedience, Phidippides' argument denies any special relation between father and son: it would apply with equal force to any two individuals. Father and son are equally judges of error and equally entitled to beat the other when he is in need of it. Mind, or knowledge, the argument implies, is the sole title to rule.[32] Phidippides has taken a position that reminds us of Oedipus, who believes that he rules Thebes because of his ability to answer the riddle of the Sphinx, i.e., because of his intelligence. Moreover, Oedipus's crimes suggest an equality between himself and his father whom he replaces through patricide and incest. When Strepsiades first mentioned Phidippides' beating him, he called his son "a patricide" and a "housebreaker" (1327). Father-beating denies the authority of the father and therefore destroys the home. Phidippides' argument clearly indicates his desire for freedom; "Why ought your body be exempt from blows, and mine not?" he asks his father, "For I too was born free" (1413–14).

Phidippides justifies father-beating also by appealing to the ways of cocks and other animals, who do not hesitate to attack fathers. Yet they are no different from us, he claims, except in not writing decrees (1427–29). But neither father nor son explore the implications of this exception. Strepsiades merely asks, "why since you imitate the cocks in all things, do you not eat dung and sleep on a perch?" (1430–31). Phidippides is appalled at the prospect. He claims, "it is not the same thing, nor would it seem so to Socrates" (1432). But why not? He fails to give an argument. And we have seen Socrates sitting on a perch, so to speak, and befouled by a lizard as he gaped up at the heavens. Phidippides has gleaned only that part of the Socratic position that is consistent with his own manliness or desire for independence. Having learned to consider the family merely conventional,

Phidippides finds a natural basis for his freedom from his father's rule—in the superiority of his mind. But the knowledge on which his superiority rests is knowledge of man's bondage to material nature. His final argument appeals to the ways of brutes. He no more escapes from necessity than his father avoids paying his debts.

Although Strepsiades is persuaded by Phidippides' argument for father-beating, he is infuriated when Phidippides tries to apply it to mother-beating. The equality between mother and son implied in such an argument would open the door to incest, which was the issue over which Strepsiades and his son began to quarrel.[33] The wretched Strepsiades now glimpses some of the implications of the influence of Socrates. Everything he holds most dear is crumbling around him. He reproaches the Clouds for leading him astray. The Clouds, evidently sensing which way the wind is blowing, claim that they entice wicked men into misfortune in order to teach them to fear the gods (1458–61).[34] Strepsiades decides to destroy Socrates.

Because Socrates can manipulate words to defend the rightness of his actions, Strepsiades would not succeed in bringing him to court.[35] He must resort to force and burn the thinkery. The abstractions of speech result in the violence of body. Strepsiades now calls for a lighted torch (1490), echoing his request for a light at the beginning of the play (18). In both cases, light reveals the extent of his indebtedness, whether it illuminates the list of what he borrowed for his son or the futility of his plan to evade payment. Strepsiades asks Phidippides to help him destroy the Socratics, but Phidippides says he will not wrong his teachers (1467). He refuses to obey Strepsiades in the end, as he refused to obey him in the beginning. Strepsiades' problem with his son surely has not been solved.[36] Although Phidippides does not join his father in burning the thinkery, neither does he warn Socrates. He appears to take no part in the conflict. Perhaps his Socratic education has not only deprived him of his manly tan, but has also made him unfit for action.

The Standpoint of Comedy

In the *Clouds*, Aristophanes portrays men imitating the tragic hero's attempt to transcend human limitation or overcome necessity. In contrast to tragedy, which reveals the nobility of such an attempt, comedy presents it as ludicrous. Whereas we might sympathize with the tragic hero and experience more strongly the desires in ourselves that make us like him, we become detached from the comic figures we see as ridiculous. Aristophanes moderates man's lofty but tragic aspirations through laughter.

Aristophanes' characters are entangled in the comic dilemma of trying to achieve something through a means that contradicts their goals. The Socratics, for example, forget about their human existence in a particular time or place. They want to know what is true at all times and in all places. Universality will bring them freedom. But man is distinguished from the rest of nature because he forms political communities. Man is a particular being with particular loyalties, limited by time, place, and circumstance. Seeking the universal or the unlimited, Socrates turns to nonhuman nature and to man only insofar as he resembles nonhuman nature. Socrates loses sight of the human, aware only of the movements of matter, whether in the whirlwinds and clouds of the heavens, in the intestines of gnats, or in the thoughts inside his own head (374–80; 160–64; 227–34). Socrates, seeking freedom in universality, discovers only that man is a slave to his own body. Caught in contradiction, Socrates is laughable.

Strepsiades and Phidippides also want to be free through the rhetoric that Socrates teaches. That rhetoric, however, provides the same illusion of freedom as Socrates' knowledge of nature. In being able to present any side of an issue, that rhetoric is not bound by the truth. Like the Clouds, rhetorical speech can take any shape. It is formless, lacking particular content. And the rhetorician, becoming free of the consequences of his actions, is no longer bound by the situations in which he is involved. In a sense, he too becomes "without content," for his rhetoric can make whatever he does and whatever happens to him appear to be other than it is. However, rhetoric frees a man from his past only to enslave him to his passions, or, as the Unjust Speech admits, to "the necessities of nature" (1075). Phidippides has been freed from the authority of his family and city through Socratic knowledge of nature and rhetoric, but, as Strepsiades points out, the actions that he is now free to do are those of cocks and other animals. We laugh at Strepsiades and Phidippides because they want to be free of the conventions of their society, yet this freedom reduces them to the level of animals. Similarly, we laugh at Socrates because he wants to be free through a knowledge of universals, yet that knowledge is of a universal bondage to body. The amorphous materiality of

the Clouds—their free-ranging slavery—is the symbol for both Socrates' knowledge of nature and the rhetoric that accompanies it.

Aristophanes defends man's particular existence against the
abstractions of the Socratics. He points out the low things—the necessities of nature—that the Socratics deny. But he is well aware that it
is the very existence he defends that leads to the destructive abstractions of the Socratics. Human life unavoidably involves a concern
with what is not strictly necessary; to be reduced to necessity is to
live the life of a brute. Even Strepsiades, who is rustic and vulgar,
knows that men should not imitate the cocks and other animals.
Unlike mere beasts, Strepsiades desires the love and respect of his son,
and he wants to be able to satisfy his son's desires. He becomes an
overindulgent father, borrowing money in order to make his son happy.
Influenced by his mother and not sufficiently restrained by his father,
Phidippides spends beyond his father's means. He wants the freedom
of an aristocratic life—the money that allows him to buy unnecessary
things and the leisure that gives him time to enjoy them. But if he
is to continue to neglect the necessities, he needs the rhetoric advocated by the Unjust Speech. Both Strepsiades' love for his son and
Phidippides' aristocratic leanings lead them to Socrates.

Man is human because he rises above mere necessity, yet there
appears to be no end to his desires. It might seem that Strepsiades'
marriage would moderate his vulgarity and elevate his tastes and, at
the same time, curb his wife's extravagance. A successful marriage
between these different types would combine an awareness of limitation with an appreciation for the refinements of life. Strepsiades and
his wife are in need of each other. But their marriage is not a success.
The completeness that their marriage promises is not realized. Phidippides, a symbol of his parents' union, combines the different elements of their marriage only in name.

In the *Symposium*, Plato has Aristophanes give an account of
love. He describes men as halves, descendants of men who were once
wholes. Each longs to be united in one body with another half, a
human being who will complete him. But it is not clear that a man's
exact mate exists. In any case, what the lover desires is impossible—
that he and his beloved be merged into one body. Lovers put their
arms around each other and eventually die from "hunger and indol-
ence," from wishing to do nothing apart (*Sym.*, 191b). According to
Aristophanes, Zeus took pity on their plight and invented sex. Through

sex, men can find some relief from their desire. This relief, although it does not give them the complete unity they long for, does allow them to turn to "the deeds of the rest of life" (*Sym.*, 191c). Aristophanes' comedies do not show men how to attain a completeness that satisfies their desires, but through laughter they offer some relief from longing so that men can turn to "the deeds of the rest of life"—to their ordinary lives, to their families, friends, and political communities. But this means that men must live within the confines of their particular, limited lives. They must accept the inconsistencies in public opinion, the irrationalities in language, and, in general, the conflicts intrinsic to human action and passion that make wholeness impossible. They must forget about the completeness and freedom they long for; they must laugh at the ridiculous Socrates and at Strepsiades and Phidippides who seek what the Socratics appear to possess. Aristophanes' solution is tenuous at best. He directs man to ordinary life as a substitute for completion, but it is in ordinary life that the desire for completeness arises. How long can laughter check desire and prevent tears? We shall see that Plato's defense of Socrates against Aristophanes' charges indicates that political philosophy is a more satisfactory response to man's incompleteness than laughter.

Part II

Political Philosophy: Plato's Response (The *Republic*)

Introduction

Plato's portrayal of Socrates differs radically from that of Aristophanes. While Aristophanes' Socrates contemplates the things in the heavens and below the earth, Plato's Socrates explores questions about how men live. He investigates such topics as courage, moderation, justice, love, and friendship. Indeed, in the *Republic*, Socrates tries to determine "a course of life on the basis of which each of us would have the most profitable existence" (344e).[1] While Aristophanes' Socrates seems neither to have nor to seek an understanding of himself, Plato's Socrates takes the Delphic "Know Thyself" as his motto (*Phdr.*, 229e). In short, Aristophanes' Socrates is a natural scientist, Plato's Socrates is a political philosopher. Since Socrates undertook investigations of nature in his youth, before raising the questions of politics and morality for which he is famous (*Phaedo*, 96a ff.), the Aristophanic Socrates appears to be a young, "pre-Socratic" Socrates, Socrates before he turned to or discovered political philosophy.[2] Because Plato, in contrast, portrays Socrates after this discovery, he shows Aristophanes the possibility of *political* philosophy, which combines the philosophical and political concerns that Aristophanes saw as antagonistic. Man finds his highest activity in knowing or contemplating, but he takes as his object human desires and activities. Plato shows us a philosophy that speaks of families and political communities, rather than one immersed in star gazing.

The *Republic* is Plato's classic work of political philosophy.[3] As such, it is Plato's defense of Socrates against Aristophanes' charges in the *Clouds*. Far from being unaware of what is going on in Athens, Socrates has gone to the Piraeus in order to see Athens' most recent change in its customs—a religious festival in honor of a Thracian divinity (327a). Rather than contemplating the heavens in the midst of a select group of students of natural science, Socrates discusses politics with young men who seem attracted to political careers. Instead of teaching a rhetoric that can speak on either side of an issue, Socrates tries to persuade the teacher of such a rhetoric that his views are wrong. Most important, the *Republic* as a whole may be viewed as Socrates' defense of justice.

Socrates describes a just city when Glaucon, one of the young men present, asks him to prove that justice is good, apart from any rewards a just man may receive. Glaucon wants to see justice as it is in itself, stripped of its consequences. At Socrates' suggestion, they look for justice in a city before trying to find it in the soul of a man. In order to satisfy a desire to see the absolute goodness of justice, they found a "perfectly good" city (427e). Existing only in the conversation of Socrates and his discussants, this "city in speech" appears to answer the question of the best political order, regardless of circumstances. Socrates thus appears to defend the goodness of justice, a defense that is necessary for the stability and decency of political life. On this level, Plato counters Aristophanes' charge that Socrates threatens political life by teaching men how to make the unjust argument the stronger.

There is evidence, however, that Plato and even the Socrates of the *Republic* do not simply approve of the city in speech. For example, there is no place in that city for the Platonic Socrates or the kind of philosophizing he practices—the constant questioning of others about the foundations of their beliefs (see, e.g., *Apol.*, 21b ff.). Far from questioning the other members of the city about their opinions, the philosophers who rule there support the public orthodoxy, including what Socrates calls a "noble lie" (414c). Nor do they share Socrates' interest in understanding man and his political life. The city gives them a mathematical education intended to turn them away from the world of change toward the world of ideas, which they contemplate outside the "cave" of political life. They must be compelled to rule, for to them "human life [does not seem] anything great" (486a). They resemble Aristophanes' Socrates, who secludes himself in the thinkery, more than the Socrates of the Platonic dialogues.[4]

Moreover, there is another obvious way in which the city in speech resembles the abstract existence Aristophanes criticizes, rather than Socrates' philosophic life, which Plato presents as its alternative. Communism, one of the city's defining institutions, resembles the Socratics of the *Clouds* in that it destroys the family. Like the men in the thinkery, those who live under communism do not identify themselves by their patronymics, for they are unaware of any con- nections to particular parents who gave them birth.[5] Serving the city's goal of unity, communism separates an individual from his origins just as it eliminates any particular relationships with others that give him an identity of his own. Like Aristophanes' Socrates, the city in speech robs fathers of their sons (cf. 540e–541a). But whereas the city in speech as far as possible treats all its members as if they were alike,[6] Socrates treats each of his interlocutors differently. As Plato illustrates in the *Republic*, Socrates takes into account the particular characters, opinions, and desires of the men he meets and addresses them accord- ingly. The city in speech aims at homogeneity, at everyone saying "mine" and "not mine" of the same things. But Socrates' philosophizing differentiates among men.

Plato thus presents two alternatives in the *Republic*: Socratic phi- losophizing, and the politics that Socrates describes. I shall argue that each of these two aspects of the *Republic* constitutes one side of his reply to Aristophanes. In the first place, Socratic political philosophy exemplifies a philosophy that does not turn away from human and political affairs but actually finds that investigating such affairs is the way to arrive at the understanding it seeks. By centering men's atten- tions on their everyday affairs and the complex possibilities that arise out of them, political philosophy can act as a moderating force on the tendency toward simplistic abstractions that Aristophanes criti- cized. Plato attempts to achieve what Aristophanes tried to achieve— a defense of human life—but by defending Socrates and philosophy rather than by laughing at them.

In the second place, by having his Socrates present the city in speech in such a way as to resemble Aristophanes' thinkery, Plato shows that the abstractions from ordinary life which Aristophanes thought were dangerous are the tendency of politics itself. Even Aris- tophanes recognized that the desire for absolutes grew out of the dilemmas faced by ordinary men such as Strepsiades and Phidippides, but he nevertheless portrayed philosophy as the natural expression of that desire and as the activity which most encouraged that desire in others. For Aristophanes, philosophy undermines political life. Plato, in response, shows the truth in the opposite possibility: not only is the desire for absolutes manifest in political life, as well as in philosophy, but that desire may become so powerful that politics forces philosophy to serve its purposes. Politics thus can undermine philosophy's ability to act as a moderating force on man's desire for absolutes and even force it to support that desire. Plato shows this happening in the *Republic*'s city in speech. He thus attributes to politics the dangerous immoderation that Aristophanes attributed to philosophy. Since, from Plato's point of view, Socratic philosophy can serve as a restraint on such immoderation, Aristophanes' ridicule of Socrates only undermines the moderation it intended to encourage.

In my discussion of Plato, I shall explore his defense of Socrates and his criticism of politics, the two major components of his reply to Aristophanes. In the first chapter, I shall argue that Book I of the *Republic* constitutes an introduction to political philosophy. There we see Socrates' investigation of a variety of opinions and desires that cannot be reconciled and thus the problems that stand in the way of the complete unity men seek. It is by revealing and exploring the complexity of human life that Socratic philosophy counters man's drive toward simple abstractions that seem to provide unity and peace. Chapter 2 will examine the gradual eclipse of political philosophy by this drive to escape complexity, a drive culminating in the city in speech. Trying to achieve an end to strife through political community, men impose simple forms and structures on human life and thereby distort its manifold possibilities. The tyranny of this endeavor does not become fully apparent until Socrates describes the equality of the sexes, the institution of communism, and the subordination of philosophy to politics. I shall discuss these facets of the city in speech in Chapter 3. Finally, in the fourth chapter, I shall show how the last three books of the *Republic* return us to Socratic political philosophy and attempt to moderate the passions which created the city in speech.

In the *Republic*, considered as a whole, Plato engages in Socratic political philosophy, exploring the alternatives between which men vacillate—the confusion and conflict stemming from the variety of human desires and opinions, on the one hand, and the simplifying action that tries to provide a way out of the conflict, on the other. Political philosophy is the best way, according to Plato, to counter the dangers to humanity that Aristophanes pointed out, whether those dangers take the form of a star-gazing philosophy or that of a homo-geneous politics. For political philosophy examines what such a phi-losophy and such a politics forget, the manifold, if irreconcilable, possibilities of the human psyche. The patient exploration of the fundamental questions guides political life, not by outlining models for cities to imitate, but by restraining man's impulses to institute cities and to accept philosophies in the belief that the fundamental questions have been answered.

Chapter 1

Plato's Introduction to Political Philosophy (Book I of the *Republic*)

Introduction

In Book I of the *Republic*, Socrates and his interlocutors discuss the meaning of justice. After Socrates refutes the definitions his interlocutors offer, he argues that justice is wise, powerful, and the cause of happiness. But he has, he admits, shown only what justice is like and not what justice is. "As a result of the discussion," he says, "I know nothing" (354b). Because Book I lacks a positive conclusion, it resembles what scholars have called Plato's *aporetic* dialogues. *Aporetic* comes from the Greek *aporia*, a state of "being at a loss," of being in a difficulty without any way out.[1] Because an *aporetic* dialogue leaves us with a variety of inadequate opinions and no apparent way of resolving the confusion, it has the appearance of a fragment rather than a whole.[2] Some scholars believe that Plato wrote his *aporetic* works early in his career and designate them as his "Socratic" dialogues. These dialogues were composed, they argue, when Plato was most under the influence of Socrates, when he had not yet formulated answers to the questions Socrates asked.[3]

Because of its *aporetic* character, Book I differs from the rest of the *Republic*, where Socrates defines justice, describing a perfectly good city and individual and the various forms of injustice. Scholars, such as Paul Friedlander, have suggested that Plato wrote Book I as a separate dialogue.[4] Friedlander argues that Plato later found this early

35

work on justice useful as an introduction to the *Republic*, since it raises questions that the *Republic* answers.[5] Because the *Republic* moves from questions to answers, it seems to reflect a development in Plato's thought—from an early stage in which questions were more obvious to him than answers, the stage of his *aporetic* dialogues, to a more mature period in which he formulated answers to the questions he raised in his earlier dialogues.

This approach to the *Republic*, however, too quickly identifies the answers embodied in the city in speech with Plato's mature position. It does not sufficiently take into account either the problematic character of the arguments Socrates gives in founding the city or the inadequacy of Socrates' responses to the objections that are raised, to say nothing of the ironies in the drama of the city's founding. Plato's presentation of justice in the city in speech and in the soul, I shall argue, does not present final conclusions; rather it implicitly raises questions about the meaning of justice.[6] Plato's political philosophy therefore resembles Socrates' more than it is its correction or completion. Moreover, after Socrates finishes describing the city, he looks at the inferior regimes and soul types. This discussion reminds us of Book I of the *Republic* because, like Book I, it reveals man's multifarious desires and the strife growing out of them. It reveals why the city in speech is both impossible and unsatisfying to men. We could say that the *Republic* resembles Book I in leaving its reader in a state of *aporia*, with the qualification that the final *aporia* is based on a better understanding of the difficulties involved in any resolution of human conflict.[7]

In my examination of Book I, I shall argue that the conflict contained in its *aporia* is not something that Plato later overcame but a reflection of the strife he saw inherent in human life. Book I reveals the tensions and conflicts that stand in the way of the peace that men desire. We shall learn from the setting of the dialogue and, more importantly, from the desires and opinions of Socrates' interlocutors that the goods men seek are in conflict with one another. We shall see the tension between thought and action, between reason or argument and experience. In Cephalus, we shall find a man who knows from experience the passions and desires that frustrate the complete dominance of reason in men's actions. But Cephalus is not sufficiently a man of reason to defend what he has learned from experience.[8] Because he leaves the gathering, his experience of man's limitations is not brought to bear on the discussion. Polemarchus and Thrasymachus, on the other hand, are men whose desires for something perfect or absolute lead them to deny the limitations inherent in human life. Polemarchus wants a perfect justice to which he can be totally devoted, while Thrasymachus seeks perfection in the self-knowledge and self-interested actions of the unjust man. Socrates' conversations with these men bring to light the problems in their attaining what they desire.

We shall see in Book I not only the complexities and tensions in human life but also man's desire to overcome or deny those complexities and tensions. That desire leads to the founding of the "perfectly good" city in speech (427e), which denies the disproportion between thought and experience, offers a perfect justice to guide men's lives, and, in general, suppresses whatever difficulties frustrate its unity. Book I thus presents the problems that lie behind the search for perfect justice.

The Setting of the Dialogue

The *Republic* takes place in the Piraeus, the Athenian port, the place where the new and the different enter into the city.[9] Socrates has gone there with Glaucon in order to attend a religious ceremony, which is being held for the first time. Athens has become interested in foreign gods, for the festivities include a ceremony conducted by the Thracians, in honor of a Thracian goddess. Plato's choice of this setting for his dialogue implicitly accuses Athens of corruption. The very charge that the city made against Socrates, that he introduced new divinities into the city (*Apol.*, 24b), Plato suggests, can be made against Athens itself, for that city introduces, or at least condones, the worship of a foreign god.[10] From a liberal perspective, Athens' interest in new customs and ways of worshipping may seem its virtue— a sign of tolerance and a condition of growth and improvement. However, a city, like an individual, may be tolerant out of weakness, as well as out of strength, and an inclination to replace its own customs with foreign ones may signify decline rather than improvement. To the extent that a city, or an individual, randomly embraces a variety of practices and beliefs that do not necessarily cohere with its traditional ones, it will lose its identity or integrity. Given Athens' own association of alien religious worship with corruption, its interest in a Thracian divinity suggests its weakness rather than its strength. The Thracians were, after all, "barbarians who [were] barely Hellenized,"[11] and they have enticed Athenians by this "all-night" ceremony (328a). Historically, Athens at this time was undergoing a state of moral and political decline.[12] The Thracian festival the Athenians are enjoying at the Piraeus is one indication of that decline.

At the beginning of the dialogue, Socrates and Glaucon have apparently seen enough of the religious festival, for they are returning to Athens before the evening's ceremony takes place. As they are leaving, Polemarchus and his group overtake them and ask them to stay. Polemarchus offers Socrates inducements to remain—an all-night festival and conversation with the young men present (328a–b). His proposal that the gathering engage in discussion inadvertently points to the coincidence of political decay and philosophy. The intellectual activity of Athenians accompanies the city's loss of vitality.[13] Perhaps the good things men strive for may be had only at the cost of other goods. Cephalus, Polemarchus' father, whom we soon meet, suggests the same thing when he explains his own condition. During the prime of his body, his desires for physical pleasures kept him away from the pleasures of discussion, but now, when those desires wane with old age, "the desires and pleasures that have to do with speeches grow the more" (328d). Cephalus' physical decline, he claims, permits intellectual activity, just as the city's political and moral decline accompanies the intellectual activity of its members. The various achievements of which men are capable do not appear to coincide.

The problems the setting reveals, however, are forgotten in the course of the evening. Rather than observe a disintegrating Athens, the company founds a city in speech, which is as unified as any city can be (462a–b). So too is the disjunction between man's political and intellectual health forgotten. In the city Socrates describes, politics and philosophy flourish together, with the city educating the philosopher and, in turn, being maintained by his efforts. In constructing the city in speech, Socrates "forgets," or leaves out of his presentation, those disunities to which the setting, and Book I in general, call attention. In more senses than one, Socrates forgets where he is: forgetting the religious festival, he does not go to the all-night events; forgetting the significance of the religious festival, he constructs a city that ignores the disjunction between political health and philosophic activity.

When Socrates forgets, he therefore suppresses the elements that cause conflict or stand in the way of unity. He does on the level of discussion what rulers do in cities when they use force against recalcitrant elements which disrupt the city's harmony. Just as Socrates makes possible the construction of the city in speech by forgetting certain truths, any attempt to construct that city in deed would be based on the use of physical force (e.g., 540e–541a). Because the unity of cities is established and maintained by suppression, whether of recalcitrant elements or obstructive truths, it is appropriate that the *Republic's* action begin with a concession to physical strength. Polemarchus proffers his invitation to Socrates to stay in the Piraeus by asking him if he is stronger than the many men present who want him to say (327c). Although Polemarchus does hold out the prospect of the festival and the discussion, Socrates merely concedes to majority will. "If it is so resolved," he says, "that's how we must act" (328b). The compulsion which Polemarchus places upon Socrates to join his group foreshadows the force the city exerts upon the philosopher to enter political life and to serve the city by ruling it.[14]

Unlike the compulsion used by the city, however, the compulsion that Polemarchus places upon Socrates is only playful. There is no question but that Socrates can return to Athens if he really wants to do so. Socrates stays to talk not so much because he is compelled by Polemarchus, or even because he is attracted by the thought of creating a unified city, but because he is attracted to conversation and the insights it might produce.[15] Socrates' protestations that he has other plans when a discussion appears imminent are more like the excuses of a politician who claims that he doesn't want to run for office than those of a philosopher-king who believes he is being drawn away from his true happiness. The similarities between Socrates and the philosopher-king, like those between the gathering at Polemarchus' house and the city in speech, are more apparent than real. When Socrates "forgets" in speech in order to show the extremes to which men may go, he can later remember. But when the city uses force against recalcitrant elements, its actions cannot always be corrected if it has a change of heart. Plato is presenting the great difference between Socrates' relations to others and the relations among the members of the city in speech.[16] Socrates accompanies the group to Polemarchus' house. Cephalus, Polemarchus' father, greets the new arrivals warmly, and we witness friendly conversation. Since Socrates speaks first with Cephalus and then with his son about justice, we can see a parallel between the *Republic* and the *Clouds*, where Socrates tries to educate another father and son on this same issue.

Socrates' Meeting with Cephalus

Socrates claims to be "delighted to discuss with the very old," such as Cephalus. Because an old man has travelled a road that other men must also take, Socrates would like to learn from Cephalus whether that road is "rough and hard or easy and smooth" (328d–e). Leo Strauss finds Socrates' question "a model of propriety." "It gives Cephalus an opportunity to speak of everything good which he possesses, to display his happiness, as it were," Strauss writes, "and it concerns the only subject of a general character about which Socrates could conceivably learn something from him: how it feels to be very old."[17] If Cephalus can teach Socrates something, it is because of his experience. However, if Cephalus can know what Socrates does not know only because he has experienced it, is it possible for Socrates to learn from him without having had that experience? Socrates seems to be trying to see how far he can learn through speech what another has learned through experience. He is implicitly pursuing the limits of reason, or the extent to which experience can be reduced to speech and conveyed to others. If learning could come through talking rather than through living, Greek tragedy might be wrong in associating learning with suffering.[18] There might be knowledge without pain or a good without any concomitant evil.

Moreover, we may wonder how proper it is for Socrates to ask an old man about old age. Rather than afford an opportunity for Cephalus to display his happiness, it reminds him of something that might be painful to him—not only old age but also the prospect of his approaching death.[19] To be sure, Cephalus discusses such matters with friends of the same age (328e–329a), but this does not mean that he would enjoy such a discussion with a group of young men, which includes his three sons, as well as some men who might be strangers to him. Socrates has asked Cephalus a very *personal* question, in a situation that almost demands *impersonal* discussion. Cephalus' reaction to Socrates' question would therefore shed light on how far the personal can be treated impersonally, or how far men can go in objectively evaluating their own situations. A Socrates, in nearing death, might well delight in speaking about his own condition, but would a less rational man who is, as Cephalus is, bothered by his fears of the afterlife (330d–331a)? Although Socrates argues in the *Apology* that it is not reasonable for a man to fear death (*Apol.*, 29a–b), most, if not all men, experience such fears. Socrates' question to Cephalus, more than "a model of propriety," an attempt to put him at ease, is a test of the limits of reason—a test that can only make Cephalus uncomfortable. Socrates, in effect, asks how far men can assess their own situations without being influenced by passion.

Cephalus takes Socrates' personal question surprisingly well. He explains that old age has freed him from the erotic desires that dominated his life (329d). It has brought him peace. Moreover, a man's character, he says, is important in his bearing old age with ease (329d). Socrates, however, continues asking Cephalus personal questions. The many would say, Socrates observes, that Cephalus bears old age so well not because of his character but because of his wealth (329e). Cephalus concedes that wealth is a necessary but not sufficient condition for his well-being (330a). He takes the position of Aristotle in the *Ethics*—that happiness requires a certain amount of external goods, as well as virtuous activity (*NE*, 1099a28–b1).

Socrates continues to demand from Cephalus an account of himself, asking him to name the greatest good he enjoys from his wealth. Cephalus claims that his money permits him to be just: it "contributes a great deal to not having to cheat or lie to any man against one's will, and, moreover, to not having to depart for that other place frightened because one owes some sacrifices to a god or money to a human being" (331b). Cephalus' statement provides Socrates with the chance to wonder if Cephalus has understood justice properly. Can justice be merely giving back what one has taken and telling the truth? Socrates asks. If a man goes mad, for example, should one return borrowed weapons to him or be obliged to tell him the whole truth (331c)? Socrates' question reveals that Cephalus' conception of justice permits cases where justice harms the just man and the one toward whom he acts. If Cephalus returns a borrowed weapon to a madman, or even tells him the truth, his act may be good neither for himself nor the madman. Does justice have such undesirable consequences? Although justice may be good for a man's soul—for it is the right thing to do—and it may even lead to rewards in an afterlife, can it also be harmful in other ways? Socrates thus raises the question of whether justice is a mixture of good and evil, as Cephalus' statement allows, or whether it is simply good.

Moreover, Socrates' example points not only to the possibly mixed consequences of justice but also to the impermanence of man's situation. A sane man may go mad. Socrates gives an extreme example of what is generally true of human life: men, and the circumstances in which they act, constantly change. Man cannot therefore possess a single rule or definition of justice that is applicable to all cases. Justice must be flexible enough to allow itself to be adapted to changing conditions. It is when men act as if justice were an unchanging rule that justice has harmful consequences—at least in Socrates' current example. By giving back the weapon that is owed, regardless of the fact that his friend has gone mad, a man may endanger both himself and his friend. Socrates' initial question about justice thus suggests that the goodness of justice cannot be ascertained apart from its consequences and that any attempt to treat justice as if it were a universally valid rule is misconceived, or at least detrimental to man's good.

Cephalus, however, does not stay around to explore these questions. He must go, he says, to offer sacrifices to the gods. Perhaps he owes something to the gods and his justice demands that he pay it. He may also recognize, however, that he cannot answer the questions Socrates has asked. He has been taught by experience—the passions he has felt, the habits he has acquired, and the conventions he has accepted. But this knowledge does not enable him to defend his beliefs. Not only his piety before the gods but his pride before younger men, including hissons, may impel him to leave. Passions again prevent his participation in discussion.[20]

Cephalus' exit precedes the serious business of defining justice. It might seem proper that he leave before the traditional opinions which he holds are called into question. After all, he is an old man, and lack of time, if not capacity, would prevent him from pursuing a philosophic consideration of the questions in which Socrates involves the young men. As Bloom argues, in order to carry on "a frank discussion about justice, . . . the philosopher must take the place of the father. . . . Socrates must induce Cephalus to leave the scene, because Cephalus is beyond reason, and it would be impious to dispute with him."[21] Cephalus, however, might have had some positive contributions to make to the discussion. Polemarchus will attempt to modify his father's conception of justice so that justice will not have undesirable consequences. Later, Glaucon asks Socrates to show that justice is choice-worthy for its own sake. Unlike Cephalus, the young men in the *Republic* seek an unqualified good in justice. They are looking for something perfect. Cephalus, in contrast, is more aware of the limitations of justice. He is trying to be just, even though his justice may not be an unmixed good for him. Not only does it take him from the discussion, but it requires money that might be otherwise left to his sons. Cephalus' experience of justice's limits might have moderated the *Republic*'s discussion.

In the second place, Cephalus knows from experience the power of man's desires, the fear of death, and the importance of property for happiness. All these things point to the limits of reason, and all of them in various ways are minimized in the city Socrates describes. Cephalus may be "beyond reason," as Bloom says, but if this means that he will not accept arguments when they run counter to experience, this may not be simply a defect. Because his long years of experience give him more to forget than the young men present, he would be less likely than they to yield to the desires that motivate the city in speech.

In the third place, Cephalus has been very erotic. He experienced his erotic desires as "very many mad masters" (329d). He felt their tyranny, or the fact that they compelled him to act in a way he would not have chosen to act. Whether for good or bad, *eros* makes a man dependent or subordinates him to something external. As indicated in the *Symposium*, eros is needy or incomplete, forever seeking what it cannot entirely possess (*Sym.*, 203c–204a). The city that Socrates and his interlocutors found, however, leaves little scope for man's eros. It denies its members' incompleteness by trying to fulfill their every need. Conforming to the requirements of the city, the discussion forgets Cephalus' eroticism just as Cephalus himself recedes into the background. Cephalus' absence might indeed have allowed the discussion to proceed in the way it does because his presence would have added a positive restraint on the discussion's excesses. Because he reminds us of considerations that Socrates' young interlocutors do not fully appreciate or comprehend, it is appropriate that his definition of justice is the only one that includes "telling the truth." When Polemarchus inherits the discussion, this aspect of his father's conception is completely forgotten.

Socrates' and Polemarchus' Search for a Definition of Justice

Throughout his discussion with Socrates, Polemarchus remains a defender of justice. Like his father, he bases his notions of justice and its goodness on his experience of honest or decent behavior, as defined by convention. But unlike his father, whose years of experience taught him that there are limits to what men can expect to achieve, Polemarchus has no counterweight to his desire for a perfect justice.[22] He will accept no qualifications to the absolute goodness of justice: he refines his father's position so that justice has good consequences; he denies considerations that show justice in a bad light; and he agrees to defend the proposition that justice harms no one at all.

Inheriting his father's argument, Polemarchus maintains that justice is giving back what has been taken, or, as he soon says, giving to each what is owed (331e). In order to avoid the undesirable consequences implied in the example of the mad friend, Polemarchus claims that we "owe it to friends to do some good and nothing bad." To enemies, conversely, we owe "some harm" (332a–b). We do not owe simply what has been taken, but what is fitting. Therefore, we do not owe a friend a weapon if he has gone mad. Although Polemarchus probably means by his answer merely that the just man is inclined to give the fitting, while the unjust man is not, Socrates assumes that he means that justice is a kind of knowledge that permits the just man to give the fitting. Socrates' assumption indicates that Polemarchus must reach beyond experience for an adequate understanding of justice. A man must not only be willing to do what is just, as he has been taught to do, but he must have some understanding of what justice demands. Socrates' questions, however, go further than merely connecting action with understanding, for they treat justice as if it were knowledge of the fitting in some particular sphere of human activity. "In what action and in respect to what work," Socrates asks, is the just man "able to help friends and injure enemies?" (332e). A doctor, for example, can give his friends health and his enemies diseases. Socrates implies that justice is like one of the arts. Polemarchus might have replied that justice is something which all the particular artisans need in addition to their arts so that they use their arts justly—in order to help friends and hurt enemies.[23] In such a case justice could not be isolated as a single art but would take on different forms as it became manifest in the variety of skills that men possess. Polemarchus, however, accepts the terms Socrates lays down and tries to define justice as a particular art distinct from other arts. By doing so, he can view justice as sufficient by itself, neither assuming different forms in different situations nor dependent on anything outside itself for its goodness.

Polemarchus locates the particular sphere in which the just man is useful to friends and harmful to enemies "in making war and being an ally in battle" (332e). But he does not mean that the just man possesses a knowledge of war; rather he is thinking of the soldier who defends his friends and attacks his enemies because of his good char- acter. Similarly, just as justice is useful in battle, in peacetime justice is useful in contracts or partnerships involving money (333a–b). The just man is the best man with whom to form a partnership not because he has knowledge of business but because he is honest. Polemarchus does not identify justice with a particular knowledge but with nobility (the courageous soldier) and decency (the honest businessman).[24] And yet, if justice is identified with nobility and decency, it does not appear to be worth defending without qualification, as Polemarchus is trying to do. Nobility and decency are not always good for an individual, as reflection on Polemarchus' own examples of war and business indicate.

Socrates pushes Polemarchus' statements about justice to absurd conclusions by continuing to assume that justice is a kind of knowledge separate from all the other kinds of knowledge. In what partnership is justice useful? he asks. In partnerships for buying or selling horses, for example, an expert on horses is most useful. Or when the concern is ships, a shipbuilder or pilot is most useful. Polemarchus again fails to reply that regardless of the particular concern, one needs a just partner—a just horseman, a just shipbuilder, or a just pilot. Allowing that experts are most useful when money is put to use, he claims that the just man is most useful when money must be kept safe. Although he is still assuming that justice is honesty—not his skill in guarding but the fact that the just man will not steal makes him useful when money must be kept safe—he nevertheless goes along with Socrates' attempt to isolate justice from the other arts and occupations. His answer allows Socrates to conclude that justice is useful when things are merely to be guarded, or when they are useless, but it is useless when things are to be used. Justice, pure and independent of the other arts, turns out to be irrelevant for use or action.

Even worse, if justice is indeed an art and the just man is the best guardian, justice also turns out to be vicious. As Socrates observes, the man best able to ward off a blow is also best able to inflict one. By the same logic, the best guardian, the just man, would be the best thief. The man who appeared useless because of his lack of knowledge of anything in particular, by a clever turn of the argument becomes a man able to succeed in all kinds of thievery. As the best thief, he can make everything his own. Justice as art necessarily leads to just acts no more than knowledge of guarding prevents a man from stealing.

Socrates has thus moved from one undesirable conception of justice—it is useless in every specific endeavor—to an opposite, equally undesirable, conception—its utility in every endeavor gives it the potential for universal thievery. Socrates' facility in speech has thus made justice move from one pole to another. As much as Polemarchus tries to do so, Socrates will not let him pin justice down. His arguments have produced a parody of justice's necessary flexibility and mocked Polemarchus' attempt to limit justice to a definition that is universally valid. Only such a definition will satisfy his desire for something permanent and secure by which he may direct his actions. Although Polemarchus is confused, he still maintains his original position while rejecting Socrates' conclusions. Socrates has not persuaded him.[25] He swears by Zeus that justice is no art of stealing. Although he no longer knows what he means, it is still his opinion, he affirms, "that justice is helping friends and injuring enemies" (334b). Throughout the twists of the argument, which he surely does not follow, he has held on to his definition, just as he wants a single standard to hold onto through the vicissitudes and changing conditions of life.

Because Polemarchus will not give up his definition of justice in spite of his inability to give a reasonable explanation of it, the discussion is at a standstill. Socrates proceeds to show the consequences of seeking the justice that Polemarchus desires. He changes the focus of the conversation by turning to the meaning of friendship. Polemarchus admits that a man chooses as his friends those who appear good to him, rather than those who are, in fact, good. But, as Socrates observes, all men make mistakes in judging others (334c). When the just man benefits his friends, should he be mistaken about their goodness, he would help those who are not good and who therefore don't deserve to be helped. And should he be mistaken in his judgment of his enemies, he would harm good men (334c–e). Polemarchus, however, denies this conclusion, refusing to accept the possibility that there is anything imperfect about justice. Instead, he modifies his conception of friendship so that the unacceptable conclusion does not follow. A friend, he now maintains, is one who both seems good and is good (334e–335a). He is not one whom a man loves according to his imperfect lights, but the one who is truly worthy of love and can be recognized as such. Polemarchus seems to have given up his friends for the sake of the purity of justice. He has certainly accepted an argument that causes men to doubt their friends and to hesitate benefitting them. He may be the fitting man to compel the *Republic's* discussion, in which Socrates constructs a city that compels men to deny friendship in the name of justice.[26]

In the next stage of the discussion, Socrates refines Polemarchus' desire for a perfect justice even further by leading him to conclude that the just man harms no one at all. When someone is harmed, Socrates argues, he becomes worse with respect to his own proper virtue; since justice is human virtue, to injure a man is to make him more unjust; but justice cannot produce injustice, no more than a musician can make men unmusical through his use of music. The just man, therefore, cannot injure anyone (335b–e). Socrates' argument assumes that good can produce only good. The harsh realities that plagued the discussion earlier are now forgotten. Socrates ignores, for example, the possibility that the man most knowledgeable in music is best able to destroy others' appreciation of music and that a doctor might use his knowledge of health to produce disease. The argument now forgets that the same thing, depending on a variety of factors, can produce opposite results. In other words, the argument forgets about complexity in order to reach the result that nothing bad can come from something good, hence, that the just man can injure no one.

In arguing that the just man can injure no one, Socrates has purged the just man of imperfect actions, just as he has freed him from imperfect friends. This perfect being, however, could not be a good citizen. A city is based on the distinction between citizen and stranger, and the preference it gives to its own often necessitates depriving strangers. Political actions that benefit some often harm others. Indeed, Polemarchus sensed this very thing when he supposed that justice was benefitting friends and harming enemies. At the very least, Socrates' argument that the just man harms no one implies that he does not go to war in defense of his city.[27] Polemarchus nevertheless does not hesitate to accept the conclusion that the just man injures no one, for it indicates the perfect goodness of justice. Since political communities harm as well as benefit, just as friends have vices as well as virtues, these arguments Polemarchus accepts lead to the destruction of friendship and politics as they appear in the world.

The drama of the *Republic* may be contrasted with that of the *Clouds*. In Aristophanes' play, it was primarily Socrates' desire for perfection—for a universal and permanent knowledge which freed him from the complexities and flux of ordinary life—that undermined politics and families. It was philosophy that encouraged such desires in ordinary men such as Strepsiades and Phidippides by making them think that such knowledge and freedom are possible and good. Plato shows in reply that ordinary men represented by another father and son, Cephalus and Polemarchus, want unchanging standards by which they can direct their lives. The impetus toward perfection and permanence comes not primarily from philosophy but from the ordinary life that Aristophanes defended, not from the denial of justice but from the pursuit of absolute justice. Moved by such a desire, Polemarchus accepts arguments that undermine friendship and politics and, in general, the experience on which his father built his life, just as Phidippides with his newly acquired knowledge finally attacks his father's deepest beliefs—the sacred assumptions which support families and political communities. Whereas Phidippides' attack stems from the teaching of the Socratics, Polemarchus' attraction to those arguments that undermine friendship and politics stems from his desire for a perfect and unchanging justice. Again in reply to Aristophanes, Plato shows through Socrates' treatment of Polemarchus that it is the philosopher who insists on change and flexibility as inevitable characteristics of human life. It is the philosopher who indicates the extreme to which Polemarchus' desire for absolute leads.

Socrates' Quarrel with Thrasymachus

When Socrates and Polemarchus agree to join "battle as partners" to defend the proposition that the just man injures no one, Thrasymachus interrupts. He objects to the discussion's "nonsense" and "inanities" and refers Socrates to the experience of the world. He believes that he knows what justice is—the advantage of the stronger, who are the men who rule cities in their own interest. He, too, like Polemarchus, seeks perfection, but he locates it in a man's knowledge of his own good and his ability to get the better of others in order to obtain it. The man most able to do this, he believes, is the tyrant who "by stealth and force takes away what belongs to others" (344a). Justice is obeying the laws of the self-interested ruler; it is, therefore, someone else's good.

Thrasymachus at first objects more to Socrates' mode of asking questions than to the specific points Socrates has made. He disdains "that habitual irony of Socrates." He had suspected "that [Socrates] wouldn't be willing to answer, that [he] would be ironic and do anything rather than answer if someone asked [him] something" (337a). Thrasymachus admires someone who has a position and defends it. It must seem to him that there is something unmanly or weak about a person who claims to be ignorant and who explores a variety of opinions without coming to a satisfactory conclusion. Without opinions or positions of his own, such a man would seem to lack strength or substance. Thrasymachus deplores Socrates' tendency to change from one opinion to another as the argument develops. Whereas Thrasymachus admires the tyrant who makes everything in the city his own, the man who questions without having answers or who constantly changes his position appears to have nothing of his own. Like Polemarchus, Thrasymachus dislikes change. The permanence Thrasymachus seeks lies in the constancy of his knowledge. If knowledge is constant, it is certain, and it results in resolute action. Thrasymachus thus approves of the man who is sure enough of himself and his own good to act decisively to obtain it. But Socrates says he does not know what the most profitable way of life is, for that is what he is trying to discover (344e). And if a man is uncertain of what he ought to do, either he does not act or his actions are hesitant and cautious. Moreover, Thrasymachus admires not only the bold but the independent. But Socrates, Thrasymachus charges, is "unwilling himself to teach" and "goes around learning from others and does not even give thanks to them" (338b). Far from ruling or subordinating others to himself, Socrates is dependent on others and, according to Thrasymachus, does not even acknowledge his dependence. Thrasymachus is indignant at what he has just witnessed.

Because Thrasymachus cannot compel Socrates to answer, he has the opportunity to do what he is eager to do anyway, which is to state his own opinion about justice. But he insists that, if he can provide a good answer about justice, Socrates should pay a penalty—a sum of money to Thrasymachus (337d). Thrasymachus offers to speak, therefore, for a number of reasons. He desires to receive money for it, but he also obviously desires to get the better of Socrates in argument. He loves victory, as well as gain. And his victory might win him reputation and students from among the young men present (345a). Moreover, his disdain for the argument's "inanities" reveals a desire for precision, for clarity, for calling things by their proper names. This man who enters the discussion, as Socrates says, "like a wild beast"

(336b), is disgusted with intellectual confusion, misperception, and blindness to the truth.[28] His many desires make him a complex man. When he first acts in the *Republic*, all his desires move him in the same direction.

Thrasymachus claims that justice is the advantage of the stronger. Do you mean the *pancratiast*, by the stronger, Socrates taunts him. In a sense Thrasymachus must mean this, regardless of the particular strength he had in mind, for *pancratiast* is literally "the one strong in all things," or "the one strong over all." Even in common usage, a *pancratiast* is not limited to only one strength, for the word designates a man who both wrestles and boxes, who combines physical might with speed. Socrates' use of a *pancratiast* as an example of strength suggests that strength might be located in complexity or comprehensiveness. The strong man may be one able to actualize a variety of human capacities, of which wrestling and boxing are only symbolic. Socrates may well wonder if Thrasymachus holds such a conception of strength, given Thrasymachus' own complexity. The possibility of such a man, however, recedes into the background in more senses than one. Thrasymachus rejects him on the literal level, indignant that Socrates can suggest that he means some athlete by the "stronger" (338d). And as Socrates and company found a city in speech, the strength of each citizen comes to reside in the possession of a single art, rather than in an actualization of a variety of potentials.

Thrasymachus means by the stronger not a *pancratiast*, he asserts, but the rulers in cities, who set down laws for their own advantage (338d–339a). He soon admits, however, that rulers sometimes make mistakes about their own advantage. The rulers' command, or justice, would then not always be to the advantage of the stronger (339c–e). Thrasymachus has contradicted himself. One of the men present tries to help Thrasymachus avoid this contradiction by claiming that justice is simply what appears to the ruler to be to his own advantage (340b). But Thrasymachus immediately refuses to accept this qualification. He admires knowledge and competence too much for that. He will not attribute strength to an ignorant or a mistaken man. He retracts his admission that a ruler can make a mistake about his own advantage (340c–341a). The ruler in the precise sense is the man of perfect self-knowledge. Like Polemarchus before him, Thrasymachus rejects what only seems to be so, in favor of what is the case. He retracts his statement that rulers enact what seems to be to their advantage, just as Polemarchus retracted his statement that a man's friends are those who seem good to him. But their motivations are different. Polemarchus modified his understanding of friend when Socrates showed him that it implied a defect in justice: the just man, helping his friends, might help those who seemed good but were not really so. A just action might benefit someone who didn't deserve it. Polemarchus could not accept this imperfection in the just action, while he was less concerned that a man could make a mistake in choosing his friends. This latter possibility would have seemed more disgusting to Thrasymachus, for he disdains stupidity. He rejects the idea that rulers enact merely what seems advantageous to them. The strong man, the ruler in the precise sense, knows his own good. The ruler who does not is not truly a ruler.

Socrates proceeds to show that the artisan in the precise sense cares for the ruled, or those with whom his art is concerned. Medicine considers the good of the sick patient, rather than that of the doctor. Horsemanship is directed to the care and the good of horses, rather than to that of the man possessing the art (342c). And so, no one who is a ruler in the precise sense "considers or commands his own advantage rather than that of what is ruled" (342e). The ruler in the precise sense is therefore selfless, as are all knowers qua knowers: "There is no kind of knowledge that considers or commands the advantage of the stronger, but rather of what is weaker and ruled by it" (342c). The knower does not dominate others, as Thrasymachus thought; rather, he serves them.

Socrates' presentation of the selfless artisan evokes a violent outburst from Thrasymachus, who asserts again that the man who understands the most about life will pursue "perfect injustice" (343a–344e). His ideal is a self-interested man of knowledge, whom he himself tries to resemble. He is engaging in the present discussion, for example, because he knows the meaning of justice and the ways of the world and because he is vigorously pursuing his advantage in seeking money, students, and victory. Since knowledge and his selfish pursuit of his own good are mutually supportive, he is self-confident and bold. Socrates' argument about art, however, shows that knowledge subordinates the knower to other men and does not lead to their subordination to him. Socrates attacks not merely one of Thrasymachus' fundamental beliefs but the union of elements that make Thrasymachus what he is. It is this union that allows Thrasymachus' resolute action.

The heat of the argument with Thrasymachus is relieved momentarily by Socrates' explanation of one of the consequences of the selflessness of art—artisans must be paid for their services. It is precisely because they serve others rather than themselves through their arts that they must be given wages for practicing their arts. Socrates thus concedes to Thrasymachus that men are selfish even while maintaining the selflessness of art. Although men may serve others through their art, as moneymakers they would compete with one another for their own advancement. In this Socrates agrees with Thrasymachus, except that he denies that knowledge can be the ground of that self-interested competition. The possibility that the moneymaker has knowledge of his own good—money, and the goods it can buy—does not arise. Moreover, since men are both selfish moneymakers and selfless artisans, there would be a potential conflict within individuals themselves.[29] Socrates emphasizes the dividedness of man throughout the remaining conversation with Thrasymachus, for he demonstrates that the qualities which Thrasymachus most desires and admires are contradictory. It is the unjust man, Socrates will argue, who is ignorant, weak, and unhappy. Thrasymachus' admiration of injustice, domination, and even tyranny, the argument implies, is inconsistent with his desire for knowledge, strength, and happiness.

When Socrates tricks Thrasymachus into placing justice in the class of art, prudence, and wisdom, and injustice among their opposites (348d), Thrasymachus blushes.[30] From this point, he is tamed, and Socrates is able to lead him around. Thrasymachus still maintains that he could give a long speech in support of his position, but, if Socrates keeps questioning, he will merely say "all right" and "nod and shake [his] head . . . to satisfy [Socrates]" (350e). He is obviously disturbed. Socrates has consistently emphasized the split between knowledge and self-interest, first through his description of the selfless artisan and now through an argument that the just man who serves others resembles the man of knowledge. If Thrasymachus is as knowledgeable as he would like to be, he cannot also be as selfish as he would like to be. But these two desires or characteristics make Thrasymachus what he is, and their coherence allows him to act. He is "tamed": Socrates has made him weak and ineffective by casting doubts on the coherence of his deepest beliefs. Socrates has undermined his unity and therefore the ground of his action.[31]

It is therefore appropriate that at this point Socrates argues that the unjust man does not possess the internal harmony necessary for action. Just as an unjust city—in which citizens act unjustly to one another—"would [not] be able to accomplish anything" (351c), so an unjust man would be "unable to act, because he is torn by faction and not of one mind with himself" (352a). Injustice therefore enfeebles men and cities, while justice, which brings harmony to both cities and individuals, makes them powerful.[32] By introducing this analogy between the city and the individual, Socrates contradicts Thrasymachus' experience of the power of injustice. Had Thrasymachus defended that experience and adhered to his original position, he might have argued that because just deeds are detrimental to a man's good, it is the just man who is torn—between his justice and his self-interest—and therefore incapable of action. Conversely, because unjust deeds are to a man's advantage, an unjust man, in contrast, suffers no internal conflict and is consequently capable of decisive action. Thrasymachus, however, is no longer inclined to defend his experience by argument. Socrates has presumably shaken his confidence in his ability to do so. Let the argument stand that injustice weakens a man, Thrasymachus says, as if his words do not have his full support (351e). He is at odds with himself, both agreeing and not agreeing at the same time. He has lost his vigor, his decisiveness, and his self-assurance.

Socrates concludes his refutation of Thrasymachus by asserting that justice is the virtue of the soul. As the virtue of the soul, that by which the soul does its work well, justice must be good and the cause of happiness (353b–354a). Although it is extraneous to the argument, Socrates describes two kinds of work or two functions that the soul performs: first, the soul manages, rules, deliberates, and all such things; and second, the work of the soul is living (353d). Socrates concludes with an argument that gratuitously reveals a duality in man. If the soul has two works and if virtue is defined as that by which a work is well done, the soul must have two virtues. Socrates nevertheless assumes that the soul has only one virtue, designating it as justice. This final argument with Thrasymachus thinly masks the complexity of man. The unity that man seeks apparently can be had only through an activity that comprehends the soul's diverse functions. The rest of the *Republic* explores the extent to which politics can do this very thing.

The Task of Political Philosophy

The discussions about justice in Book I of the *Republic* reveal various tensions or conflicts in human life that stand in the way of the unity or perfection that men seek. Even the setting itself, the activities taking place in the Piraeus, intimate the decline of a political community and a disjunction between man's intellectual development and his political life. Cephalus soon suggests an opposition between life and thought, for when he was in the prime of life, his desires kept him from the pleasures of speech. But even when old, Cephalus does not stay to discuss; his concern for life in the next world draws him away from the conversation. The activities relating to life do not seem conducive to thought. Because Cephalus is so concerned with life, and even near death is preparing himself for a future life, he will not bring his long experience of man's conflicting desires to bear on the discussion.

Socrates must therefore search for the meaning of justice with Cephalus' heir, Polemarchus, a man devoted to justice and ready to maintain its value regardless of what the argument concludes. Lacking his father's experience, he is not aware of the difficulties of attaining the perfection he seeks. Attempting to give a formula or definition of justice that is universally applicable and to save justice from the undesirable consequences implied in his father's conception, he claims that justice is helping friends and harming enemies. He has difficulty, however, in specifying the particular area in which justice is manifest and the kind of knowledge that the just man possesses. When justice is conceived of merely as knowledge, it does not seem to result in the good acts that Polemarchus associates with justice. Socrates finally shows that for Polemarchus to have a justice to which he may be completely devoted, he must give up his friends and political community for its sake.

Thrasymachus' ideal is the man who knows his own good and acts decisively to obtain it. Given the imperfect world of conflicting interests, this will be the unjust man who pursues his own interests by harming others. Thrasymachus thus reacts to the conflict that he experiences by presupposing the possibility that a man can attain a perfect knowledge of his own good and that his action can be in perfect harmony with his knowledge. He denies the conflict between activity and the pursuit of knowledge, which Cephalus admitted, and the difficulty in joining knowledge to activity, which frustrated Polemarchus' attempt to define justice. Socrates again reveals the problem with the harmony his interlocutor seeks, now arguing that knowledge is selfless or directed toward the good of others rather than that of the knower.

Socrates admits that an artisan is not only a knower and caretaker of the good of others but also a self-interested wage earner. Man himself is torn like Thrasymachus, who admires both the ruthlessness of the tyrant and the competence of the knower. Socrates' final argument against Thrasymachus asserts that man's soul has two separate functions. As suggested throughout Book I, man is in a state of potential conflict and thus in need of some unifying principle. Socrates now calls this principle justice, which he claims is the virtue of the soul. He does not explain, however, how man's two functions can share the same virtue. It is not even clear whether justice integrates in some unexplained way the various elements in man or whether Socrates is hiding the conflict in man under the cloak of justice.

In spite of Socrates' final statement that justice is the virtue of the soul, Book I as a whole is inconclusive. Although Socrates has "proven" that justice is wise, mighty, and the cause of happiness, he admits that he has shown only what justice is like and not what justice is, "so that as a result of the discussion I know nothing" (345b). The argument has not arrived at any understanding of justice on the basis of which men can live. The disproportion between discussion or thought and life or action remains. The stage is set for the founding of the city in speech, which attempts to overcome that disproportion.

In Book I, Plato presents in another form the problem portrayed in the *Clouds*, in which Aristophanes criticizes thought for being divorced from life and even for undermining life. Aristophanes' Socrates spends his time contemplating the heavens; consequently, he is unaware of the limitations inherent in human life and teaches a rhetoric that purports to free men from those limitations. He seeks a universally valid and permanent truth but, as a result, wreaks great havoc. Moreover, he seems oblivious to the harm that he causes. Plato, in contrast, shows that philosophy is aware of the dangers of thought and examines this problem in his dialogues. Plato's Socrates reflects upon himself, as Aristophanes' Socrates never did. And although Socrates sees that the desire for perfection and permanence underlies much of previous Greek philosophy,[33] he also finds that it is one of the primary motivations of politics. This desire leads men to forget or deny the necessary complexity and conflict of life in order to attain a state of perfect harmony and peace. This very forgetting, we shall see, results in the tyranny of the city in speech and that city's forcing philosophy into its service. It is Socrates who reminds men of what they desire to forget—the imperfections of their activity and knowledge. We have seen in Book I, for example, that Socrates continually suggests the limits of man's reason, as well as the limits of his experience. And we shall see that after Socrates describes the perfectly good city, he insists on looking at the decline of regimes and the conflicting passions in the human soul that make perfection on the political level impossible. Moreover, Socrates emphasizes the incompleteness of his own knowledge. He admits that he knows nothing at the end of Book I. Similarly, at the end of the *Republic* when he is completing his defense of the simple goodness of justice, he confesses that they have not yet seen the "true nature" of the soul. They have only "gone through its affections and forms in this life," where the soul is distorted by its union with body (611b–612a). The complexity of man, his combination of body and soul, makes perfect knowledge impossible, just as it makes impossible any perfect ordering of political life. The Socratic political philosophy that Plato presents pursues knowledge and order without losing sight of man's complexity and the limitations implied in that complexity. Political philosophy is the Platonic alternative to a philosophy blind to that complexity, a philosophy that finds unity either in the peaceful contemplation of the heavens or in political action culminating in tyranny.

Chapter 2

Justice in the City and the Soul (Books II–IV of the *Republic*)

Introduction

When Glaucon and Adeimantus ask Socrates to show them that justice is good in itself, Socrates proposes that they look for justice in the city before they try to find it in the individual. Once they find justice in the city, it will be easier to see it in the individual, for the city is the individual writ large. The three of them found a city in speech, with Socrates describing its principles and institutions, and Glaucon and Adeimantus offering suggestions and asking questions. The end of the city is unity, especially for its soldier class, whose members must believe that they have no interest distinct from the city's. To this end, the city gives them a strict education, banning any poetry that strengthens their sense of their separate or private lives. The city also establishes communism of property for its soldiers, thereby depriving them of the external goods that distinguish them from others. Through such means the city tries to give its soldiers a sense of wholeness and completeness, so that they remain satisfied citizens and do not need to look outside of politics for their fulfillment. Life in the city will be secure, unchanging, and apparently complete. Socrates defines justice as each part of the city doing its one job that determines its place in the city and contributes to the good of the whole.

After Socrates completes his description of this "perfectly good" city (427e), he draws a parallel between it and the soul in order to

57

locate justice in the individual. Justice in the soul, as in the city, is each part's doing its proper job, which contributes to the smooth functioning of the whole. Each part of the soul, like each part of the city, minds its own business. As the harmony of the soul, justice is good in itself, regardless of any consequences. Socrates has proven the desirability of justice, since it is the virtue that guarantees a man's internal harmony. The man who possesses this internal harmony in his soul, the just man, Socrates maintains further, will be just by all "vulgar standards." If "each of the parts in him minds its own business," Socrates explains, the just man will not filch gold or silver, betray his agreements, or fail to care for his parents or the gods (442e–443b). That a man refrains from these deeds, unjust by conventional standards, is obviously good for a city. The good of the individual, his internal harmony, is therefore completely compatible with the good of a city.

The city that the *Republic* presents, however, is plagued with difficulties. We shall see that it is primarily Glaucon who is the driving force behind this search for perfect goodness, which necessitates a harmony between man's individual or private good and his communal life. His brother, Adeimantus, acts as a foil, raising objections to provisions that Socrates and Glaucon lay down. One of his most important questions is whether the communism of property, so necessary to the city's unity and happiness, does not prevent the individual on whom it is imposed from being happy. He explicitly questions whether what is good for the city is also good for the individual, and Socrates fails to give a satisfactory response. In general, Adeimantus is concerned with the private pleasures of men that the city appears to eliminate. His concerns suggest that the city is actually tyrannical, in that it takes from its member everything he has or treats him as if he has no integrity that constitutes a limit to what it might do. Moreover, in order to maintain the harmony between the individual's good and the city's, Socrates must ignore the tensions and the conflicts that emerged in the discussion in Book I. That earlier discussion indicated the disharmony rather than the harmony among the goods men seek. We saw a possible conflict, for example, between a man's own good and the good of others. By ignoring the results of the earlier discussion and by maintaining the simple goodness of justice, Socrates has adopted the perspective of the city, which assumes an identity between its good and that of its members in order to demand their absolute loyalty. Such a perfect harmony between the individual and the city will satisfy Glaucon's desire for perfection, which is the impetus behind the founding of the city.

To eliminate the conflict between the city and the individual, the city must weaken men's attachment to their particular relatives and friends, which it does through its education in music. Its noble lie further weakens the bond between a man and his parents by teaching that all the men in the city owe their birth and nurture to the same mother, the earth. The communism of property finally removes one of the strongest supports for a man's private or separate existence. In all these ways, the city removes man from the ordinary human life that Aristophanes defended. It leads him to an abstract existence, in which he is related only to the whole city. This tendency can be seen not only in the provisions of the city in speech but also in Socrates' defense of justice as absolutely good. That defense requires Socrates to locate justice in the soul—as the internal harmony of its parts. Such a definition stands in contrast to a definition of justice which locates justice in the proper relations among men and which therefore necessitates their involvement with others. According to Socrates, when the parts of the soul each do their own jobs, men do their own jobs in the city. By concentrating solely on their own business, the members of the city contribute to the functioning of the city as a whole. They are, in effect, removed from any interactions and relationships with particular individuals so that they can become merely members of the city. They lead abstract lives. Plato thus shows that the abstract existence that Aristophanes attributed to philosophy is actually a result of an unqualified defense of justice and political life, a defense that denies the conflict between the individual and the city.

Glaucon and Adeimantus

Although his discussion with Thrasymachus has not shown him what justice is, Socrates thinks that he is "freed from argument." But Glaucon, "most courageous in everything," demands more from Socrates. Socrates needs better arguments, Glaucon says, if he is "to truly persuade us" that justice is good (357a). Glaucon is "at a loss," for "countless" men have told him of the advantages of injustice, but he has yet to hear an argument on behalf of justice that satisfies him (358b–d). He would like to hear such an argument from Socrates. Specifically, he wants Socrates to show that justice is good in itself, not because of its consequences. A just man, for example, might acquire a good reputation, but this benefit that comes from justice does not prove that justice is good in itself. Glaucon asks Socrates to reveal what justice is and "what power it has all alone by itself when it is in the soul—dismissing its wages and its consequences" (358b). Glaucon, in effect, desires Socrates to isolate justice from the world in which it can be seen, since in the world all actions, including just and unjust ones, have consequences. Actions are related to other past actions, which they must take into account as limitations, and to future events, which they may take into account as possibilities. Glaucon seeks to isolate justice from the context of the actions and events in which justice is visible. He wants to look below the surface, or beyond the appearances, into the soul, in order to see something pure, or simple, unmixed with the complexity of relationships that characterize human life. He seems ready to dismiss the world, with its multiplicity of appearances, just as he is ready to dismiss the opinions of countless men if he can hear from Socrates the one argument that satisfies him.

Glaucon's desire for something simply good underlies his desire for simplicity. He is ready to reject the world because he cannot find what is simply good there. Although he asks Socrates to show the power of justice apart from its consequences, he accepts Socrates' opinion that "the finest kind" of good is one that we desire both "for its own sake and for what comes out of it" (357c–358a). He wishes that justice were such a good, but he has heard opinions to the contrary. In particular, the opinion that justice is drudgery but beneficial to us because of its consequences is among the ones he wants refuted. If that opinion were true, justice would be a mixture of good and bad. Moreover, he fears that justice does not even have good consequences. Although the reputation for justice is beneficial, it does not necessarily follow from justice. In fact, the unjust man might be able to acquire a reputation for justice more easily than the just man (360e–362c). Desiring perfect goodness, Glaucon is repelled by a world in which the just man suffers and the unjust man prospers. Glaucon is therefore ready to reject the world of action, as long as he perceives that good acts have undesirable consequences. He wishes that the world were one where good acts do have good consequences, or that "the finest kind" of good existed. He would be attracted both by the philosopher-kings' escape from the cave to a world of perfect beings and by their reentrance into the cave in order to transform it into an image of those perfect beings (540b).[1]

In order to hear the praise of justice he desires, Galucon offers to praise injustice so that Socrates can refute him. He begins with an account of the origins of civil society. Men realized that although they profited from doing injustice to others, they suffered more from the injustice that others did to them. They therefore agreed not to do injustice so that they would not have to suffer it. The laws supporting this agreement and preventing injustice are called just. Glaucon thus arrives at "the genesis and being of justice." It is, he says, "a mean between what is best—doing injustice without paying the penalty— and what is worst—suffering injustice without being able to avenge oneself" (359a). Justice therefore benefits the weak, who band together to compel the strong to obey their laws. The justice that Glaucon is now deprecating is a mixture of good and ill: justice is good for a man because the law prevents others from getting the better of him, but it is bad for him because he is prevented from getting the better of others. The disadvantages of justice that Glaucon describes accompany its advantages. The situation is different for the unjust man, the one "truly a man" (359b), who is "courageous and strong" (361b). He does not have to depend on the law for protection from others, nor is he prevented by law from doing injustice to others. Glaucon has found his unmixed good in injustice. No disadvantages are attached to the actions of the unjust man. Although Glaucon's praise of injustice is "not at all [his] own opinion," it reveals what he longs for. In order to praise injustice, he describes it as unmixed good.

If the just man has license to do injustice, Glaucon continues, he will do so. He is just only because he has no choice. Glaucon tells the story of an ancestor of Gyges, as an example of a man who chances upon the opportunity to do whatever he likes. In the midst of an earthquake, a chasm opens in the earth. In the chasm, the hero of the tale finds a hollow, bronze horse within which there is a naked corpse, larger than human size (359d). He steals a ring from the corpse's finger and later discovers that the ring permits him to become invisible. With the help of the ring, he commits adultery with the queen, kills the king, and seizes the throne (360a–b).[2]

Glaucon's story is an adaptation of one told by Herodotus. In Herodotus' tale, the king forces his servant Gyges to view his wife naked in order to fully see her beauty. Gyges at first resists, for, as he says, a man should look "upon his own."[3] The queen, when she discovers what has been done, is appalled that her privacy has been violated. She enlists Gyges' aid in revenging herself upon her husband. This original story of Gyges therefore involves the sanctity of an individual's privacy and even teaches that privacy cannot be violated without disastrous results. Glaucon's story, in contrast, ignores such issues. His hero violates an individual's privacy by looking upon his naked corpse and even robbing it. But Glaucon does not question this violation of privacy; in fact, it is his hero's means to success and even to further violations of privacy. The magic ring, making him invisible, allows him to be present during the private conversations of others (359e–360a). Finally, as tyrant in the city, he takes from others whatever he likes. Glaucon's story thus revises the one Herodotus tells, for it eliminates any suggestion that the privacy of others should serve as limits upon a man's actions. In this, Glaucon's story foreshadows the city in speech: like Glaucon's unjust man, the just city eliminates privacy.

The actions of the hero of his tale, Glaucon contends, are those that anyone, whether just or unjust, would perform if given the opportunity (360b). If we could see the hidden desires of even the man who appears just, Glaucon says, we would see a man who craves the power of a tyrant. Glaucon is like his hero in attempting to see into the desires and intentions of men that ordinarily remain hidden from sight. A ring that makes its wearer invisible appeals to him not so much because he wants to remain hidden from others but because he wants nothing to remain hidden from himself. A communistic city in which men have no private lives and which presupposes that nature places no limits on what men can know of one another would therefore appeal to him. One of the blessings of injustice which Glaucon enumerates near the end of his speech is that the unjust man will probably be dearer to the gods than the just man, since he can make magnificent sacrifices and votive offerings to the gods (362c). Glaucon's reference to sacrifices suggests nothing of Cephalus' fear of divine punishment or the subservience that comes from fear. Rather Glaucon would like to find a way to guarantee the gods' friendship. If there were a way to do this, he could understand and control even the gods. Glaucon would like everything to fall within his knowledge and power. He resembles the tyrant who makes everything in his city his own. Neither allows anything to remain private, unknowable, or alien.

Glaucon concludes his speech with sketches of an absolutely just man who suffers miserably because he is believed to be unjust and of an absolutely unjust man who prospers because he has acquired a reputation for justice. His sketches assume that men can appear completely different from the way they are, or that there can be an absolute disjunction between truth and appearance. Nettleship makes the sensible point that what Glaucon imagines is impossible: "the appearances and the reality of justice cannot be kept separate throughout every part of life"; and the "consistently unjust man must somewhere drop the appearance of justice, and the man who consistently maintains the appearance cannot always escape the reality."[4] Socrates himself may suggest that Glaucon's portraits have an unreal finish when he observes that Glaucon is polishing the just and unjust men as if they were statues (361d). Although Glaucon's sketches may portray what is impossible, they confirm our interpretation of his character. His presentation of a radical disjunction between reality and appearance is based on his belief that appearances hide the truth and implies a contempt for the world as it appears to men. Moreover, if the unjust man can manipulate appearances so greatly that he appears just, a remaking of the world might be possible.

Glaucon's desire for perfection is therefore deeper than the desires we saw in Polemarchus and Thrasymachus. Like Polemarchus, he seeks a perfect justice, but he is much more aware of the difficulties involved in finding what he desires. He has heard countless opinions that imply that justice is not good in itself, as well as others that claim that it has bad consequences for men. Moreover, he has observed the harsh facts of the world that suggest that nothing simply good can exist. He would like, therefore, to find a way to deny the opinions he has heard and the experience he has had. He would like to find a reality unknown to the opinions that sadden him and irrelevant to the appearances he perceives. Not sharing Polemarchus' naive assurance that there is an unchanging standard by which he can guide his life, he all the more intensely desires such a standard. He is harder to satisfy than Polemarchus.

Nor is Glaucon as easily satisfied as Thrasymachus. Thrasymachus accepts the experience he has of the world and the conflict he perceives. He is content with successfully manipulating that conflict in his own interest. Although Glaucon may be tempted by such manipulation, it is finally unacceptable to him, for it concedes the impossibility of the perfect goodness he longs for. He does not want to perfectly manipulate experience as much as to purge experience of its imperfections. Although he resembles Thrasymachus in longing for a perfect knowledge of his own good, he believes he cannot know his own good without also knowing what lies at the bottom of things. He therefore believes that knowledge of one's own good is more complicated than Thrasymachus thinks, just as he knows that perfect justice is more problematic than Polemarchus supposes. Consequently, at the same time that he possesses Polemarchus' desire for perfect justice and Thrasymachus' desire for perfect knowledge, he doubts that these desires can be satisfied.

Glaucon's brother Adeimantus finds Glaucon's praise of injustice inadequate and undertakes to complement it with a speech of his own. Although he echoes Glaucon's request to see justice stripped of its consequences and to understand the truth of things rather than their appearances, there is a different emphasis in his speech. Glaucon's speech, as we have seen, consists primarily of a story of the origin of justice, a revision of a tale from Herodotus, and sketches of perfectly unjust and perfectly just men who have reputations for being exactly opposite of what they are. His speech is creative and original. Adeimantus' speech, in contrast, is primarily a discussion of the opinions he has heard. Far from merely accepting those opinions, however, he analyzes them in order to see their implications. His analysis is his own. His intelligence and his inclinations lie in a different direction from his brother's. Rather than strike out on his own, he stays closer to common opinion but, consequently, can analyze it with more care than Glaucon.

Specifically, Adeimantus is troubled by those who praise justice for its rewards (363a). By doing so, they imply that justice is not good in itself. Glaucon, in contrast, is troubled by more radical but less subtle depreciations of justice—the simple praises of injustice that he hears (cf. 361e and 363e). And yet Glaucon is ready to dismiss these countless opinions that worry him (358c–d), unlike his less extreme brother. Similarly, Adeimantus appears to admire the self-sufficient man less than Glaucon does. He is more concerned with the lives of others, especially the effects their opinions have. He laments, for example, what the popular sayings about justice "do to the souls of the young men who hear them" (365a).

Moreover, Adeimantus is interested in the consequences of justice in that he would like them to be pleasant. We can see what he values from what he remembers to have heard men praise as the rewards the gods give to the just. He mentions primarily private pleasures— the produce of the earth in abundance, sheep laden with wool, and a tribe of descendants. He even mentions one poet who makes it seem that the reward of the just is "an eternal drunk" (363b–d). Adeimantus differs from his brother in being more interested in private happiness than in ruling.[5]

Another thing which Adeimantus hears which troubles him is that justice is noble but "hard and full of drudgery," while injustice is "sweet and easy to acquire" (364a). He quotes Hesiod's verse that the road to virtue is long, rough, and steep (364d). When Glaucon complained that justice was said to be drudgery, he disliked the implication that justice resembled medicine and therefore was not to be chosen for its own sake (357c–d). He was not repelled by drudgery so much as the thought that what he was working to achieve with so much difficulty was not simply good. He is a tougher man than his brother. He wants to see the goodness of justice even though the just man suffers tremendously for it (361b–c). For Adeimantus, in contrast, justice cannot be good if the just man suffers greatly. He wants what is easy and pleasant. Even when he argues that one should do injustice and try to get away with it, he seeks ways to make it easier to do so: "We'll organize secret societies and clubs, and learn rhetoric from teachers of persuasion" (365d). While Glaucon praises injustice by presenting it as a good unmixed with evil, Adeimantus praises injustice by arguing that it is easier, more pleasant than justice.

Adeimantus seems much more ready to accept the limitations against which Glaucon rebels. He takes more seriously than Glaucon the opinions of men and, unlike Glaucon, even shows a concern for the welfare of others. Moreover, he reveals a desire for ease and pleasure that plays little role in Glaucon's character. Glaucon loves perfection too much to accept limits, whether they are imposed by others or come from himself. Adeimantus shows no signs of desiring the self-sufficiency that attracts Glaucon, who describes the almost absolute control which the perfectly unjust man achieves in the city (362a–c). Not surprisingly, Adeimantus is able to sympathize with other men and their weaknesses: he imagines a man who knows that justice is best and who consequently "has great sympathy for the unjust and is not angry with them" (366c).[6] Given these tendencies of Adeimantus, it is not clear whether, when he seconds his brother's demand to see justice apart from its consequences, he is acting out of his own concerns or following the lead of his bolder and more striking brother.

The rest of the *Republic* constitutes Socrates' answer to the charges of these two men. Socrates speaks with one and then the other as different topics attract them into the conversation. Plato gives us a fuller view of their characters as the dialogue proceeds, although the differences that emerge even in these first speeches help us to understand their objections to some of Socrates' proposals, as well as their ready acceptance of others. As we shall see, just as Glaucon is the first to ask that the discussion continue, he gives the discussion its direction. The satisfaction of his desires requires the extremes which the just city represents. Adeimantus, on the other hand, acts as a foil. Just as his own praise of injustice brought up considerations that Glaucon's speech omitted, his discontent with the city's communism reveals the ultimate incompleteness of political life and the price that absolute justice demands of men.[7]

The City of Pigs and Its Deficiencies

After Glaucon and Adeimantus speak in praise of injustice, Socrates agrees to succor justice as best he can. He offers first to investigate justice in a city rather than in a man, for in the larger entity justice may be easier to see. Socrates' move to examine a city is at first surprising: since he had been asked to show justice all alone by itself, apart from the consequences, we might expect him to isolate justice in the soul rather than to describe political life. Glaucon has revealed a desire for purity and simplicity, whereas a city seems necessarily complex. But, as we have seen, Glaucon's desire for purity is a manifestation of his dissatisfaction with a world in which good cannot be separated from evil, in which the just suffer and the unjust prosper. Although Glaucon wants to escape such a world, he would also like to strip that world of its imperfections. He longs not simply for a pure soul but for a perfectly good city. Socrates' search for justice in the city will transform the world to Glaucon's liking, just as it makes a normally complex entity, a city, as simple as possible. Although Socrates turns from the individual to the city, as he says, for the sake of viewing a larger picture, it is only a larger picture that can satisfy the thirst for perfection. Ultimately that larger picture will include not merely a political community but a cosmos as well.

Socrates begins his description of the city by observing that it comes into being "because each of us isn't self-sufficient but is in need of much" (369b). One man provides one of the necessities, and other men provide others. A man should not neglect the others, Socrates says, and "produce a fourth part of the food in a fourth part of the time and use the other three parts for the provision of a house, clothing, and shoes, not taking the trouble to share in common with others, but minding his own business for himself" (369e–370a). Adeimantus observes that the situation of sharing that Socrates describes is easier (370a). Socrates adds that it is also more efficient, for the man who practices only one art does "the finer job" (370b). The man who gives all his attention to one art, then, becomes a better artisan and hence a more useful member of the community. Socrates maintains further that this efficient arrangement is according to nature. "Each of us is naturally not quite like anyone else, but rather differs in his nature; different men are apt for the accomplishment of different jobs" (370a–b). Socrates thus grounds the city he is describing on the principle that each individual possesses only one job by nature. This city is based on the simplicity of individuals: a man, even potentially, is only one thing.[8]

Because men are simple by nature, they fit conveniently into the city. Although nature makes men different in giving to them the potential for different arts, she treats all equally. She favors no man more than others by giving him a potential for more than one art, nor does she disfavor any by giving him no potential for an art at all. Having the potential for only one art, a man does not have to decide which occupation or way of life is best for him. His activity cannot be a source of confusion or doubt, for he has no other options or possibilities that it precludes. While a man may deliberate about how to improve his art, he does not have to deliberate about fundamental questions. He does not have to choose his way of life, for it is provided by nature. This simplicity serves the interests of the city, since it is conducive to unity or harmony in the city. As Ernest Barker points out, if each abides within a single sphere and concentrates upon his own work, no one will come into conflict with another. Civil dissension is rendered unlikely when each has a "settled" function and a "regular place."[9]

Although the men in the city practice different arts, they are all fundamentally like one another: each aims merely at satisfying the same basic needs—food, clothing, and shelter.[10] Given the simplicity of their needs and therefore of the way of life that satisfies them, their way of life can be transmitted without change to their descendants. The members of the city will, Socrates says, "live out their lives in peace with health, and at last dying as old men, they will hand down other similar lives to their offspring" (372d). The harmony of the city renders it unchanging.

In spite of Glaucon's desire for simplicity, he is not content with this harmonious city of artisans. He objects that Socrates has described a city of pigs, who are being given feasts without relishes (372c). Although Socrates complies by giving them both relishes and desserts, Glaucon states again that they have no relishes (372d). He does not seem sure what he wants or what is missing from the city.[11] To be sure, the city of artisans differs radically from the city he described in his praise of injustice. Far from serving the common interests of its members, that city served the interests of only the weaker members of the community and was therefore potentially divisive. Socrates' account of the city of artisans substitutes an egalitarian view of men as artisans equally in need of one another for Glaucon's division of men into the weaker and the stronger. Glaucon's dissatisfaction with the city of artisans reflects his knowledge that the world is not as harmonious as Socrates describes it, that the interests of men do not coincide, and that conflict among citizens and among cities necessitates rule. Although Glaucon desires harmony and simplicity, he senses that they cannot be found in the easy way Socrates proposes.

Socrates suggests that Glaucon wants a "luxurious" or "feverish" city, possessing what goes beyond the necessities, and that the city must go to war to acquire the surplus necessary for a luxurious life (372e–373e). The city therefore needs a soldier, or guardian, class to which nature assigns the art of war. None of the men present notices that, as soon as the city must go to war, nature is found to produce men with an aptitude for fighting—a group of men who would have no place in the city of pigs. Nature conveniently produces what the city needs. This gives us grounds for suspecting that the one-man, one-art formula is not as natural as Socrates claims but that it serves the needs of the city.

Glaucon is surprised that the city will have a soldier class, for he imagined that its citizens were "adequate [for war] by themselves" (374a). They should not have to depend on others to do their fighting for them. When Socrates reminds Glaucon of the one-man, one-art principle, and also of the skills necessary for waging war, Glaucon no longer mentions the citizen army, for he is eager to discuss the character of the warriors. He similarly forgets the relishes or luxuries he introduced into the city. His interest in war indicates that he does not want relishes or luxuries because he is soft or self-indulgent. Luxuries indicate self-reliance, for a man with a superfluity of goods depends on himself rather than others to meet his needs. But self-reliance typifies even more a warrior who can defend himself and those to whom he is attached.

Although a good fighter shows the self-dependence Glaucon admires, Glaucon is not attracted to war for its own sake. He deplores a world of strife, where just men suffer and unjust ones prosper. He would find it hard to accept the chances of war that treat just and unjust, deserving and undeserving, alike. War does, however, lead to power over others, a power that might seem to its possessor to afford security from the vagaries of chance. War is for the sake of peace, and the manly Glaucon is interested in war as a means to power, control, and security.

In summary, Socrates has described a city with which Adeimantus appears content. Life in it is easy going; each man has a specific task, and his needs are provided for. Men are needy, but their needs are easily satisfied. The one-man, one-art formula upon which the city is built renders men dependent on the city, which makes exchange possible. Moreover, the formula ensures that everyone in the city has one and only one place. This is the true city, the healthy city, Socrates says. It limits the development of individuals so that everyone can benefit from a common life together. Glaucon's desire for something more than this city offers destroys its simple harmony. Socrates nevertheless tries to satisfy him. He is led by Glaucon to introduce more complicated desires and conflict into his description of political life. The "feverish" city nevertheless is an extension of the original city that Socrates and Adeimantus founded, rather than an alternative to it. We have seen that the one-man, one-art principle, by which the original city was constituted, is still applicable in the city Glaucon demands. In spite of its new perspective and concerns, that city continues to impose on its members the order it requires. Its aims remain essentially the same—peace and harmony. But due to the complex desires that Glaucon has introduced into the city, its peace and harmony, in comparison with the simple harmony of the city of pigs, will be attained with much greater effort and at much greater cost.

The Nature of the Guardians

The good guardian, Socrates says, should resemble a "noble puppy." Both need qualities useful in war—"sharp senses, speed to catch what they perceive, and, finally, strength if they have to fight it out with what they have caught" (375a). The guardian's courage, moreover, must be supported by a quality of soul that Socrates calls "spiritedness," which is "irresistable and unbeatable . . ., so that its presence makes every soul fearless and invincible in the face of everything" (375a–b). But if the guardians have such natures, which are required if they are to "fight well," Socrates wonders, "how will they not be savage to one another and the rest of the citizens?" (375b). Socrates here states the problem of the guardians' nature: how can they be both "gentle to their own and cruel to enemies," for "a gentle nature is opposed to a spirited one" (375c)? The problem thus lies in the guardians' inflexibility, for their character seems to permit only one kind of action.

Homer's portrayal of Achilles in the *Iliad* is in the background of Socrates' search for good guardians. In the first place, Homer's Achilles surpasses the other heroes as a fighter because he possesses both speed and strength—qualities which no other hero combines.[12] The military capacities of Socrates' guardians, who have both speed to catch their enemies and strength to fight it out with them, are modelled on Achilles. More important, Achilles is cruel to both strangers and his own. He illustrates the danger which Socrates says the guardians hold for the city. When his commander deprives him of the slave woman he was awarded as a prize for valor, Achilles not only refuses to fight the Trojans but he also seeks revenge upon the Achaeans. Because he thinks he is the best of the Achaeans, he feels the insult more keenly than an ordinary soldier might. He asks the gods to let the Trojans win so that the Achaeans feel his absence. The very strength that makes him so valuable to the Achaean army— his personal prowess that permits him to fight the Trojans almost single-handedly—renders Achilles independent of the army. His virtue is the source of his danger to his people, for it leads to pride. He can be cruel to his own, a threat to his army, or to his city. Socrates' search for guardians with appropriate natures must overcome the danger that a man like Achilles holds for a city.

In fearing that the guardians might turn on those whom they are supposed to guard, Socrates acknowledges the experience of the world to which Thrasymachus referred him—those who care for the sheep are the ones who devour them. But in searching for proper guardians, he is trying to find a way in which this harsh fact will not apply to his city. And he is soliciting Glaucon's help in checking this predatory element in man's nature. In this praise of injustice, Glaucon sympathized with the strong man, whose interests were opposed to the weak who founded cities. Socrates is asking Glaucon to help him discover how the strong man can be prevented from harming the weak with whom he is linked in political community.

Socrates declares that the noble puppy, with whom he originally compared the guardian, is both gentle towards its familiars and hostile towards strangers and that this proves that these opposite characteristics can coexist in the same nature. Whether the puppy is gentle or harsh to others depends on his familiarity with them. Socrates' suggestion that the guardian could resemble this simple puppy obviously ignores the more complex nature of a man like Achilles. Achilles has an awareness of his own virtues and a concomitant sense of his difference from others that a puppy would not. Achilles turned on his commander when he felt insulted by him, but the noble puppy, as Socrates says, never turns on his master, even if his master mistreats him (376a). Unlike the puppy, Achilles understands himself as independent of his familiars. He has choices to make in which his good may be distinguished from theirs; for example, he wonders whether to choose a private life and stay out of the fighting or to win immortal glory for himself by fighting the Trojans. He can imagine an alternative to his service to his army—a private life with family and friends in the country of his birth. Achilles is independent because he is not merely an Achaean. And yet, in a way, Achilles would not be Achilles if he did not fight on the side of the Achaeans. He is a tragic figure, unable to reconcile his independence from his fellow Achaeans with his similarity to them.

Socrates' comparison of the guardian to the puppy indicates the kind of men the city needs. They must be simpler men than Achilles. To guard against the dangers of a man like Achilles, the city tries to raise men who conform to its needs, who are gentle to their own and cruel to strangers. It therefore provides an education and institutions that eliminate the guardians' sense of independence from the city at the same time that it prevents them from forming bonds with relatives or friends of their own. It is such personal bonds, like Achilles' tie to his slave woman, or even to his family and friends, that pull him away from his military duties. Like the noble puppy, who identifies with only one master, the guardians must identify with their city as a whole, their familiar master to whom they are gentle, and to whose enemies they are cruel.[13]

Although the guardian might seem to be complex because he is both gentle and harsh, he is in fact simple. Like the dog to whom Socrates compares him, he reacts differently to familiars and strangers, not because he reflects on what actions are appropriate in different situations, but because he has extended his self-love to his familiars.

Both in his gentleness and his harshness, he is protecting his city against the alien. His different responses are therefore due not to a flexibility given by the understanding but to an inflexibility produced by habit or custom. Socrates even admits that the puppy, with whom he is comparing the guardian, is angry when it sees someone it doesn't know, "although it never had any bad experience with him," and greets warmly whomever it knows, "even when it never had a good experience with him" (376a).

Because the puppy, and the guardian who resembles it, react out of habit rather than understanding, it is surprising that Socrates describes them as "philosophic" (375e–376a). The puppy "distinguishes friendly from hostile looks by nothing more than by having learned the one and by being ignorant of the other." Therefore it is a philosopher, "since it defines what's its own and what's alien by knowledge and ignorance" (376b). This conception of philosophy that Socrates introduces here does not apply to Socrates himself. Socrates might indeed define his own and the alien by knowledge and ignorance, but he does not rest content with what he already knows—with what he is familiar. He does not resemble the puppy or the guardian in repelling the unknown, as if it were his enemy; rather, he is attracted to the unknown, which he is constantly trying to understand. If a man thrusts the unknown away, he never learns anything more than he already knows. If he is hostile to everything unfamiliar, he does not grow or change. Nor could he acquire new friends. Satisfied with the familiar, he would be content with what he is and what he possesses. He would think himself self-sufficient rather than perceive his incompleteness. Socrates is attributing a closed or static character to the philosopher and to the guardian he is calling philosophic. By identifying the philosopher with the spirited guardian, Socrates is presenting philosophy so that it is consistent with the requirements of the city. This philosopher is not cruel to his own city by questioning it, for example. Rather, he maintains its public orthodoxy. Socrates introduces philosophy in the *Republic* as a support for the city. The city, which forces all the manifestations of life into forms consistent with its own welfare, not only tries to reform Achilles but demands that philosophy become its servant. Just as the city will attempt to educate a guardian who does not resemble Achilles, it will eventually try to educate a philosopher who does not resemble Socrates.[14]

Socrates' treatment of philosophy is consistent with the one-man, one-art formula on which the city is built. That formula implies that human nature is closed to variety, novelty, and change. As long as a man is only one thing, with no potential for becoming anything else, then man does not change or develop, except in the limited sense of becoming more adept at a single task. If the city necessitates such stability, as is implied both by the distortion of philosophy and the one-man, one-art formula, it would have no place in it for philosophy, as embodied in the Socratic way of life.

Glaucon accepts Socrates' description of the philosopher. Desiring perfect knowledge and control, he too would be angry at the unknown or at whatever eludes his grasp. He does not pursue knowledge so much as the certainty that knowledge affords. Although the city tries to level the strong man whom Glaucon admires, it satisfies Glaucon in a deeper sense, for it provides the security he seeks. In its public tales, the city purges the afterlife of its shadows and fears (386a–387c). Ultimately, the city offers knowledge of simple and eternal ideas as a substitute for the uncertain understanding necessary in a world of complex and changing objects. In both its music and philosophy, the city removes ambiguity. The guardian's strength, or his spiritedness, serves to maintain a world that can be perfectly known and controlled. Achilles' pride, in contrast, leads him to inaction, during which he considers the different possibilities open to him. He becomes aware that the choice of one possibility precludes the choice of others. There is no unmixed good for him. Glaucon may sympathize with Achilles' strength, but he fears Achilles' dilemma. He is the perfect founder of a city in which spirited fighters will not have to face that dilemma.

The Guardians' Education in Music: The Public Tales

Having argued that the natures required by the guardians are possible, Socrates turns to the education that will produce those natures. He first considers the tales the guardians will be allowed to hear. Adeimantus, who had earlier revealed a concern for the effect of speeches on "the souls of young men" (365a), now replaces Glaucon as Socrates' interlocutor. Socrates begins by censoring stories of quarrels among the gods. For, if the guardians take fighting gods as their models, Socrates observes, there will be strife within the city (378c). They will fight their fellow citizens—the very thing Socrates was seeking to avoid in his search for the natures proper to guardians. This censorship aims at promoting domestic peace, which characterized the first city Socrates described.

If the public tales are not permitted to depict gods who quarrel, what understanding of the divine must they convey? The god, Socrates argues, is absolutely good. As a consequence of his goodness, he cannot cause any evil, for the good causes only good (379e–380c). Moreover, because whatever is in the best condition is least transformed by something and least given to transforming itself, the god who is in a perfectly good condition does not change (380d–381d). That condition is one of simplicity, for the more composite something is the more vulnerable it is to decomposition (381a). Through this public theology, the city takes as its model complete goodness and simplicity. In discussing the divine, Socrates has replaced the various gods of the Greek pantheon with the god. If gods are absolutely good and simple, they would in no way differ from one another. A number of gods would no longer be needed. The unity of the divine thus follows from its goodness and simplicity.

The rules which the poets must follow in depicting heroes aim at giving the citizens heroic models of goodness and simplicity—more human manifestations of the god of the public theology. Socrates censors tales of the horrors of Hades, fearing that they will make men softer than they ought to be (387c). Similarly, he excises "the laments and wailings of famous men," both because they suggest that death is a terrible thing and because the man who grieves shows his need for the one who has died. But the model for Socrates' citizens "is most of all sufficient unto himself for living well, and, in contrast to others, has least need of another. . . . For him it is least terrible to be deprived of a son, or a brother, or money, or anything else of the sort" (387d–e). Socrates is educating a man whom, it seems, nothing will affect, and who therefore must be detached from other particular human beings. He is like the god previously described in that he least undergoes change due to circumstances and accidents of time. He "laments the least," Socrates observes, "and bears it most gently when some misfortune overtakes him" (387c). In praise of divine simplicity, Socrates observed that even the composites in the best condition "are least altered by time and other affections" (381a). The man least in need of another not only forms no close ties with his nearest kin but he also forms no close friendships. Achilles' laments for Patroclus are the next lines of verse Socrates censors (388a).

Socrates is educating the guardians to be independent of others. They will not form close attachments either to friends or relatives, and they will be largely unaffected by external circumstances. But although their education seems to make them self-sufficient, they are still members of a city of artisans, on whom they depend for the necessities of life. The guardians are even more dependent than the others, for each artisan can provide one thing for himself—food, shoes, or clothing, for example. But the guardians' specific art is the art of war. Although that art maintains the city against threats from enemies, it does not have a particular product, as do the other arts in the city. Rather than produce something new, the guardians' art preserves what already exists.[15] If the city is as it ought to be—perfectly harmonious within and strong enough to deter potential attackers—the guardians will not need to exercise their art. Socrates gives the guardians nothing to do in times of peace (cf. Aristotle, *Pol.*, 1265a16). Paradoxically, his self-sufficient guardians are completely dependent on the city, as will become even more obvious when Socrates describes the community of property: guardians will be given the necessities as they are needed, neither more nor less than they need (416d–e). They are public wards.

This paradox of the guardians is a more radical version of the one that defines the city's artisans whose independence of others in their practice of a single art renders them more dependent on others for the satisfaction of their physical needs. Similarly, the guardians' independence of others, or their self-sufficiency, is in the service of their total devotion to the city. If they were attached to particular human beings within the city, they would be less inclined to sacrifice themselves for the city as a whole. Detached from others by the tales they are told, the guardians are related to the whole city rather than to any of its parts.[16] They have no particular identities stemming from particular relationships, or even from the particular products of their arts, as do the other artisans. Having no particular identities, they have no lives of their own; they are simply the city's instruments. They are men whose dependence becomes more total as their independence becomes more complete.[17]

To censor the laments of heroes and their grief at the death of those they love is, in effect, to ban tragedy from the city. Tragedy makes men aware of how vulnerable they are, how they may lose those things to which they are attached. It reminds them of their own incompleteness, which no city can entirely fill. But the city, demanding its citizens' total dedication, pretends to be their complete good—the whole that completes them and with which they must identify. Its guardians are not to see tragedy, which brings men into contact with their own insufficiency and therewith the incompleteness of their political community.

Just as the heroic models are not to be depicted as grieving, they are not to be depicted as laughing. Having attacked tragedy, Socrates attacks comedy. "Noteworthy human beings" must not be portrayed as "overpowered by laughter," he says, "for when a man lets himself go and laughs mightily, he also seeks a mighty change" (388e). Socrates does not explain the mighty change which laughers seek or why seeking such a change is objectionable in the city's guardians. He does, however, give the example of the gods laughing at the lame Hephaestus as he hastens through the halls (389a). A man laughs at the ridiculous, the ugly, the unexpected. More specifically, he laughs at the imperfect, or at the disproportion between what he sees and what he hopes for or imagines to be proper. A god, who should be perfect, should not have his pace slowed by a limp. A lame god is laughable. He is like the boaster, who is a traditional comic figure. The boaster claims to possess qualities he does not actually possess. We see how far short he falls of what he pretends to be and laugh at the disproportion between the defects or vices he manifests and the perfections he claims are his. In the *Clouds*, Aristophanes portrays Socrates as a boaster. There, Socrates claims to be akin to ethereal objects, yet his mind is so material that it can be weighed down by the pull of the earth. His material nature thus seems to triumph over his rationality at the very moment that he acts as if his material nature were of little consequence. As an ethereal being upon whom matter impinges, Socrates is as ridiculous as an imperfect god.

Although our laughter at the suspended Socrates or the lame Hephaestus indicates our pleasure, our laughter does not completely overcome our pain at the disproportion between the comic figure and his aspirations. To try to overcome that disproportion is to seek a mighty change. Socrates implies that Aristophanes' comedy is insufficiently conservative, for it leaves men dissatisfied and hence desirous of change. The public poetry of the city in speech will differ from the tragedy and comedy Socrates criticizes. Arousing neither grief nor laughter, it evokes no longing that might prevent men from being content with their lives as citizens.

Implicit in Socrates' description of these tales is that the city and those in charge of the city are perpetrating a lie—that the city is the whole that completes a man. It is therefore fitting that Socrates now brings up the necessity of truthfulness and makes an exception for the city's rulers. While it is a great fault for a private man to lie to his rulers, it may be "appropriate for rulers . . . to lie for the benefit of the city" (389b–c). This is the first time that Socrates mentions the rulers of the city.[18] He had been speaking of the guardian class that defended the city with its military strength. It is now explicit that these self-sufficient guardians are to be subordinate to others. Similarly, when Socrates makes his final recommendation for the guardians' tales, he defines moderate men as "being obedient to the rulers, and being themselves rulers of the pleasures of drink, sex, and eating" (389d–e). There are rulers for these self-rulers.[19]

Socrates links self-mastery with obedience to rulers in his definition of moderation. The city obviously needs both in its warriors: self-indulgence would sap their courage, while disobedience would make them dangerous. Socrates' definition of moderation assumes that the virtues the city needs belong together. The problem of Achilles, however, still lurks in the background. Are men who are strong enough to master themselves likely to accept other masters over them?[20] The city's need for moderate guardians reminds Socrates of Achilles. He now criticizes Homer for attributing to Achilles "illiberality accompanying love of money" and "arrogant disdain for gods and human beings" (391c). Socrates' criticism of Homer, however, is not entirely accurate. Although Achilles was arrogant toward gods and human beings, he was at times a liberal man, showing little concern for gain and magnificent in the bestowal of his own possessions on others. Homer's portrayal of Achilles suggests that arrogant disdain may be a concomitant of liberality. A man's freedom from small or petty concerns may be at the root of both liberality and arrogance. If arrogance typically accompanies liberality, the city faces a perhaps intractable problem. Its guardians must be liberal—free from small concerns, unpossessive, and mindless of their own gain. At the same time, they must not share Achilles' disdain for others. The virtues the city needs in its members must not be accompanied by the vices that threaten it. The city requires that good not be mixed with evil. It requires divine simplicity.

Having discussed the place of grief, laughter, truthfulness, and moderation in the public tales, Socrates brings up justice. He claims that they cannot decide how the tales should treat justice, for they have not yet determined "what sort of thing justice is" (392c). As Strauss points out, however, Socrates has placed courage and moderation in the public tales without any investigation of what sort of things they are.[21] The public tales, for the most part, encourage independence of men from all others in the city, while making them devoted to the city as a whole. But from any common sense perspective, justice involves a man in relationships with particular human beings.[22] The discussion of justice must await Socrates' argument that justice in the city is nothing other than each part's doing its own job and that justice in the soul is each part's performing its proper work. Socrates will arrive at a conception of justice which, as we shall see, abstracts from the just man's involvement with others without contradicting his absolute service to his city.

The rules for the poets that Socrates lays down reveal what the city asks men to become—detached from others but totally dependent on the city and aware of no incompleteness that makes them look beyond the city for their satisfaction. The city and the city alone provides its members with identity and purpose. Socrates indicates the hostility of the city to both tragedy and comedy, for both make men aware of their complexity and therefore uncomfortable with the simple identity the city gives them. Socrates is showing Aristophanes that a complete defense of the city requires sacrificing much more than Aristophanes thought. Not only does the city ultimately repress a man's desire to transcend the limited life of his own city but it also severs his ties to family and friends, abolishing the relationships which Aristophanes believed that the city supported. Socrates is replying to Aristophanes that the city itself leads to the abstractions from ordinary life that he attributed to philosophy.

The Guardians' Education in Music: Further Considerations

Socrates turns from the content of the tales to their style. There are two styles of speech, narration and imitation. A poet narrates when he recounts what his characters say without quoting them directly, but he imitates his characters if he lets them speak directly. In order to determine which style of poetry to permit in the city, Socrates examines "whether our guardians ought to be imitators or not" (394e). The issue of whether poets should be imitators is inseparable from whether guardians should: the imitations of the poets produce like imitations in the souls of their audience. Guardians should not be imitators, Socrates argues, because imitation violates the one-man, one-art principle. In the first place, no man is able to imitate many things as well as he can imitate one. Moreover, Socrates says, "human nature looks to me to be minted in even smaller coins than this," so that a man is unable both to imitate and "to do the things themselves of which imitations are in fact only likenesses" (395b). Each man has his own activity, but the man who imitates takes on another task and becomes "a double man," or even "a manifold one" (397e). Although Socrates finally allows poets to imitate good men (396c–d), the effect of the discussion is to condemn imitation. This is confirmed in Book X, when Socrates refers back to this earlier discussion, claiming that they were right "in not admitting any part of [poetry] that is imitative" (595a). The poets of the city, being members of the city, are themselves good men; hence, their imitating the actions of good men is not likening themselvs to what is different from themselves. The words they speak through their good characters would be their own words, if they found themselves in the circumstances in which they placed their characters. Imitation, by which a man likens himself to what is different from himself, is therefore totally banned. No one in the city is to be other than himself, and each is simply one thing.

Socrates' ban on imitation reenforces the stability, or the static character, of the city. Imitation is a means of changing. Men eventually come to resemble what they imitate. As Socrates says when describing the deleterious effects of imitating bad men and actions, "imitations, if they are practiced from youth onwards, become established as habits and nature" (395d). Socrates speaks as if nature is indistinguishable from habit and is therefore malleable. Imitation is dangerous precisely because nature does not restrict man's ability to change. The imitator is a double man, who is both what he has been and what he will become. Imitation opens a man up to a variety of possibilities. Socrates concludes his discussion of imitation by exiling from the city the poet who is able "to become every sort of thing and to imitate all things" (398a). Imitation reveals complexity, and complex things, we learned from Socrates' discussion of theology, are liable to change. Unlike the exiled poet, the members of the city have identities which are fixed and unchanging. After banning imitation, Socrates restricts the modes, rhythms, and musical instruments permitted in the city to those which are simplest and least promote change (398c–400c).

Socrates concludes his discussion of music by making the artisans conform to the standards imposed on the poets. Not only must poets be "compelled" to impress "good harmony, good grace, and good rhythm" upon their poems, but all craftsmen must be "supervised" so that they impress these "on images of animals or on houses or on anything else that their craft produces" (401b). If the craftsmen are successfully supervised, the young "dwelling as it were in a healthy place, will be benefited by everything" (401c). When the guardians experience the world, they experience an artificial world produced by poets and craftsmen.[23] The city's healthy environment is the work of its artisans. The community of artisans that began as an attempt to overcome the natural scarcity of life's necessities has developed into an attempt to eradicate nature's ugliness entirely. In the nature of bodies and the rest of "the things that grow" (*ta phuta*, connoting "the things that are by nature"), Socrates says, one finds "grace" and "gracelessness" (401a). But in the city created by compelled poets and supervised artisans, one finds only the former.

The guardians, educated on images of grace and beauty, come to recognize and love beauty as something akin to themselves, for they have come to possess such images in their own souls. Harmony results because each recognizes every other as like himself. Socrates indicates that no divisive affections for particular human beings will intrude upon this love for all by observing that immoderation and licentiousness are inconsistent with the beauty and gracefulness that prevail. The man indulging in sex, or love of the body, is subject to blame as "unmusical" and "inexperienced in beautiful things" (403c). Love is love simply of souls. But since all the guardians have the same nurture, and it is nurture that produces good dispositions and natures (401d–e), all are alike in their souls. The equality of the city of pigs, implied in the commensurability of the artisans' products, has developed into the equality of the guardians, who are educated in an environment created by artisans, supervised from above. Commensurability has developed into sameness. Socrates is well on his way toward communism.

Socrates has completed his account of the guardians' education in music, and the artificiality of the city has become more apparent. The ban on imitation is a ban on complexity and change, as is the selection of the modes, rhythms, and musical instruments which are to be permitted in the city. The city provides a common life for men by imposing order on the anarchy of unlimited possibility, as represented by the exiled poet, who indiscriminately imitates every kind of thing. In contrast to this poet, whose soul is open to diversity, the city demands sameness. In the city's politics, art imposes simplicity on the complexity of nature.[24]

The Gymnastic Education of the Guardians

Socrates begins his discussion of the gymnastic education of the guardians by asserting that "a good soul provides the body with its own virtue, so as to make it as good as it can be" (403d). In assuming that the condition of the body is a consequence of the condition of the soul, Socrates treats the body as if it were not an independent element that had to be taken into account. The gymnastic education that he prescribes for the guardians attempts to assure the validity of this assumption, for it aims at a conquest of the body.

The guardians' gymnastic must be simple, akin to their simple music. Their diet, for example, appears to be without relishes or desserts; at least, the guardians will have no "Syracusean table," "Sicilian refinement at cooking," or "the reputed joys of Attic cakes" (404c–d). Glaucon, who is again Socrates' interlocutor, does not object. He has come to approve of moderation (cf. 399e). This should not surprise us. As I have argued, Glaucon was attracted to relishes not because they are pleasant but because they are signs of freedom and independence. In desiring a perfectly controlled world, Glaucon seeks mastery over himself, as well as mastery over others. The purging of the city required by moderation is therefore in keeping with his character. Moderation controls the desires that obstruct order in the city. It is a means toward a perfectly controlled world, in which Glaucon can feel at home. It necessitates the harsh suppression of everything not conducive to order and of everything that does not conform to the city's arrangements.

This harshness appears in the medical practice that is part of the city's gymnastic. If a man is too sick to do his job, doctors should refuse to preserve his life (406b–407a). Socrates derives this practice from Asclepius, who "knew that for all men obedient to good laws, a certain job has been assigned to each in the city at which he is compelled to work, and no one has the leisure throughout life to be sick and treat himself" (406c). Socrates gives no indication that the assignment of jobs and the compulsion that keeps men working at them comes from nature. The city that he is founding increasingly appears to be an imposition on nature rather than a development of it. But there may be good reason for art to replace nature. Socrates gives the impression that the simple medicine he advocates interferes very little with nature and that nature is therefore good. However, the example he gives of medicine's allowing nature to take its course is a case where nature produces disease that the medical art cannot cure. In that case nature prevents a man from performing the tasks assigned to him; nature makes it impossible for man to conform to the institutions art has established for man's good. The harshness of the medical art is therefore made necessary by the harshness of nature.

The harshness of nature underlies Socrates' ludicrous description of medical education. Doctors, in order to understand the illnesses they cure, "should themselves suffer all diseases and not be quite healthy by nature" (408e). Suffering is <u>necessary for knowledge</u>. Socrates contrasts the doctor with the judge who need not experience what he seeks to know. The judge, Socrates says, knows the evils in souls without possessing them, making use of "knowledge, not his own personal experience." Because he knows the various evils as "something alien in alien souls," he learns without suffering, just as Socrates tried to learn from Cephalus about old age. The harshness and ugliness of nature, with its many diseases of body as well as soul, leads men to desire knowledge without experience. They would like to know without being affected by their knowledge. In order to diminish their suffering, they found cities as a protection against nature. The judge, whose knowledge is divorced from experience, is modelled on the city, while the doctor who accepts experience will under normal circumstances be destroyed by it. Socrates' recognition that medicine cannot cure all the body's diseases intimates the ultimate impossibility of the city's attempt to escape the evils of nature.

Glaucon makes no objection to Socrates' account of medical education. Perhaps he does not like to pay much attention to the concerns of the body. It was Glaucon who agreed with Socrates that a good soul imparted its own condition to the body, as if little consideration needed to be given to the body (403d–e).[25] Moreover, if the condition of the body follows from that of the soul, no bodily disease is ultimately significant. The soul determines a man's condition. Only by minimizing, not to say ignoring, the effect on a man of his body's condition can Socrates depict a doctor who learns all the diseases by suffering them himself. Socrates now thrusts the body even further out of consideration. He asserts that gymnastic is not for the sake of the body but, like music, for the sake of the soul (410c). Later, when Socrates turns to consider how seeing justice in the city helps him to see justice in the man, he looks only at a man's soul (435c; cf. 368e). He speaks as if man were merely his soul.

Gymnastic is the counterpart of music, Socrates says, because both contribute to the proper balance of hardness and softness in the soul (410c–412a). While gymnastic hardens, making men savage and cruel if carried to an extreme, music softens. While the proper amount of music, balanced with gymnastic, makes men gentle, an excessive exposure to music produces "a feeble warrior" (411b). Socrates illustrates the proper effect of music with the flute's "sweet, soft, wailing harmonies," which soften a man's spirit as iron is softened, and make it "useful from having been useless and hard" (411a). Glaucon, who is more inclined to the hard than the soft, does not seem to remember that Socrates has banned the flute and the wailing harmonies that now seem necessary to make the soul gentle (399d). Indeed, in discussing the public tales, the core of the guardians' education in music, Socrates was more concerned with restricting those that made men "softer than they ought [to be]" than those that made men too hard (387c). He banned portrayal of heroes overcome by grief or laughter (387c–389a) and offered truthfulness and self-control as appropriate poetic models (389b–391e). Moreover, he included the warlike harmonies in the guardians' education in music (399a). All this suggests that their education in music aims at hardening, not softening, as Socrates now maintains. Socrates nevertheless concludes that his education has produced the proper balance, but, as Aristotle was to remark later, Socrates has made the guardians fiercer than they ought to be (*Pol.*, 1328a8–12).

The guardians' education in both music and gymnastic aims at hardening them against nature, so that they will not be affected by its evils. Just as the guardians' music education tries to preserve them from grief at the death of their nearest relatives, their gymnastic seeks to minimize the influence of their bodies on their lives. The city attempts to protect man from nature, but it does so at the price of closing him off from everything external that might affect him. A man's love of his relatives and friends would cause him to be affected by them and by what happens to them, but the public tales depict heroes who are least in need of other human beings and least affected by grief. So, too, does a man's acquisition of knowledge necessitate that he be affected by the external world as he comes to understand it. And his experience, which brings him into contact with people and things outside himself, influences what he is. Through knowing and experiencing, as well as through loving, man is affected by the world. But just as the city tries to protect its members from the effects of love, it tries to minimize the effects of knowledge and experience. In accordance with the city's strict demands, Socrates assumes that the judge will not be affected by his knowledge of evil and that the doctor will not die from his experience of every kind of disease. And, as we shall see in the next section, Socrates begins to interpret the love possessed by the guardians so that it is consistent with the requirements of the city.

The Unity of the City: Its Noble Lie and Communism of Property

Having completed his account of the guardians' music and gymnastic education, Socrates now distinguishes those guardians who will rule from the other guardians, or "auxiliaries." Obedience to rulers, as we have seen, was one aspect of the moderation sought through the guardians' education. But who are these rulers, and what guarantees their loyalty to the city? If they are to "care for the city" or "love" it, Socrates says, they must believe that "the same things are advantageous to it and to [themselves]" and that "if it did well, [they] too would do well along with it, and if it didn't neither would [they]" (412d). The city can rely only on completely public men, who have no interest apart from the city's. The rulers will derive support for their identification of themselves with the city from what Socrates calls the "noble lie" (414c).

The men in the city, Socrates says, must be persuaded that they were "fashioned and reared" under the earth, which they must defend as their mother and nurse. Their actual rearing and education they must regard merely as dreams. The noble lie thus asks men to substitute an invisible and alien world for their ordinary experience and to give their lives for it as their true home and the source of their existence.[26] By teaching that the earth is the mother of all the citizens, the noble lie severs the connection between a man and his particular parents. Since the earth is the mother of all and all are brothers, the lie indicates the homogeneity of all the members of the city.

The god, however, does separate men into distinct classes. According to the noble lie, the god "fashions" the men in the city, mixing gold in the souls of rulers at birth, silver in the auxiliaries, and iron and bronze in the farmers and craftsmen (415a). The city's classes are produced by divine art.[27] They are as permanent as a man's possession of his one art. If children of one metal happen to be born in a class of another, rulers must transfer them to their proper classes (415b–c). Socrates assumes that qualities of soul are discernible at an early age. No relevant changes occur over time, and every man fits simply into one class or the other. The god makes men simple, allowing no such complexity as a man belonging to more than one class or to none of the simple classes the god fashioned. The arrangement assumes that there are no individuals, only classes. It leaves no place for a man who is, or who at least would like to be, in a class by himself.

In spite of the noble lie, the city's soldiers still endanger the city. It would be terrible "for shepherds to rear dogs as auxiliaries for the flocks in such a way that due to licentiousness, hunger, or some other bad habit, they themselves undertake to do harm to the sheep, and instead of dogs become like wolves" (416a). Neither their noble lie nor their education is adequate to the problem. You should not be too sure that the auxiliaries have been finely educated, Socrates warns Glaucon (416b). To alleviate the danger of the auxiliaries, Socrates now proposes communism of property. The auxiliaries will live and eat together, own no property in private, and own no more property in common than they need. As a consequence, they will not suffer the passions that exist where there is private ownership of property, where there is "hating and being hated, plotting and being plotted against" (417b). Moreover, it will be difficult for men living under communism to steal from one another, even if so inclined. Since "no one will have any house or storeroom into which everyone who wishes cannot come" (416d), an auxiliary would have no place to hide any stolen goods.

Glaucon accepts the communism of property without comment. Perhaps it satisfies his desire for purity or simplicity, for the auxiliaries under communism have no private lives that conflict with their public duties. They are only one thing—citizens of the city. And what they are is completely visible, for men living under this communist regime have no privacy in which they can remain unseen. They cannot appear to be what they are not. This communism should appeal to Glaucon, who objected to a world in which men can deceive others. Glaucon can see everything about the guardians, just as the ancestor of Gyges could peer into the private lives of others.[28]

Adeimantus, in contrast to Glaucon, is uncomfortable with an institution that deprives men of the goods they typically seek. He charges that Socrates is making the guardians unhappy, for under communism, they will "enjoy nothing good from the city as do others, who possess lands, and build fine big houses, and possess all the accessories that go along with these things, and make private sacrifices to gods, and entertain foreigners, and, of course, also possess what you were just talking about, gold and silver and all that's conventionally held to belong to men who are going to be blessed" (419a). To be happy, Adeimantus thinks, men must own land, fine houses, and all the goods that go with them. In a system of communism, he misses "private" sacrifices to gods and the means to "entertain foreigners." He seeks private pleasures, as well as something of his own that distinguishes him from others. Communism undermines a man's separate identity. If the guardians want the things Adeimantus wants, and are forced to live under communism, they will be disgruntled, if not rebellious, citizens. Communism would be a cause of contention in the city rather than a support for unity.

Socrates defends communism by arguing that "in founding the city we are not looking for the exceptional happiness of any one group among us but, as far as possible, to that of the city as a whole" (420b). We are fashioning "the happy city—a whole city, not setting apart a happy few and putting them in it" (420c). In assuming that the city can be happy although its parts are not, Socrates is acting as if the happiness of individuals in the city is irrelevant to the happiness of the city. Consistent with this is his proposal of communism. That institution abolishes private property, which protects and nourishes a man's individuality and his independence of others. If he has property of his own, a man is not simply a citizen, indistinguishable from other citizens, a part that has no existence separate from the whole.[29]

After Socrates dismisses the happiness of the auxiliaries in light of the happiness of the whole, Adeimantus wonders if the city, lacking wealth, will be able to wage war. Socrates' defense of communism has forced Adeimantus to seek a different justification for the pleasures he desires. If wealth is necessary for the city's wars, then the happiness of the whole city might require the guardians to possess the goods

Adeimantus desires. Socrates, however, argues that wealth is not nec-essary for success in war.

Soldiers can wage war against rich neighbors by appealing to one part of the enemy city against other parts. In particular, they can make allies of the poor in enemy cities by offering them the power and the money of the rich (423a). All cities, Socrates claims, except the one he has just founded, are torn by conflict between those who possess wealth and power and those who desire to do so. In his city, in contrast, there is no class which, possessing both wealth and power, would be a cause of envy and strife. It is not clear, however, that all the classes of the city in speech are as content as Socrates implies. Why would its artisans differ so radically from the poor of the typical city? They may desire the power of the guardians, as well as more wealth than the moderate amounts they are allowed to possess (421d–422a). Moreover, until he introduced communism, Socrates admitted that the powerful guardian class of the city posed a threat to the rest of the city which it was supposed to protect.[30] And Adeimantus' recent objection to communism evinced a desire for the blessings of private wealth—a desire which the city's guardians might also possess. The rulers of an enemy city might foment discord by appealing to either class in Socrates' city, while other cities typically have at least one class, the wealthy and the powerful, who want to preserve the status quo. In Socrates' city, it is true, no part is favored at the expense of another part. Although the city attempts to satisfy only the whole, it does not clearly satisfy anyone.

Socrates has completed his description of the city. It is composed of three classes: the class of farmers and artisans, the soldiers, and the rulers. The latter two classes are subdivisions of the guardian class. Socrates has thus far shown the most concern for the education of the guardians, which aims at producing the kind of men necessary for the city's security. The guardians must be independent of all other men so that they may be completely devoted to the city. But to that end, their public tales are insufficient, even when combined with a gymnastic education that hardens their souls against adversity. Soc-rates proposes that they believe a "noble lie." Men's differentiation into classes, which the city obviously requires, is not as fundamental in the lie as the homogeneity: the differences are fashioned by a god and imposed upon men who are brothers by birth. Moreover, even though there are classes, there are no individuals. Men are distin-guished only by the gold, silver, and bronze or iron metals the god placed in their souls. But as long as property remains, men are distinguished from others by having something that belongs to them and to no one else. Socrates therefore attempts to produce unity in the city by establishing communism.

Through his presentation of Glaucon, especially of Glaucon's ready acceptance of the communist arrangements, Plato indicates the passions that support the city and its demands. Glaucon's desire for perfection, for example, makes him eager to escape the conflicting demands of public and private life that necessitate imperfect compromises. Moreover, because of the simplicity of all the men in the city, they are easily known, and their education gives their educators extensive control over what they will be. This city satisfies Glaucon's yearning for complete knowledge and control. In Adeimantus, on the other hand, especially in his objection to communism, Plato presents the passions that obstruct the city. Adeimantus desires private pleasures and things of his own which distinguish him from others. At the conclusion of the founding of the city, his objection and Socrates' unsatisfactory answer to it point to unresolved problems with the city's unity.

Locating Justice in the City

Socrates now tries to find justice in the city, in order to see it more clearly in the soul. If the city has been correctly founded, Socrates says, it is "perfectly good." The virtues of wisdom, courage, moderation, and justice are therefore to be found in it. Socrates assumes that if he can locate these first three virtues in the city, justice will be "the remainder" or "what's left over" (427e–428a). None of the interlocutors objects to this strange procedure. Even scholars do not object strongly. James Adam, for example, comments, that it "is undeniable that this method is much more likely to lead us astray in ethics than in mathematics or the natural sciences, owing to the nature of the subject; but it is valid if our analysis of the phenomena is exhaustive and exact."[31]

But, in the first place, we have no reason to believe that Socrates' present list of virtues is exhaustive. Why are the virtues limited to only four, and why to these four in particular? Elsewhere, in the Platonic corpus, Socrates speaks of five virtues which appear to have coequal status—the four he mentions in the *Republic*, as well as piety.[32] The Greek word we translate as piety (*hosiotēs*) usually connotes a man's conventional relations with the divine, such as ritual sacrifice, communal worship, or obedience to prescribed laws, but the Greeks also had a concept of reverence or awe for the divine (*eusebeia*).[33] Is piety in neither sense to be found in the city in speech? Socrates' omission of piety is puzzling, especially since the city is formed by a public theology that teaches the simplicity and goodness of the god and a noble lie that tells how the god fashioned men to belong to the city's different classes. Holding such beliefs apparently does not constitute piety.

Piety is traditionally associated with the family, for the family depends on the sacred prohibition against incest. But the city's noble lie, and later its communism of women and children, destroy the family. Socrates' omission of piety from among the virtues in the city foreshadows the incestuous character of the city's communism.[34] Moreover, just as piety shows the need for limitation and restraint through its prohibition of incest, piety also gives a man a sense of his own incompleteness through worship of the divine. The city, however, denies the incompleteness of its members, who are supposed to feel complete or self-sufficient through identifying with the city. The divine model of simplicity and goodness serves after all as a paradigm for the guardians (especially through the tales of self-sufficient heroes) rather than a reminder of the perfection they lack. Similarly, the god of the noble lie fashions men so that they fit perfectly into the city's classes and therewith into the city. There is no element in their natures, no desire in their souls, that leads them to a divinity beyond political life. Piety is therefore out of place in the *Republic*'s city.

More important than the question of whether Socrates' list of the virtues is complete, however, is whether this procedure, often valid "in mathematics and the natural sciences," is at all applicable in ethics. Assuming that there are only four virtues in the city, Socrates tries to find justice by seeing the remainder after the other three are separated off. He is proceeding as if goodness can be broken down into a limited number of parts and as if each can be separated from the other parts. He is assuming that goodness is no more than the sum of its parts and that each part can be isolated without losing its identity. Socrates' mathematical procedure would necessarily fail should any part of goodness acquire its identity in relation to other parts of goodness and to goodness as a whole.

This mathematical calculation of justice thus treats each virtue as if it were as self-contained as the members of the city, whether they are viewed as artisans with potentials for only one task or as men who belong to one and only one of the city's classes. The city that Socrates founds presupposes that both human beings and the characteristics that constitute their goodness are simple. This would mean that both men and their virtues are knowable in themselves rather than through the complexity of their appearances—in relation to a variety of other entities or in the various actions they undertake. Simplicity would seem to be necessary for an entity to be wholly knowable, for a simple entity does not change. It is only what it is. Should an entity be known, on the other hand, only through its appearances—its relationships and activities—it would be complex, and it would change over time. One could not have complete knowledge of it, for it would be open to infinite variations as its activities proceeded and its relationships developed. Socrates' treating each virtue as if it were complete in itself, like his omission of piety from the virtues in the city, assumes a simplicity and completeness that make the world as Glaucon would like it to be. If goodness can be broken down into its four parts—if it is no more than the sum of its parts—it contains no mystery for man; it can be grasped through knowledge of its parts. Socrates' assumptions satisfy Glaucon's desire to arrive at a plain and simple truth.

Socrates shows Glaucon the virtues in the city. Wisdom, found in the rulers, is good counsel about the city's affairs. Courage, found in the soldiers, preserves their opinion about which things are terrible and which not. Moderation, by mastering pleasures and desires, keeps men in their proper places. Moderation is shared by all in the city when they hold the same opinion about who should rule. But when Socrates and Glaucon look for justice, it seems nowhere to be found. Socrates dramatizes its discovery by shouting "alas, alas," and claiming to have sighted its track (432d). Justice, he declares, is nothing else but the rule they set down at the beginning—each man's doing the job for which nature has most fitted him, or each man's minding his own business (433a). For carpenters, carpentry is justice, for doctors, medicine, and so on.

Socrates' definition of justice is as general as Polemarchus' conception of justice as helping friends and hurting enemies. When Socrates pointed out that each of the arts benefitted friends and harmed enemies, Polemarchus was unable to identify the particular benefits and harms the just man produced. He might have said that the particular arts were forms of justice, each benefitting and harming in its own way. But that would have seemed to be the disappearance of justice rather than its discovery, since justice would have been nothing in particular. And here, too, justice seems to have disappeared. Socrates still speaks of justice as "what's left over" after the three other virtues are found (433b–c). But if the city possesses the three virtues, with rulers exercising wisdom, soldiers courage, and all classes agreeing as to who should rule, each class is doing its own job. There is no remainder.[35] Socrates now speaks as if justice were the sum. It is identical to perfect goodness, and the other virtues are forms of justice. Socrates has given Glaucon the perfection he sought in justice, for there is no good thing outside of it. And yet it seems to be nothing that one can grasp, for it is no particular thing. Particular acts are wise, courageous, or moderate, but there are no just acts as such. The search for perfect goodness leads to an abstraction that has no content.

Drawing a Parallel to the Soul

Having found justice in the city, Socrates will proceed to find it in the soul. That procedure assumes that a man's virtue can be seen by looking within his soul and therefore in abstraction from his relationships with others. It assumes, in other words, that a man needs nothing external for human excellence—not even others toward whom he must act or refrain from acting.

Socrates shows that his understanding of justice in the city can be applied to justice in the soul by demonstrating the soul's similarity to the city. He argues that the soul has three parts, corresponding to the three parts of the city. "We learn with one, become spirited with another of the parts within us, and desire the pleasures of nourishment and generation and all their kin with a third" (436a). The alternative to this partitioned soul is that "we act with the soul as a whole in each of [these three things] once we are started" (436b). Socrates attributes no merit to this alternative.

In order to show that the soul has distinct parts, Socrates first supposes the case of a man who is both thirsty and unwilling to drink. There must be something in his soul bidding him to drink and something forbidding him to do so. What forbids proceeds from calculation, Socrates says, while what draws is due to affections and diseases (439c–d). But why is this result necessary? A man might calculate the propriety of going forward, and a state of disease might cause him to hold back. Ignoring this possibility, Socrates arrives at the existence of two parts of the soul: the "calculating," and the "irrational," or "the part with which it loves, hungers, thirsts, and is agitated by the other desires" (439d). His description of these two parts of the soul indicates that all desires and loves are irrational and that it is the job of the calculating part of the soul to hold them down. Socrates thus depreciates the desires—the part of man which "longs to take something" and "embraces" in favor of that part which "rejects" or "thrusts away" (437b). Longing and embracing reveal incompleteness: a man longs for and embraces what he lacks. Rejecting and thrusting away, on the other hand, suggest sufficiency: a man does not need what he rejects. Socrates presents a soul that suppresses its desires for externals, particularly those involving physical need, which it views as "irrational." The conflict between calculation and desire, as Socrates presents it here, comes to light as a conflict between a man's attempt to be self-sufficient and his inevitable dependence.[36]

Socrates next establishes the existence of a third part of the soul— "the part that contains spirit and with which we are spirited" (439e). Spiritedness first appeared in the *Republic* as the force which dominated the guardians, making them willing to fight and to stand firm. As we have seen, Socrates argued that a spirited man would be gentle to his own by comparing him to a noble puppy, who both wards off strangers and defends his acquaintances. Spiritedness thus appeared as the force that preserved the city, closing it off to the unfamiliar— to everything that might lead to decay, as well as to growth and development. Because it maintains what is given, against both dissolution and improvement, spiritedness is central to the city. It again receives prominence when Socrates, after giving an account of the city, discusses the soul the city was intended to reveal.

When Socrates now mentions the spirited part of the soul, Glaucon at first associates it with the desiring part (439e). In order to teach Glaucon that there is a difference between spiritedness and desire, Socrates tells him the story of Leontius. When Leontius is overpowered by his desire to look at corpses left by the public executioner, he is disgusted with himself and angry at his desire. This disgust and anger, according to Socrates, is a sign of his spiritedness. Socrates does not explain why Leontius wants to look at the corpses or why he struggles against his desire. Why does a man want to look at death, at the apparent end of human life and the dissolution or decay that accompanies it? Spiritedness rebels at the sight of human mortality, fighting for the strength and dignity undermined by the vision of the corpses. Just as it defends the integrity of the city, it defends the integrity of a human being. It is therefore directed especially against desire, for desire reveals incompleteness or insufficiency. This is true of the desire for food and drink, which Socrates mentioned when he first spoke of the desiring part of the soul, but also of the desire to view human mortality.

The particular corpses that Leontius wants to see, moreover, reveal that men come into conflict with their city. Here the conflict is so great that men are publicly executed. Just as spiritedness rebels against death, the decomposition of the human being it tries to maintain, it may also rebel against the truth that man is not wholly satisfied by the city, or that he needs something for his satisfaction that goes beyond what he can create and control. On different levels spiritedness tries to hide man's vulnerability. Socrates' example of spiritedness allows us to identify it as the passion we have seen in Glaucon—his drive for control, independence, and self-sufficiency. Spiritedness is potentially violent. Socrates even imagines that it operates in beasts (441b; cf. Aristotle, NE 1116b31–32). Leontius' spiritedness would, if it could, root out his desire to look at the corpses. It strikes at his eyes, as "damned wretches" who will look no matter what (440a).

In spite of the violence of spiritedness, Socrates associates its action with reason: spiritedness turns against desires, he says "when desires force someone contrary to the calculating part [of his soul]" (440a–b). Socrates goes so far in arguing that spiritedness "becomes the ally of reason," that he asks Glaucon, "as for [spiritedness] making common cause with the desires to do what reason has declared must not be done, I suppose you'd say you had never noticed anything of the kind happening in yourself, nor, I suppose, in anyone else" (440b). Although Glaucon agrees—the more elevated spiritedness is in the soul, and the closer ally it is to reason, the more justified is Glaucon's own spiritedness[37]—his initial association of spiritedness with desire suggests that it might also ally itself with desire. A man's spiritedness, for example, might react against his reason when reason prevents him from indulging his desires. Anger when desire is frustrated is surely as common as self-reproach for yielding to desire. But whether spiritedness sides with reason or desire against the other, spiritedness tries to maintain man whole, unified, complete, and invulnerable to the outside. It may react against desire, which indicates a man's longing for something external. Or, it may react against reason when reason's frustration of desire keeps a man in a state of longing or need. Even its attack on reason is more fundamentally an attack on desire, for it attacks reason when reason makes the desires more painful and obvious by denying their satisfaction. Socrates is therefore justified in describing spiritedness as the ally of reason against desire.

Socrates' description of the soul as tripartite makes it comparable to the city, with its three classes. The calculating or reasoning part corresponds to the rulers, the desiring part to the farmers and artisans, and the spirited part to the warriors. Just as Socrates gave most attention to the soldiers in his description of the city, he has given the most attention to the role of spiritedness in the soul. In both cases, the existence of this middle element appears the most problematic: Glaucon had not imagined that the city needed a separate class to fight its wars, nor that there was a third part of the soul, distinct from calculation and desire (374a, 439e). Spiritedness preserves the unity of the soul, just as the soldiers preserve that of the city. But as preservers of unity, neither is clearly part of the unity. If unity existed naturally, or without force, neither spiritedness nor soldiers would be necessary. Both attempt to overcome the natural disunity with which they are confronted. There were no soldiers in Adeimantus' city of pigs, where men quietly accepted death, passing on their lives to their descendants in quiet contentment. But because man is too complex to belong to the harmonious city of pigs, spiritedness is necessary to provide structure or order in which men can live. Spiritedness makes politics possible: it creates coherence or community out of a variety of elements. Similarly, it gives identity to a man, by suppressing the desires that impel him in opposite directions or that lead him to embrace what is alien. It holds a man's course to particular directions and prevents him from pursuing other desires or actualizing other potentials. It might make even him believe, for example, that he possesses one and only one art by nature. In maintaining identity, it would tend to defend the familiar and ward off what is alien. It is opposed to change and novelty.

Because the parts of the soul correspond to the parts of the city, Socrates can define the virtues in the soul as he has in the city. Wisdom resides in the calculating part, and courage in the spirited part, when that part acts as reason's ally in making war against the soul's enemies. Moderation is the agreement of all parts that reason should rule in the soul (442b–c). The just man, finally, is the one who doesn't let "the three classes in [his] soul meddle with each other" but requires each class to perform its own job (443d). Justice has, then, "in [no] way been blunted so as to seem to be something other than when it came to light in the city" (442d). Justice is the sum of the three other virtues; each part of the soul of the just man performs according to its proper virtue or virtues. The just man "harmonizes the three parts, just like the three notes on a harmonic scale, lowest, highest, and middle" (443d). He is perfectly self-contained. His excellence depends on nothing outside but consists in the perfect working of his parts. Justice exists, as Socrates says, "not with respect to a man's minding his external business, but with respect to what is within, with respect to what truly concerns him and his own" (443c–d). In the just man, spiritedness appears to have succeeded in maintaining an internal harmony uninfluenced by anything outside. Socrates has described the self-sufficient man Glaucon longs to be.

The **Republic's** *Defense of Justice and Aristophanes'* **Clouds**

Like Strepsiades in the *Clouds*, Adeimantus appears to accept the necessities of life and to be content with the simple and easily attained pleasures they allow. Just as Strepsiades' rustic manner of living contrasts with the more flamboyant life of his son Phidippides, Adeimantus acts as a foil for his brother Glaucon. Glaucon shares with Phidippides the desire Phidippides inherited from his mother—to live without having to consider the necessities. Glaucon is as little content with the city of pigs, the city that stays within the confines of the necessary (372d), as Phidippides is with the limitations of his father's life. Both Phidippides and Glaucon are spirited; the former is especially interested in horseracing, the latter in war. Phidippides disdains everything effeminate (*Clouds*, 119–20), while Glaucon is the "most manly in everything" (357a). Both desire freedom and independence. Phidippides is converted to the unjust rhetoric Socrates teaches when he learns that it promises a greater freedom than he had ever conceived. Like Phidippides, Glaucon becomes a companion of Socrates and hopes that Socrates can show him the way to freedom. The freedom that Glaucon wants, however, takes the form of a perfect justice, the goodness of which is unqualified by the necessities of human existence, the imperfect actions and complex relationships men ordinarily experience. What Phidippides wants through injustice, Glaucon wants through justice. Plato has reenacted the situation of the *Clouds* but in such a way as to show that Aristophanes has not correctly identified the problem. Not the unjust demands of men, but their admirable human qualities are the source of the evils against which Aristophanes warns.

Aristophanes' warning is dangerous because it misleads men into a complacency about their pursuit of justice, leaving them unaware of its perils. By defending justice and the political life justice makes possible, Aristophanes allows men to think that justice is simply good for an individual or that man's personal life is in perfect harmony with his political life. He tries to make men forget about cravings or longings that cannot be satisfied by politics. He ridicules Socrates' "ethereal" aspirations. He is like the Zeus in his *Symposium* speech who tries to turn men away from erotic desires that cannot be satisfied to the deeds of ordinary life. Socrates' description of the just city and soul which resembles it can be considered a reply to Aristophanes. It is dangerous, Plato warns, to defend justice and politics, without clearly indicating their limits; but, to the extent that justice and politics are limited, the aspirations that lead men beyond any given political order are legitimate. Plato presents the ultimate result of an unqualified defense of justice and politics—a politics that distorts human nature by insisting that the city alone is its complete fulfillment and a soul whose eros is restricted if not denied. It is a city and a soul which Aristophanes himself would find appalling. The city undermines the close attachments within families that he saw as a source of human happiness. The noble lie, for example, has the effect of separating children from their parents, and the education in music attenuates the bonds between relatives, as Aristophanes accused Socrates of doing. And the soul Socrates describes is self-contained and consequently isolated from the relationships Aristophanes defended. The perfectly just city eliminates the distractions and complications of particular relationships, while the defense of justice as perfectly good isolates the soul from the imperfect world of action.

At the beginning of the *Republic*, Socrates, like Leontius, is "going up" from the Piraeus (cf. 327a and 439e), which is a scene of decay.[38] In the Piraeus, Socrates has the chance to view not the decay of human bodies but the decline of a city. That decline is manifest especially in the all-night festival the group plans to attend. Like Leontius, Socrates also turns away from decay; instead of going to the all-night festival, he looks at a perfectly unified city and an individual in perfect harmony with himself. If Socrates' spiritedness forces him to look away from decay, it, like Leontius' spiritedness, wins out only "for a while" (439e): Socrates intends to look at vice, with its unlimited number of forms, and the imperfect regimes and souls (445c). But the young men present refuse to let him turn away from the "perfectly good" city he has established. They want to hear more about the communism of women and children (449c). Socrates' account of the city's communism and of the philosophy that makes it possible, allows us to see the extent to which spiritedness can go in forcing divergent elements into a whole—the tyranny to which a defense of absolute justice can lead.

Chapter 3

Communism and Philosophy (Books V–VII of the *Republic*)

Introduction

In the next three books of the *Republic*, Socrates reveals in greater depth the institutions and the principles of the city he has founded. He discusses equality of the sexes, the communism of women and children, and the rule of philosophy. Because there are no natural differences between the sexes, Socrates argues, men and women should share equally in the jobs the city requires, and communism of women and children should replace the family, with its differentiated sex roles. Communism, which results in the citizens' saying "mine" and "not mine" of the same things, is the greatest good for the city, since it "binds [the city] together and makes it one" (462b–c). This city can come into existence, Socrates says, only if philosophy comes to power. He explains what philosophy is and how the philosophers must be educated.

In describing the equality of the sexes, the communism of women and children, and the rule by philosophers—"three waves" which Socrates thinks might overwhelm him—Socrates reveals more completely the city's attempt to impose homogeneity on its members. It is a homogeneity that comes from a denial of the body, for, as Socrates admits, only the body stands in the way of complete unity (464d). Man's corporeality guarantees his separate identity. A man's separate identity, necessitated by his body, develops or matures into character

99

through his choices, actions, and relationships with others. Because a man has a character, he is distinct from others, and cannot be reduced to the material or bodily existence that belongs to all men. The city's denial of the body paradoxically results in the reduction of men to body.

The city in speech thus reproduces the mistake Aristophanes attributed to the Socratics. In the *Clouds*, the Socratics attempt to be free of bodily limits by discovering what is universally true. By ignoring the differences among men that grow out of their different political and familial situations, they ignore the human characteristics that emerge when men respond to their particular circumstances, such as man's natural capacity for a rational choice among alternatives. They miss what is distinctively human. The universal knowledge they acquire is of the pervasiveness of material nature, a knowledge that reduces man to a brutish existence.

Just as the Socratics in the *Clouds* seek freedom from material nature by knowing what is universally true, the city in speech tries to achieve a unity free of the individual differences and conflicts that arise out of particular human situations. Through its education of the guardians and their communistic property arrangements, and now even more vigorously through the equality of the sexes and the communism of women and children, the city tries to conquer the body and achieve an absolutely common existence for its members. But, as in the case of the Socratics, the city's denial of body leads to a reduction of men to body. The city's guardians, for example, no different from one another, are treated merely as bodies to be manipulated. We shall see this in the city's marriage arrangements and its provisions for raising children. Because the guardians have no individual identities, they have no distinct characters that rulers must respect. Nothing prevents the city from becoming tyrannical.

Moreover, Plato shows how the city and its passions distort philosophy itself. The city educates its most promising members in a mathematical philosophy that prepares them for tyranny over the city. That education leads to a simple unity—a "one equal to every other one, without the slightest difference betweem them and containing no parts within itself" (526a), a one independent of tangible or visible bodies (525d). It is a philosophy that abstracts from experience of a complex world in order to arrive at an undifferentiated unity, beyond experience. It differs radically from Socratic political philosophy which tries to give an account of experience as it explores the diversity and complexity of men. The mathematical philosophy of the city is appropriate for philosophers who must impose communism on the city, for communism renders each human being as much as possible like the mathematical oneness the philosopher seeks—to the extent possible each is like every other, without the slightest difference between them. Insofar as the city succeeds in becoming homogeneous, it approaches the simplicity of the mathematician's unity—"containing no [differentiated] parts within itself." Certainly the members of the city are not supposed to look upon themselves as separate or independent from the others but to identity themselves with the city as a whole. The city even tries to be "independent of tangible or visible bodies," which it either attempts to conquer through training and institutional arrangements or depreciates as mere appearances. The philosophy of the *Republic*'s city is, therefore, a reflection of the city itself. To support the city, philosophy must be politicized. Plato thus replies to Aristophanes that if philosophy can undermine politics, politics can also corrupt philosophy.

Socrates' Reluctance to Speak

Socrates mentioned the communism of women and children in passing, as he completed his description of the city (423e–424a). No one seemed to notice the proposal at the time. Knowing that Socrates would identify justice after he finished describing the city, Socrates' listeners may have been so eager to hear the conclusion of the discussion that they did not want to stop to examine details, even one as important as the communism of women and children. Now, once justice has been defined, they ask to hear about the arrangements for women and children. Adeimantus, speaking for himself and Polemarchus, claims that Socrates is "robbing us of a whole section of the argument" (449c). It is not clear whether he wants more explanation because he has reservations about the communism of women and children or whether he is merely curious. But given his disapproval of communism of property, we might assume the former.

When Socrates is reluctant to speak about the city's communism, Glaucon and Thrasymachus add their voices to the demands of Adeimantus and Polemarchus, suggesting that the majority is voting for Socrates to do what they are asking (450a). The situation thus parallels that at the beginning of the *Republic*. Just as the majority forced

Socrates to stay in the Piraeus, it now compels him to enter this stage of the discussion as an unwilling speaker, forced to share his thoughts with the company. Again, the dramatic situation seems to foreshadow the city's compelling the philosopher to rule. Just as the city claims that it is being wronged if the philosopher whom it educates refuses to rule, Adeimantus claims that they are being robbed if Socrates does not give them all of the argument.

As at the beginning of the dialogue, however, the dissimilarities between the dramatic situation and the one in the city are more important than their similarities. Far from intruding upon the privacy of Socrates, Adeimantus is actually defending his own independence. If he is to support the city and its institutions, he has a claim on the argument that defends them. It is wrong of Socrates to try to persuade, he assumes, without the explanation necessary for a rational decision. Adeimantus' objection to Socrates' robbing them of a section of the argument thus constitutes an implicit objection to the city in speech, which does not treat its members as if they have a capacity for reasoned choice. Socrates must not treat them, Adeimantus is saying, in effect, as the city treats men. His demand that Socrates not deprive them of what belongs to them is therefore an appropriate beginning for the discussion of an institution that forces men to give up their privacy.

Socrates is reluctant to speak, he says, because he fears that he will be unable to persuade the group that the communism of women and children is possible. "The argument might seem to be a prayer" (450d). Socrates knows that the young men, especially Glaucon, will not be satisfied unless they believe that the good can be actualized. Moreover, he hesitates to speak because he is not sure that his position is sound, and he may therefore deceive the group about the justice and goodness of laws (451a–b). Not only might the city described in speech, along with its justice and its laws, be impossible; it might not even be good. Glaucon insists that, if they are harmed by the argument, they will pardon Socrates. Whereas Adeimantus showed a concern that in presenting the argument Socrates treat him and the others justly, Glaucon tells Socrates to press forward regardless of the consequences. He does not stop to wonder how, if they are deceived by the argument, they will know they are deceived and so be able to pardon Socrates. He acts as if the harm inflicted on a man's soul is as easily detected as injury done to his body.

Although Socrates proceeds with the argument when Glaucon insists, he has given notice about his uncertainties. He does not act like the city, proclaiming the truth without questioning its knowledge. He has tried to warn them. He will now describe the institutions of the city—equality of the sexes, communism of women and children, and rule by philosophy.

Common Natures, Common Jobs

The communism of women and children among the warriors serves to unify the city. All say "mine" and "not mine" of the same things and hence feel joy and sadness at the same times. Communism therefore tries to make men alike, moved by the same desires and affected by the same passions. The communism of women and children will produce a "community of pleasures and pain" (462b). It is another manifestation of the city's drive toward homogeneity. We have seen that drive in the one-man, one-art principle, which guarantees that men are simple and have commensurable roles in the community they serve. The drive toward unity, however, applies to the city as a whole, not merely to the simple artisans and to the warriors, whose way of life is communistic. In the noble lie, the common origin of the city's members is more fundamental than their differences. All the citizens have the same mother, and their differences, fashioned by the god, have an artificial character (415a). In war, Socrates claimed earlier, the unified city he was founding had the advantage over other cities, whose different classes made them "very many cities but not a city" (422e). The unity shared by the city as a whole becomes most visible in the most visible of the city's classes, whose communistic arrangements help them to identify with the city which they defend with their lives.

If men and women have different natures, however, the human beings in the city would be divided in such a way as to belie the city's homogeneity. This city, in accordance with its principles, therefore treats men and women as if they had the same natures. According to Greek tradition which was formed primarily by the poets, however, there were natural differences between men and women.[1] Socrates recognizes this tradition when he tells his listeners that the city's equal treatment of the sexes will appear ridiculous to the men of his time (452a–e). When Socrates asks Meno to define virtue in Platos' *Meno*, Meno appeals to this common opinion about the sexes, claiming that men and women have different virtues (*Meno*, 71e). Although Meno does not develop the argument, tradition seems to have traced the differences in the natures of men and women primarily to their different functions in procreation.[2] Because of women's role in childbearing, they were thought to have closer ties to physical nature, to their offspring, and hence to the limits imposed upon human beings by their particular existences. Unlike men, women are tied down by pregnancy and the nursing of children. They were therefore thought to acquire a moderation due to their closeness to natural limits that men did not; they would be less likely to yield to their desire for something universal or to their desire to be free of the limits of a particular time and place. According to this same reasoning, males would be more likely to transcend their particular contexts and to attain broader visions and achievements. From this perspective, the *Republic*, in its search for the regime that is everywhere and at all times the best, or even in its search for justice unconnected to its consequences, is particularly unwomanly.

If such differences between the sexes exist, they would present a greater barrier to the city's homogeneity than the differences among the artisans. These latter differences are subordinate to the same bodily needs, which the different arts are needed to fulfill. Similarly, the differences among the classes in the city are fashioned by the god. They are arbitrary distinctions made for the sake of the city's survival. The members of all the classes of the city are supposed to want the same thing, the good of the whole. There is no tension between them; they are all "of the same mind," as Socrates says (432a). But the differences between men and women that Greek tradition acknowledges, although they originate in bodies, develop into differences in character and perspective—differences that make men and women "of two minds" rather than one.

It would be desirable if the feminine and masculine elements the tradition describes could balance each other. The male would provide the drive toward the formation of political communities, which endure beyond the present and in which human beings transcend their immediate particular lives and come to see what they have in common. The male might moderate the woman's excessive love of her own, which stands in the way of community.[3] The female, on the other hand, might restrain man in his attempt to overcome the limits of nature. By her awareness of the natural force of particular attachments, she would check a city's drive for unity at the expense of the individuality of its members. She might therefore act as a moderating force on such manly efforts as the city in speech.

Socrates, however, does not harness any feminine characteristics in the city he is founding.[4] In fact, he even denies that there is anything peculiar to women (455a–b).[5] Because women make no contributions of their own, Socrates claims, they have capacities for the same arts that men practice. It is true that people think that men and women should have different jobs because they have different natures, Socrates admits. However, they are not making correct distinctions when they distinguish men from women, any more than when they distinguish bald-headed from long-haired men. They are not using "dialectic," which "separate[s] [the matter under discussion] into its classes" (454a).[6] Dialectic, for example, separates the class of doctors: "a man and a woman whose souls are skilled in the doctor's art have the same nature" (455c–d). When dialectic arrives at a class, Socrates' example indicates, dialectic ignores the visible bodily differences, in order to uncover sameness. And just as men and women may both have a doctor's nature, they may both be fit for guarding a city. The same education assigned to men with natures suited to guarding therefore should be assigned to women with such natures.

The common education given to men and women goes even to their exercising together naked in the gymnasium. Socrates admits this might seem absurd to men now but points out that, in past times, it seemed ridiculous even for men to see each other naked. That view of the shameful was overcome "when it became clear . . . that to uncover such things is better than to hide them" (452d). Common exercises in the nude, however, would uncover the obvious physical differences that stand in the way of homogeneity. Even when the bodily differences between men and women are most apparent—when they are naked—they can be rendered unimportant by a dialectic that uncovers sameness below the surface appearances.

Although the equality of the sexes that this dialectic uncovers reveals a common humanity between men and women, it is one without particular content. Men and women are alike in that the different natures that suit human beings to particular arts are found similarly among both. Humanity breaks apart into a number of artisans. In discovering the same abilities for the different arts beneath the visible differences, this dialectic finds only the human capacity to compensate for nature's lack of provision. There appear to be no natural ends to which humanity is directed other than the satisfaction of the bodily needs served by the arts. It is therefore appropriate that Socrates gives the example of medicine as an art which both sexes can practice (455c–d). Nor does this dialectic find any natural limits that might restrict the use of human beings in the arts the city requires, such as would be suggested by natural differences between the sexes. Socrates almost suggests that both men and women can nurse babies (460b–c). Rather than discover nature, dialectic denies nature. It finds no limits to the conquest of body, but, since there are no natural ends beyond body, the conquest of body, or the arts, serves only the body.

Ironically, dialectic tries to discover what men are by considering their souls in abstraction from their bodies, but, in doing so, it subordinates men all the more to their bodies. If there were differences between the sexes, as the traditional view maintained, those differences would provide a basis for a view of a naturally good human life—one that comprehended in some way the different perspectives to which each sex was inclined. Nature would then indicate, although in broad outlines that allowed for any number of possibilities, the ingredients of a good life. Without some such natural end that serves as a goal and therefore as a limit, men are merely bodies that can be manipulated. The dialectic that supports the institutions of the city has the same character as the Socratic philosophy that Aristophanes condemns: in the *Clouds*, Socrates' attempt to escape his body results in bondage to the body. As Strepsiades asks his son when he returns from Socrates' school, "since you imitate the cocks in other things, why do you not eat dung and sleep on a perch?" (*Clouds*, 1430–31). It is not surprising that in the *Republic* Socrates will soon take the breeding of dogs and cocks as the models for the matings of men and women in the city (459a–b).

Communism of Women and Children

The arrangements for marriages and the rearing of children are very strict. Rulers determine which men marry which women. Such marriages last only until procreation occurs. Since they aim at producing the best offspring, only the best men are mated with the best women and only the offspring of the best marriages are raised (459d–e). Children are taken from their mothers at birth and reared in public nurseries. Neither parents nor children know each other. Mothers, "full with milk" are brought to the nurseries, but nurses "[invent] every device so that none will recognize her own" (460c–d).

In explaining that the best men are to be mated with the best women within the soldier class, Socrates admits that there are natural differences within that class. Nature produces distinctions that are inconvenient for the city, whose unity would be better served if each class were simple. As long as there are better and worse members of this middle class, the absolute distinctions between the classes themselves are less clear. If some soldiers are not as good as others as soldiers, would they be better artisans, for example? And would the best soldiers have any capacity for rule? To the extent that the classes are complex, the simple lines the city draws between them are less justified. The city applies simple categorizations to what is complex by nature.

Moreover, the differences within the soldier class create practical problems for the city. Should the warriors become aware that some are singled out as superior to others, there might arise envy or ill will. The policy of mating the best men with the best women and of rearing only the offspring of the best contradicts the equality that is supposed to exist among the warriors. Consequently, this policy must be hidden from them. For example, "certain subtle lots must be fabricated so that ordinary men will blame chance rather than the rulers for each union" (460a). The control that rulers have in the city is so great that it extends even to the quality and quantity of offspring (460a). Like all-powerful gods, their manipulations lie behind what others perceive as chance.

The warriors do understand that they are treated unequally, however, when the rulers give those "who are good in war or elsewhere" "the privilege of more abundant intercourse with the women." "Under this pretext," Socrates says, "the most children will be sown by such men" (460b). Presumably the risk of envy this practice could produce is not as great as the advantages secured by it. The end of giving women as prizes of war is not to distinguish one guardian from another but to serve the good of the whole city by the production of good offspring. And although some are rewarded, their rewards are transitory. Since marriages are brief, there can be no Achilles in the city who refuses to yield his war prize when the law demands it. Those singled out for reward, it turns out, have only more to give up.

The brevity of the marriages prevents the formation of any attachments between men and women. Similarly, women do not grow fond of their children, since children are immediately taken to the nurseries. The city weakens as much as it can the bond between mother and child and, with it, the woman's connection to nature. Neither men nor women fear that chance may deprive them of those they love, for they don't love anyone in particular.

When men and women are beyond the age of procreation, they may have intercourse "with whomever they wish." There is, however, one restriction—incest will not be permitted (461c). Of course, parents and children, and brothers and sisters, will not know each other, since children are immediately removed from their mother. So that incest will not occur, men and women will consider some of the members of the city as their parents and others as their offspring. They will consider as their children all those who are born seven to ten months after their matings. These children, in turn, will call these men and women their mothers and fathers. Brothers and sisters, grandparents and grandchildren will be designated in a similar way (461d). The law will not permit intercourse between those who recognize each other as parents and offspring or as siblings.

As we saw from Strepsiades' reaction to Phidippides' new learning, men feel repugnance at the thought of incest between brothers and sisters but, more especially, at the thought of incest between parents and children. Indeed, the prohibition against brother-sister incest seems to serve as a means of strenghtening the prohibition against incest between parents and children. By refraining from incest, a man shows respect for his parents as the cause of his being. He acknowledges his dependence, his incompleteness, and even, on some level, the mystery of his existence as a particular, contingent being. Because the incest prohibition fosters this awareness of incompleteness and sense of mystery, it provides support for piety. The incest prohibition is commonly regarded as sacred. The man who commits incest rejects the natural relations between himself and his parents, as well as the dependence and incompleteness which that relation implies. The crime of incest is therefore often linked with that of patricide, as in the case of Oedipus.

The incest prohibition, however, could no longer serve its purpose in the communistic society of the *Republic*. Communism removes a man from his particular family and thereby destroys the natural relation between generations that the incest prohibition protects. Communism does not merely render the incest prohibition meaningless, but, by denying the natural relation between children and parents, it imitates incest itself. Because the city is incestuous in this deeper sense, it is appropriate that its prohibition of incest in the literal sense is soon broken. That prohibition was supposed to be guaranteed by requiring men and women to call certain guardians sons, daughters, fathers, mothers, grandparents, and siblings. With these close relatives, a man was forbidden to have sexual intercourse. However, the unity of the city necessitates that "with everyone he happens to meet [a guardian] will hold that he's meeting a brother, a sister, or a father, or a mother, or a son, or a daughter, or their descendants or ancestors" (463c). Every marriage from the city's point of view constitutes incest, since it joins a man with someone whom he considers a close relative. The city has no reason to prohibit incest, for it itself severs the bond between parents and children that the incest prohibition protects.[7]

In summary, the communism of women and children prevents the formation of close family ties between men and women, parents and children. Men are isolated from those with whom they might form close bonds through procreation, in order that they may be attached solely and completely to the city. Although the provisions for the marriages recognize inevitable inequalities, communism tries to give the appearance of equality and sameness. The link to particular origins that Oedipus severed through his crimes of patricide and incest is severed for the men in the city by the institution of communism. As we will see even more clearly by examining its philosophic rulers, the communistic city is akin to Aristophanes' thinkery, whose denizens also deny the special relation between parents and offspring and the dependence which that relation implies. Plato is criticizing politics for the same things for which Aristophanes criticized philosophy. By veiling man's natural origins and denying man's incompleteness, the city destroys man's connection to nature.

The Philosopher-Kings

Socrates has persuaded Glaucon that the communism of women and children is best for the city because it produces unity, the city's greatest good (464a–b). It then remains to be considered whether or not this communistic city is possible. Socrates argues that the city would come into being if philosophers became kings or if kings philosophized. For philosophy to be united with kingship, Socrates adds, "the many natures making their way to either apart from the other are by necessity excluded" (473d). Although Socrates' philosophic life may be called "political" in contrast to that of philosophers who study the physical universe (see also Gorg., 521d), Socrates is obviously not making his way to kingship along with his philosophizing. Very soon, he will explain to Adeimantus his luck in not being involved in politics (496c; see *Apol.*, 31d). If the men pursuing philosophy apart from kingship are to be excluded from the group of philosophers selected to rule, Socrates himself might be excluded. Here at the outset of his discussion of philosophy, Socrates implicitly raises the question of his own place in the city he is founding. As we shall see, Socrates will leave little room for his own way of life in his description of philosophers.[8] It is therefore for good reason that he suspects that his account of the coincidence of political power and philosophy will "drown [him] in laughter" (473c). By placing philosophers in a class which excludes himself, he acts like a comic figure, whose lack of self-understanding involves him in contradiction. His definition of philosophy, contradicted by his own existence, illustrates that he has forgotten himself. This self-forgetting, however, is in the service of finding appropriate rulers for the city he founded in speech. By forgetting himself, Socrates does the very thing which the city demands of its guardians through its imposition of communism on them. Only by such a self-forgetting can Socrates support this city.

Because philosophic rulers are needed to bring the city into existence, Socrates will undertake a description of who they are. These philosophers are useful to the city, and useful for action. Their role in the city resembles that of art, since art brings something into existence that does not exist of necessity (see Aristotle, *NE*, 1140a12–16). Philosopher-kings will produce for mankind what otherwise would be left to chance (see Aristotle, *NE*, 1140a19–20).

To define philosophy, which means literally "love of wisdom," Socrates defines love. When a man loves something, Socrates says, he doesn't "show a love for one part of it and not for another, but much cherish all of it" (474c). As Socrates illustrates, "all [boys in the bloom of youth] seem [to the lover] worthy of attention and delight" (474d). Lovers of wine love every kind of wine, and lovers of honor, loving "honor as a whole," love honor bestowed by both greater and lesser men (475a–b). When a man desires something, "he desires all of that class," Socrates says, rather than "one part of it and not another." Socrates' account of love is rather odd, for it assumes that lovers have no preferences. But surely the erotic man has his favorite, the wine lover hates poor wine, and those most desirous of honor disdain honor coming from those they believe unworthy of bestowing it (see Aristotle, *NE* 1124a5–12). And yet the city's communism could be successful, only if Socrates' account of love were true: only if the guardians love all the members of a class—all the other guardians—will the "community of pleasures and pains" exist (464a). More particularly, should a guardian have a preference for one woman over another, he would be dissatisfied with marriage arrangements that did not take his preference into account. Socrates has defined love to comply with what the city's institutions require.[9]

Glaucon surprisingly accepts Socrates' account of love. Experience should have taught him that lovers single out particular human beings on whom they bestow their affection. But Glaucon has revealed himself to be a man of excessive spiritedness, who is disgusted with the imperfect appearance of things. Love of something complete, such as all of a class, might be more appealing to him than love of a particular human being.[10] It is not clear that this spirited man is very erotically inclined. In asking Glaucon to confirm the theory that lovers desire all of a class, Socrates does call Glaucon "an erotic man" (474d). But Glaucon says cautiously, "If you want to point to me while you speak about what erotic men do, I agree for the sake of argument" (475a).

After claiming that lovers love all of what they love rather than a part, Socrates considers philosophers, who love all of wisdom or learning and are "willing to taste every kind of learning with gusto" (475c). This implies, according to Glaucon, that "many strange ones" are to be counted among the philosophers, such as "lovers of sights" and "lovers of hearing," who although they are unwilling to attend a discussion "run around to every chorus at the Dionysia" "just as though they had hired out their ears for hearing" (475d). Glaucon disdains these lovers of the pleasures of the senses, among whom he includes men who take pleasure in tragedy. He himself obviously dislikes tragedy and does not run to every chorus at the Dionysia. Tragedy, as Socrates made clear in his discussion of the guardians' music education, reveals men's weakness, their inability to control their situation, and their vulnerability. It makes men aware that undertakings like cities of perfect goodness may fail. But Glaucon is engaged in such an undertaking and would like the city they are founding in speech to be possible. He is disappointed when he thinks that Socrates is including lovers of tragedy among the philosophers who will rule in the city.

Socrates relieves Glaucon's disappointment by refining his conception of the lover of wisdom. The lovers of sounds and sights "delight in beautiful sounds and colors and shapes and all that craft makes from such things," while the philosopher delights "in the nature of the beautiful itself" (476b). He loves the "idea of the beautiful itself, which always stays the same in all respects" (479a) and, similarly, other ideas such as goodness and justice (476a).[11] Socrates thus answers Glaucon's concern, for it is not all learning that the philosopher loves, but learning the universal characteristic that all the particular things that appear to the senses have in common. Socrates has changed the object of love from all the members of a class to the class itself. He is not contradicting his first statement about love, however; he is, in fact, explaining it. If a man loves all the members of a class, he loves them because they embody some characteristic they have in common rather than because of characteristics peculiar to each member. All seem worthy of attention and delight because nothing distinguishes them. To love all the members of a class is to love none of them in particular—to love the class rather than its members. The refined statement of love would be even more acceptable to a spirited man like Glaucon, whose desire to escape the imperfections of the world would resonate with Socrates' depreciation of the objects grasped by the senses and whose demand for perfection might find satisfaction in such universal characteristics as "the beautiful itself."

In clarifying what the philosopher loves, Socrates distinguishes knowledge, opinion, and ignorance and their respective objects. Just as a man knows what is, Socrates says, he is ignorant of what is not. And opinions, which fall between knowledge and ignorance, have as their object what falls between existing and not existing—everything which comes into being and passes away—the world we know through our senses.[12] The objects which cannot be fully known are merely those which delight lovers of sight and hearing, the many beautiful things, for example, which, falling short of beauty itself, partake of its opposite as well—if they are not simply beautiful, they are also ugly (479a–b). This account of what philosophers love trivializes complex and changing objects and the opinions men form of them. Moreover, since what is not fully knowable is not some inaccessible reality behind the appearances but the appearances themselves, it constitutes neither a threat to the fundamental intelligibility of the world nor a source of awe.[13] Socrates has, in effect, satisfied Glaucon's desire for a magic ring, which permits him to thrust aside the imperfect appearances in order to know a truth that lies beyond them. In contrast to these appearances, the objects that are knowable are unmixed with their opposites; they are simply what they are. In a sense, Socrates is providing Glaucon with what he asked for when he began to play a major role in the discussion—something good that is not mixed with its opposite, as would be the case if justice had harmful consequences.

On the basis of his distinction between philosophers and lovers of opinion, Socrates argues that the former make the best rulers. Looking to what is always and everywhere the same, they are able to give laws to the city about what is beautiful, just, and good (484c–d). To one who "contemplates all time and all being," Socrates adds and Glaucon agrees, "human life [does not seem] anything great" (486a). One might wonder, however, whether those who do not consider human life very great are the best ones to provide for human life by ruling in the city. Is their vision of "what is always the same in all respects" (484b) really useful for managing a city, where one finds complex and changing affairs? Adeimantus also is uneasy about turning the city over to philosophers. "In speech," he cannot refute what Socrates says about them, but "in deed," he sees that philosophers are useless and vicious (487c–d). He uses Socrates' most recent argument as an example of what is wrong with philosophy. When men trust Socrates' arguments, they forget that what happens in the world contradicts Socrates' conclusions. Adeimantus accepts the world of experience more readily than Glaucon, who seems willing, and even eager, to escape it.

Socrates admits that what Adeimantus says about philosophers is correct, but he blames it on the current corruption of cities. In a good city, he implies, philosophers would be neither useless nor vicious (492a–497a). He thus imagines a situation that never existed in order to contrast it with the experience Glaucon would like to reject. He argues further that there are sophists who give philosophy a bad name by usurping its place. Believing human affairs to be the greatest things, they desire to rule in cities more than anything else. And they rule by manipulating the multitude, having observed what gives it pleasure and causes it pain. Philosophers, in contrast, contemplating what is always and everywhere the same, can mold the dispositions of men in light of their contemplation (500d). They "take the city and the dispositions of human beings, as though they were a tablet, which, in the first place, they would wipe clean" (501a). Socrates speaks of them as painters who look to divine patterns and draw them on their cleaned tablets. The experience the sophists acquire of the pleasures and pains of men is therefore unnecessary. And love for human life, it seems, would only prevent philosophers from doing what is best.

Their political art wipes clean the tablet or erases human life as men experience it. Their lack of knowledge of complex and changing affairs does not, therefore, disqualify them from ruling in the city. Their rule requires, not action in the midst of complexity and change, but a transformation of the world into something as simple and as unchanging as possible.[14] Acquiring knowledge of what is always the same in all respects is the necessary preparation for their political activity. The politics described in the *Republic* thus necessitates the kind of knowledge its philosophers attain.[15] Although Socrates answers Adeimantus' objection to the rule of philosophers, his answer constitutes greater cause for alarm.

Socrates' next revelation about philosophy, moreover, should make Adeimantus all the more cautious about philosophic rule. The philosophers' greatest study is the good, Socrates says, which "every soul pursues and for the sake of which it does everything. The soul divines that [the good] is something but is at a loss about it and unable to get a sufficient grasp of what it is" (505d–e). But only with the greatest certainty and knowledge should a man wipe the tablet of human existence clean and draw new patterns upon it. If the philosopher-king is at a loss about the good, can he be trusted to rule the city? As Socrates says, "those best men in the city, into whose hands we put everything, [should not be] in the dark about a thing of this kind and importance" (505e–506a).

Moreover, because of this uncertainty about the good, Socrates says, his earlier description of the virtues in the city and in the soul was inadequate (504b). Socrates seems to have shown what justice is without knowing "in what way [it is] good," but he "divine[s] that no one will adequately know the just and fair things themselves before this is known" (506a). The discussion is at a standstill, and the soundness of everything previously agreed about justice and the other virtues has fallen into doubt. As at the beginning of the second book, when Socrates claims to have proven that justice is good without knowing what it is, it is Glaucon's insistence that moves the discussion forward. "You're not going to withdraw," he now says to Socrates, for "it will satisfy us even if you go through the good just as you went through justice, moderation, and the rest" (506d). Socrates complies with Glaucon's request and returns the discussion to its former level. The soul's incomplete knowledge recedes into the background with Glaucon's reentrance into the discussion.

In order to help his listeners understand the good, Socrates compares it to the sun. Just as the sun in the visible realm provides light so that objects can be seen, the good in the intelligible realm provides the truth so that objects can be known (507c–509a). It is goodness that makes an object intelligible to men. What is not good would be unknowable, just as what is unillumined by the sun remains unseen. The analogy between the good and the sun establishes the goodness of knowledge. Socrates is presenting Glaucon with a world in which he may be completely at home—in contrast to the world that Glaucon portrayed in his praise of injustice, the dissatisfying world in which the truth was ugly and a man's goodness worked to his detriment.[16]

Moreover, the sun is not only like the good, Socrates says, it is the "child" of the good (506e, 508b). His language of generation suggests that the visible is created by the intelligible, at least in this most important instance. Hitherto, Socrates was appealing to Glaucon's disdain for the senses, and his desire to penetrate behind the appearances of things, by offering an escape from the sensual world of appearance. But now, when arguing that philosophers must rule in the city, he speaks of the visible world as if it were the offspring of that purer world behind the appearances. If the world is a child of the good, then man can be secure in it.

Socrates further explicates the visible and intelligible realms by asking Glaucon to locate them along a line. Each of the two realms is divided into two, so that there are four segments on the line. The lower segment of the visible realm contains images of the objects in the higher segment of the visible, the natural and the artificial objects that men perceive around them (510a). In the lower segment of the intelligible realm are the objects that "fall under geometry and its kindred arts" (511b). Mathematicians, when dealing with the things men see, treat them merely as images of the objects in the intelligible realm. They view the round objects in the world, for example, as images of the perfect circles about which they make their arguments (510d). In their eyes, the visible world is one of images, which fall short of the perfect objects with which they are concerned. It would be easy for them to understand the visible world as a cave filled by images of the ideas contemplated by the best men.[17]

Indeed, this is how Socrates has been presenting the world since he began describing the philosophers the city needs. As we have seen, when Glaucon feared that Socrates was including the lover of sights and sounds in the class of philosophers, Socrates distinguished the lovers of these sensible objects from philosophers. The latter love only the universal characteristics of the objects men perceive, such as the ideas of the beautiful and the just, rather than the beautiful and just objects in the world. The philosopher thus loves perfect ideas analogous to the perfect figures which mathematicians take as their objects.[18] He is as little concerned with the imperfect embodiments of the ideas he loves—the mere appearances which most men love—as the mathematicians are with the imperfect figures that reflect their perfect objects. Socrates' description of the third segment of the divided line lets us see that the philosopher who rules the city looks at the world as if he were a mathematician, as if there existed perfect ideas of the qualities imperfectly represented in the objects and actions of experience. This mathematical outlook on the world depreciates the complex objects available to experience. Like the mathematician, the philosopher to whom Socrates is turning over the city is concerned primarily with abstractions.[19]

Socrates describes a fourth and final segment of the line. It "make[s] no use of anything sensed in any way, but using ideas themselves, going through ideas to ideas, it ends in ideas too" (511b–c). These ideas, unlike mathematical objects, apparently have no images in the visible world. It is not clear how man could ever come to know them. Socrates, however, is not returning to the thought that the highest things remain outside man's grasp. Although he does not explain how men can reach this final knowledge, he leaves the impression that it is possible by making it the fourth stage of a progression from objects like images and shadows to objects that are supposed to be more and more intelligible. The gap between sensible objects and those on the fourth section of the line is not between man's mind and the highest objects but between the highest kind of knowledge open to man and his ordinary experience. Progress along the line leads man farther and farther away from the visible world that had seemed to be his home.

Socrates creates the impression in another way as well that the objects on the highest segment of the line are accessible. By giving no example of these highest ideas, he allows us (and his interlocutors) to suppose that they are identical to the ideas he spoke of earlier— ideas of the beautiful, the just, the big, the little, the light, the heavy— ideas that become manifest in visible objects (479a–c).[20] But if these are the ideas residing on the highest segment of the divided line, the highest kind of knowledge resembles mathematical knowledge—

abstractions from the world of appearances.[21] This in fact is what Socrates' earlier description of the objects loved by philosophers indicated. The move away from the concrete world of experience, which the divided line suggests, is the move made by mathematics. Any hints of a philosophy aware of its own limits are dropped, and philosophy is reduced to mathematics.

Mathematical objects, Socrates indicates, are not like those which both are and are not, which come into being and pass away; they are simply what they are. The square with which the geometrician is concerned is perfectly square. Mathematicians are the most obvious examples of men who deal with things that are simple. But the desire for simplicity motivates the founding of the city. The god of its public theology is simple: it does not change its shape or deceive men in any way. And the men in the city, in various ways, resemble the god, for they too are only one thing. Each has only one art by nature; there are no "double" or "manifold" men in the city (397e), nor are there men who could belong to more than one class. The poet, who is complex enough to imitate a variety of things, is exiled (398a–b). And communism aims at making men simply one thing—public men, who are identical, for they have no families or property of their own which distinguish them from one another. The simplicity which the mathematician finds in his objects is supposed to be possessed by members of the city, who are simply what they are. Politics, as Plato presents it, aspires to the simplicity of mathematics. While the mathematician looks away from himself in order to find simplicity in his objects, the citizen seeks his own simplicity through politics. He forgets his various desires and possibilities in order to become one thing, supported by the institutions and the public understanding of his city.

Moveover, the simplicity sought in both mathematics and politics leads to understanding and control. If objects can be counted and measured, they can be understood enough to be manipulated. And if men possess only a single art, their contribution to the community is readily intelligible, and rulers can place them in the community to good advantage. Mathematics and politics lead to power. Both make men forget their incompleteness and dispel the confusion arising because the good is divined but imperfectly known.

Socrates illustrates man's situation in relation to the divided line with an image of a cave. The visible realm is like a cave, he says, in which men are bound so that they see only in front of them. A fire burns behind them, and between them and the fire men carry artifacts that cast shadows on the wall of the cave. The prisoners of the cave, men like us, Socrates says, see only these shadows. When some men, the philosophers, are forced outside the cave, they at first look only at shadows, then at the phantoms of human beings and other things in the water, then at the things themselves, and finally at "the things in heaven" (516a–b).

Socrates indicates even more strongly in his image of the cave what he implied from the beginning of his discussion of philosophy—he himself is not like the philosophers who are suited to rule the city in speech. In contrast to these philosophers, for whom the city is a cave they escape, Socrates gains clarity within the city.[22] He even denies in the *Apology* that he investigates "the things in the heavens" (*Apol.*, 19b–d)—the final objects the philosophers in the image of the cave see and therefore the culmination of their knowledge. Indeed, far from resembling Plato's Socrates, the city's philosophers are like Aristophanes' Socrates, who contemplates the things in the heavens rather than the political life of men (*Clouds*, e.g., 95, 225, 228). Plato's Socrates investigates "the things in the cities," moreover, through discussing with men what most concerns them, as he is doing in the *Republic*. The philosophers in the cave image, however, do not engage in discussion. The only discussion Socrates mentions in the image takes place among the prisoners, who discuss the shadows on the walls of the cave (515b). It is not surprising, then, that Socrates claims that the prisoners are "like us," but refers to no affinity between himself and the philosophers who ascend from the cave.

Although Socrates is unlike the philosophers who escape political life to dwell among "the things in the heavens," he transcends his own political community in ways the philosophers of the cave image do not. In spite of the authoritative answers his city provides, Socrates recognizes his own ignorance (354b–c). He seeks to discover the most profitable way to live (344d–e). He wants to know his own good and whether he is attaining it. He even characterizes his philosophic life as an attempt to know himself (*Phdr.*, 229e). Socrates' awareness of the incompleteness of his knowledge is a sign of his eros, as well as of his complexity. An erotic man, inasmuch as he is incomplete, is both what he is and what he might become. He transcends any given city in his longings and his possibilities.

No such awareness of insufficiency explains why the philosophers in the cave image pursue philosophy. Indeed, they are not attracted to philosophy at all.[23] They must be "compelled" to look toward the light and "dragged . . . by force" into the sun's light (515e–516c). They are not characterized by any erotic striving that urges them out of the cave, any intimation that there is anything dissatisfying about their life there, or any sense of insufficiency. In the image of the cave, Socrates thus ignores the soul's divination of the good, about which he was beginning to tell Adeimantus. He presents philosophers as nonerotic, moved by external compulsion rather than by their own motion.[24] Moreover, these philosophers do not understand themselves. When they look away from life in the cave, they look away from themselves, for as human beings that life they seem to escape is at least in part their own. Socrates admits that the prisoners of the cave lack self-knowledge, for they see nothing "of themselves or one another" (515a). But their defect is not entirely corrected in the city's philosophers. Although these philosophers do see human beings outside the cave as they ascend toward knowledge of higher things (516a), they never see themselves. As Annas points out, their knowledge is "impersonal; individual scrutiny of self plays no role at all."[25] These philosophers, unerotic and unlike Socrates, belong in the city in speech. Although they ascend from the cave in which men live, they accept the horizon of the city that rears them. They deny ordinary experience and do not question the abstractions on which they are educated. They learn only what is necessary for them to become the kind of rulers their city requires. The pure world outside the cave serves as a model for the purified politics of the city in speech.

Although their knowledge fits them to rule the city in speech, these philosophers must be compelled to return to the city (520a), just as they were forced out of the city. Echoing Adeimantus' objection that the city mistreats the guardians in instituting philosophy among them, Glaucon objects that making the philosophers rule is "to do an injustice, and make them live a worse life when a better one is possible for them" (519d). But whereas Adeimantus objects to the lack of privacy and ultimately to the lack of personality resulting from communism, Glaucon objects to the city's depriving philosophers of their impersonal contemplation. Socrates' answer is similar to the one he gave to Adeimantus earlier: the end is the good of the city as a whole, rather than of any one of its classes. And the philosophers will rule because they owe their education to the city. They rule because of obligation.[26]

The education that compels the philosophers to ascend from the cave aims at drawing them from becoming to being (521d). For such an education Socrates seeks a "common thing that all kinds of art, thought, and knowledge use as a supplement to themselves" (522c). That supplement, not surprisingly, is "number and calculation." The philosophers' education will be a mathematical one. Although number is supposed to draw the soul from becoming to being, Socrates' example of number shows that it is a means by which man arranges and manipulates the materials he finds in the world in order to make them more suitable to human life. By discovering number, Palamedes claimed, he "established the dispositions of the army at Ilium and counted the ships and everything else" (522d). Number seems particularly useful in war.

To show how mathematics draws the soul from becoming to being, Socrates explains that sensation is defective because it "doesn't reveal one thing more than its opposite" (523c). Any perceived object, for example, is larger than some objects but smaller than others, or harder than some objects but softer than others. Man's intellect must determine that largeness and smallness, for example, are two separate things. It must "[do] the opposite of what sight did" (524c), for sight presented largeness and smallness as existing together in the same object, insofar as the object is compared to other objects both larger and smaller than itself. The intellect is to move from the sensed world of relationships to simple things that are what they are without coming into relation to anything outside themselves. The intellect that Socrates describes does not so much build upon sense, moving from hard objects to hardness itself, as it denies the evidence of the senses, moving from complexity to simplicity. The number that Socrates proposes as the key to the philosophers' education is the prime illustration of how man abstracts from the evidence of the senses. For sensation, "nothing looks as if it were one more than the opposite of one" (524e). "We see the same thing," Socrates says, "at the same time as both one and as unlimited multitude" (525a). That is, each thing looks as if it were one thing and also as if it possessed many opposite qualities, such as largeness and smallness, or hardness and softness. The study of number aims at discovering a one that is not susceptible of further division—a one that is not composed of an infinite multitude. Number and calculation should not be taken up as they are nowadays, Socrates concludes, for mathematicians "[discuss] numbers that are attached to visible or tangible bodies" (525d). Philosopher-kings, in contrast, will seek a one "equal to every other one, without the slighest difference between them, and containing no parts within itself" (526a).

The unity sought by the philosopher-kings' mathematics thus abstracts from all the differences among the things counted, just as it abstracts from the particular attributes that distinguish one object from another. It is therefore the fitting preparation for philosophers who are to introduce communism in the city.[27] The simple men in the city, for whom there is no privacy, are each equal to every other one, without the slightest difference between them. The politics of the *Republic*'s city, like the philosophers' mathematical education, finds few limits in visible or tangible bodies, whose particular identities constitute limits to the city's absolute unity.[28]

The other mathematical studies in the philosophers' education are all supposed to have the same effect—turning philosophers away from becoming toward being, until they are able to grasp the good itself (532a–b). Dialectic, which usually refers to the conversations in which Socrates directs his words to particular interlocutors as they explore the numerous sides or facets to the phenomena they are discussing, is included among the mathematical studies on which philosopher-kings are educated. The dialectic learned by the city's philosophers, however, does not appear to involve shared speech, for through it they attain the being of each thing "by means of argument (*logos*) without the use of any of the senses" (532a). Their dialectic is therefore inaudible, private, and not limited like a Socratic conversation by the presence of an interlocutor.[29]

After dialectic leads philosopher-kings to the good, they "use it as a pattern for ordering the city, private men, and themselves" (540b). By instituting communism in the city, as well as by depicting models of self-sufficiency in the public tales, however, the rulers go further than merely using the good as a pattern for ordering the complex affairs and human beings in the city. They try to endow what they find in the city with the simplicity of their model. But to impose simplicity on complexity is to destroy complexity. Several times in the discussion of mathematics, Socrates acknowledges that the study is useful both for contemplating being and for making war (522c–d; 525b–c; 527c).[30]

Socrates concludes his discussion of the genesis of the city by describing how it is founded by true philosophers: "All those in the city who happen to be older than ten they will send out to the country;

and taking over their children they will rear them—far away from those dispositions they now have from their parents—in their own manners and laws that are such as we described before" (540e–541a). In rearing children apart from their parents, philosophers remove them from what most obviously distinguishes them from others, just as the mathematician concerns himself with units that are undifferentiated. Socrates does not mention how parents "sent out to the country" and deprived of their children will react. He speaks of exile, although the situation calls for mass murder. The tyrannical drive for absolute certainty and control ends in perfect horror.[31]

The Dangers of Politics

Socrates has explored the character of the city by arguing that men and women, having the same natures, should perform the same jobs, that communism of women and children is the chief good for the city, and that the city will come into existence only if philosophers rule. In each case, his argument bypasses the limitations that natural differences impose on man's desire for absolute unity. Dialectic places men and women in the same class, denying that their physical differences indicate anything about their natures. Communism of women and children, which compels men to say "mine" and "not mine" of the same things, produces a community of pleasures and pains. Communism therefore imitates the crime of incest, attacking its members' ties to their particular families—ties that would make the homogeneity at which the city aims impossible. Finally, the philosophers who rule the city assume men to be a slate which they can wipe clean. There are no natures in the world of the cave that limit their rule. This view of the world is fostered by their mathematical education, which abstracts from individual differences in order to impose its vision of unity. These characteristics of the city indicate that it is animated by spiritedness. Just as Leontius' spiritedness tries to prevent his looking at the decay of the human body—at man's mortality and thus his inevitable limitations—the spiritedness driving the city tries to blind man to his dependence and incompleteness, to all that stands in the way of a simple unity that is unassailable because it is simple.

The city in speech that Socrates describes thus possesses attributes that Aristophanes located in the Socratics, particularly their search for absolutes and their desire to free men from their particular, contingent existences, plagued by tensions and conflicts. The Socratics, blinding themselves to the human characteristics that emerge when men respond to their limited and particular circumstances, ultimately reduce men to bodies. So too does Plato's city in speech become tyrannical. It denies the independence of its members; it tries to manipulate them as if they were animals. In denying particular differences, the city ultimately denies nature. Plato replies to Aristophanes that the dangerous propensities he attributed to the Socratics arise out of politics itself.

Aristophanes tries to defend the city by criticizing philosophy and diminishing its influence on man's life. But Plato shows that the city will be led inevitably to philosophy. Experience is not sufficient to answer the perplexing questions that arise in political life. But unless politics is moderated in its demand for perfect knowledge and control, politics will go as far as to corrupt philosophy itself. Socrates indicates this very corruption in his description of the philosopher-kings and the spirited reduction of philosophy to mathematics. In response to Aristophanes' portrayal of the dangers of philosophy for politics, Plato portrays the dangerous influence of politics on philosophy.[32] What is needed is not the ridicule of philosophy that Aristophanes offers but a philosophic understanding of the city's legitimate needs, as well as of its dangerous tendencies. Philosophy must be political, in order to avoid being politicized. In the next books of the *Republic,* Socrates looks at the decline of the city into a variety of regimes. He examines the conflicting and chaotic passions of men that not only make the unity sought by the city impossible but also demonstrate why men desire that unity. This comprehensive vision of the city that Socrates provides—of its tyrannical tendencies and of what justifies or explains them—is the best way to minimize the city's dangers. Plato replies to Aristophanes that Socrates' political philosophy is man's best means to guard against the harmful abstractions Aristophanes criticizes.

Chapter 4

A Return to the Socratic Perspective (Books VIII–X of the *Republic*)

Introduction

In the last books of the *Republic,* Socrates looks at the complex desires of men that thwart the perfect unity which the city tries to achieve. He describes the decline of the city he founded in speech into timocracy, oligarchy, democracy, and tyranny. At each successive stage, man's private and selfish desires become stronger and erode the communal life that holds the regime together. Consequently, the regimes become less and less able to provide coherence and stability for human life. As the regimes become more fragmented, so do the men who live under them. Socrates does not mention any statesman-ship that improves a regime or even slows the speed of degeneration. Man appears to be unable to mitigate the chaos of his situation.

Plato thus presents two major political alternatives in the *Republic*: the unity of the city in speech, and the chaotic politics arising out of the breakdown of that city into conflicting parts. He contrasts the homogeneous unity of the city in speech with a situation having almost no unity. The conflict and chaos that emerge out of the city in speech is hardly a satisfactory alternative to that city's tyranny. In fact, the miseries of degeneration that Socrates presents explain and, to some

125

extent, even justify the city in speech. They show the necessity of ordering or controlling the conflicting elements that man encounters in the world and in himself. And Socrates' account of the dependence that stems from eros—the disgusting and even pitiful life of the tyrant—explains man's spirited suppression of his erotic longings. If man vacillates between the tyranny of the city in speech and the chaos of its decomposition, his situation is tragic.

In addition to Socrates' account of the city in speech and its decline, however, Plato also presents Socrates' own activities. The community Socrates forms with his interlocutors, since it takes their different characters into account, is an alternative to the communistic city in speech. But because Socrates does exercise rule, patiently guiding the discussion and encouraging its participants in their common endeavor, the community he forms with his interlocutors is also an alternative to the undirected regimes into which the city in speech deteriorates. The dialogic community held together by Socrates combines the unity and the diversity left asunder in the politics described in the *Republic*. Since Socratic philosophy understands man's pretensions, such as the city in speech and its philosophy, but itself escapes their tragic potentials, it is closer to comedy than tragedy. But because it avoids tragedy through understanding or philosophy, it differs from Aristophanes' comedy, which mocks the pursuit of knowledge.

Not only does Plato answer Aristophanes by defending philosophy, his presentation of a philosophy that understands political life makes possible a defense of justice. After describing the final degeneration of the regime into tyranny, Socrates asks Glaucon to judge between the orderly or just life and the unjust life of the tyrant. Socrates presents three contests between the two ways of life, from which the just life emerges as victor. Plato thus reenacts the agon of the *Clouds*, but now justice wins the contest. The just man who wins, however, is the lover of learning rather than the just man of Book IV, whose internal harmony is as perfect as that of the city in speech. As a lover of learning, he is aware of his own incompleteness. He is therefore not as likely to succumb to the attractions of an absolute justice either by locating such a justice in his own soul or by trying to impose it upon the world. In his awareness of his own limits, the just man actually resembles Socrates himself.

Finally, Socrates reopens the question of poetry, this time criticizing it, not from the perspective of the city, but from that of political philosophy. Far from revealing man's complex nature and possibilities, poetry, Socrates now argues, may bind a man to a single vision or perspective, by presenting that perspective as complete and arousing passions against whatever threatens it. Poetry can support the city founded in the *Republic* and attack political philosophy, which shows men the variety of their possibilities and the numerous perspectives that contain part of the truth. Socrates' criticism of poetry in Book X is thus an implicit criticism of the city in speech, which resembles the narrowing poetry Socrates describes. Socrates concludes with a poetic myth, which both presents a cosmic wholeness and thus acknowledges men's need for unity but also allows for the diversity that his own political philosophy reveals. The myth, however, raises more questions than it answers. Man cannot arrive at a final or complete understanding. His search for knowledge is as endless as the lives of the souls in the myth, lives of infinite cycles of deaths and rebirths. Moreover, the combination of unity and diversity found in the myth of Er is only mythical. We are left with the question of whether the dichotomies the *Republic* presents—unity and diversity, wholeness and partiality, spiritedness and eros—can ever be overcome.

The Degeneration of Regimes and Human Beings

Socrates returns the discussion to the point from which it digressed when Adeimantus asked for a fuller explanation of the city's communism. At that time, he was planning to look at "four forms" of regimes "whose mistakes are worth seeing" and the men who are like them. Only when they have seen these will they be able to judge "whether the best man is happiest and the worst wretched, or whether it is otherwise" (544a–b). To Glaucon, the effort seemed unnecessary. The just man, he thought, is obviously happy, if justice is the good condition of the soul. Life would hardly be worth living, he says, when "the nature of the very thing by which we live is confused and corrupted" (445a–b). Although Socrates agreed, he insisted that they look anyway (445b). They must see justice, not merely by looking at it by itself, but by seeing it in relation to things unlike itself. They must see by way of contrast. Socrates was about to see by way of contrast when the group insisted on hearing more about communism, an institution that eliminates the individual identities of its members and therefore makes it impossible to see by way of contrast. To bring that institution into existence, a philosophy was needed that transcended the contrasts revealed by the senses, which perceive objects as, for example, both beautiful and ugly in their relation to objects more and less beautiful than themselves. That philosophy rises to beauty itself, absolutely unmixed with its opposite. By insisting on seeing by way of contrast, Socrates rejects the philosophy which, like mathematics, views things only in their purity and simplicity. In spite of this "detour" to the communistic city and its philosophy, Socrates now "go[es] back to the same way" as he originally intended (543c).

Although there are "an unlimited number" of forms of vice (445c), Socrates is going to limit his discussion to four—timocracy, oligarchy, democracy, and tyranny. Other regimes are "somewhere between these" (544d). There might also be men who are "somewhere between these," for regimes arise "from the dispositions of the men in the cities" (544e). Regimes, and perhaps also their citizens, are complex, and do not fit simply into one class or another. And the "in-between" regimes are numerous, for, Socrates says, they exist among the barbarians as well as the Greeks (544d). There are "many strange ones," Glaucon adds (544d), showing his typical dislike of diversity. Socrates nevertheless plans to speak of the different regimes "in the order that each appeared to [him] to pass from one to the other" (449a). The regimes therefore change, and, because they change, they are not simply one thing. It is possible for them to become other than they are.

As Socrates describes these four regimes and the souls of men that correspond to them, each appears inevitably to give birth to the regime and soul type below it on the scale. It seems to be impossible for men to return to the more satisfactory order of things that their fathers enjoyed. Nor does Socrates mention any success men have had in holding off degeneration for any period of time. He paints a picture of human life that is void of human control. Men do not exercise choice. There is no statesmanship in these regimes and among these soul types—no arranging of either the individuals or material elements of the city in any pattern in accordance with human purpose.[1] Pieces come together and break apart, and man does not control the process.[2] Just as there is little lasting cohesion among the elements of the city as it changes from regime to regime, there seems to be no abiding identity in the human soul. While Glaucon's impetus provides the direction for the city in speech, Socrates discusses the inferior regimes and soul types with Adeimantus. It fits Glaucon's character that he plays a minimal role in this discussion, for these regimes embody the imperfections he seeks to escape. Such a discussion of the complexity of the soul and city, on the other hand, is appropriate for Adeimantus, who had reservations about both communism and the city's philosophic rulers.[3]

Socrates asks the Muses to describe the fall of the city in "their high tragic talk" (545d–e).[4] The city's fall occurs when its rulers lose the knowledge necessary to arrange proper marriages. This knowledge, however, is not an understanding of the different characters of human beings, as we might expect matchmakers to possess, but mathematical knowledge. As Socrates says, a "whole geometrical number is sovereign over better and worse begettings" (546c–d). Although Socrates' account of the so-called nuptial number is obscure,[5] the rulers apparently determine matings by calculations that "render everything conversable and rational" (546b). In their goal they thus resemble Aristophanes' Socrates, who also searches for "the most beautiful measure," and tries to impose a rational simplicity on the city's conventions, as in his proposals for language reform. But, as Plato's Socrates suggests, the mathematical rationality of the city encounters such difficulties as "irrational diameters" (546c). Moreover, this mathematical rationality cannot indefinitely be forced upon the human materials it attempts to unite in a stable community. Mixed types are inevitably produced—a "chaotic mixing of iron with silver and of bronze with gold" which leads to irregularity and strife (547a).

The iron and bronze elements, now existing in the ruling classes, pull the regime toward moneymaking and private property; the gold and the silver pull it toward virtue and the ancient establishment. The leading men are torn between a desire to make things their own and a desire for unity that supports the city in speech. This tension culminates in "a middle way"—a warlike regime devoted to victory and loving honor (547b). A timocracy honors men for their total devotion to the public good, especially for the sacrifice of their lives during war. At the same time, however, it awards men honor for distinguishing themselves from others. In its concern with honor, the regime therefore combines public and private elements. Moreover, the regime is torn between its love for virtue and its secret desire for money, another private element (547d–548b). Because it combines these diverse elements, the regime is unstable, and neither individual nor community is truly served. The rulers' desire to have something of their own is not completely satisfied through honor, for which they may have to sacrifice their lives, nor do they serve the community well by forcing the regime to "[spend] all its time in making war" (547e–548a). The timocratic man who resembles this regime is born out of the tension between self-denial and self-assertion. He is the son of a father who cares little for asserting or even protecting his own and of a mother who seeks preeminence and wealth for her own family (549c–d).

As a result of the expansion of the private or selfish element and the contraction of the public one, the inferior regimes are less able to provide an identity for men or a horizon in which they know their place and their purpose. Timocrats need others to recognize their worth. They acquire their identity, not from their fixed place in the community, as might an artisan or guardian in the city in speech, but from the fluctuating opinions that others hold of them. While a timocracy makes a man's place depend on opinions, oligarchy, which comes into being when the timocrats' desire for money gets the upper hand, leaves a man's place open. Out of its pursuit of gain, an oligarchy permits the same man to farm, make money, and go to war (551e–552a). But, to the extent that a man derives his identity from his occupation, a man who has a variety of occupations seems to have a variety of identities. Moreover, in an oligarchy, a man's place depends on his financial status, which is subject to change. In the worst case, the dynamics of oligarchy produce men who have no place at all. In their greed to have more, oligarchs allow men to sell all they have. And then the destitute man "live[s] in the city while belonging to none of its parts, called neither a moneymaker nor a craftsman, nor a hoplite, but a poor man without means" (552a). This is "the greatest of all evils" for cities, Socrates says, for men who live in cities without means are fomenters of revolution, since the regime in which they live has no place for them (552c–d).

Just as oligarchy comes out of timocracy, an oligarchic man arises when the son of a timocratic father sees his father lose all his property, becomes "frightened," and turns greedily to moneymaking" (553b–c). He enslaves all other desires in order to satisfy only his "necessary" ones (554a). He is driven by his fear that he will have nothing. Since he wants money itself, rather than the luxuries and comforts that wealth affords, it seems he is most concerned with security or the preservation of his life.

The breakdown of cohesion in both the regime and the soul is carried even further in democracy. This regime emerges when the poor realize the weakness of the rich and displace them (556c–557a). Offices are awarded by lot and are consequently shared "on an equal basis" (557a). Democracy makes no distinctions among men on the basis of their possessions, as do oligarchies, or of their deeds, as do timocracies. Freedom reigns along with equality, for there is "license in [the city] to do whatever one wants" (557b). Because "all sorts of human beings come to be" in a democracy, a democratic city "contains all species of regimes." A man organizing a city would go to a democracy, Socrates continues, in order to "choose the sort that pleases him, like a man going to a general store" (557d). The regime is nothing in particular because it has something of everything.

Socrates has described a democracy that could not actually exist, for it has no principle of cohesion. Nothing binds its members into a community, neither principle nor force. Democracy, Socrates says, compels no one to make war or keep peace (557e). Not even are those condemned by law punished (558a). Socrates himself, however, was later condemned to death and also executed in the comparatively tolerant Athenian democracy.[6] In contrast to this actual democracy, the democracy Socrates is describing does not seem to be a regime at all. The absolute homogeneity the city in speech attempted to maintain has dissolved into random elements that form no community.

Socrates claims that democracy is "probably the most beautiful of the regimes." Its beauty lies in its variety, for it is like "a many-colored cloak decorated in all hues" (557c). By attributing beauty to democracy, Socrates reminds us that he also called the city in speech a "beautiful city" (527c). The beauty of that city evidently lies in its purity or its lack of diversity. Although there are grace and gracelessness in all natural things, the city's artisans create an artificial environment by representing only nature's grace, only its beauty (401a). These two standards of beauty that appear to have nothing in common reflect the tension in human life that the *Republic* reveals. On the one hand, man's urge to homogeneity is manifest in the city in speech and its mathematical philosophy. On the other, man's attachment to his own, an attachment that preserves diversity, underlies the other regimes. Given the differences between Glaucon and Adeimantus, it is appropriate that Socrates addresses Glaucon when he refers to the city in speech as "your beautiful city" (527c) and that it is Adeimantus who agrees with Socrates' statement about democracy's beauty.[7]

The unnecessary desires that his oligarchic father held in check are unleashed in the democratic son. Like the democratic city, which treats equally all the different ways of life that develop in it, the democratic man treats all his desires equally. He is "all-various and full of the greatest number of dispositions" (561e). Just as the democratic city does not discriminate between its members, the democratic man exercises no choice. He permits everything. He does not choose among his possibilities but keeps them all open. There is nothing in his soul—or his city—that forces or encourages him to be some one thing. He is as formless as the city he resembles.[8]

The democratic man's openness to all possibilities degenerates into the tyrannic man's pursuit of every possible physical pleasure. The tyrannic man lives among "feasts, revels, parties, prostitutes, and everything else of the sort" (573d). Just as the democratic man refuses to limit himself to a single way of life, so the tyrannic man will not bar himself from any deed that he thinks will satisfy his desires, even cannibalism and incest (571c). A slave to his desires, the tyrannic man becomes a slave to those whom he needs to satisfy his desires. He is thus like a city ruled by a tyrant: its people desire the wealth of the few, elevate a leader who promises to give them what they desire, and soon become his slaves (564a ff.). As Socrates says, "if [tyrannic men] have need of anything from anyone, they themselves cringe and dare to assume any posture, acting as though they belonged to him" (575e–576a).

The erosion of community—its distingegration into private or selfish pursuits and its inability to give its members a sure place or identity—ends in the extreme selfishness of the tyrant. By showing that the absence of the harsh restraints imposed by the city in speech results in the evils of tyranny, Socrates shows how those restraints benefit men. The city in speech attempts to escape the chaotic struggle of selfish individuals by giving them a place in a larger community. This conflict, which the city in speech attempts to overcome, derives from man's bondage to his body, the source of his private or particular existence. This bondage is most manifest in the tyrannic man, in whom we can see the most unattractive form eros can take—the complete subordination of the soul to the body and its pleasures. Once we view the degrading life of this man, whose love for particular concubines and boy friends encounters no restraint, we can more fully understand Glaucon's spirited attempt in the city in speech to overcome man's dependence on his body and to suppress love for particular human beings. The confusion, instability, and selfishness of the declining regimes are little more desirable than the extreme represented by the city in speech. By describing these alternatives, Socrates tries to steer men away from them.

The Contest between Justice and Injustice

When Socrates begins to "sum up" the character of the tyrannic man, Glaucon breaks into the conversation (576b). Glaucon likes to be in on conclusions, on pulling together the various strands so that they can be seen at once. Socrates continues to speak with him and asks him to compare the happiness of the tyrant with that of the man with the well-ordered or just soul. Socrates stages three rounds of a contest between the two. In each round of the contest, in different ways, Socrates suggests the incompleteness of man. Socrates tries to connect Glaucon's choice of justice to an acceptance of the limits inherent in human life.

Socrates begins the first round of the contest by pointing out that, in the tyrannic city, the tyrant enslaves the multitude. As he says, "a small part" of the city is master, while almost "the whole of it and the most decent part is slave, without honor, and wretched" (577c). By analogy, the erotic part of the soul of the tyrannic man is master while the most decent part is slave and wretched. The erotically ruled tyrant is therefore as unhappy as the tyrannically ruled city. But is the opposite sort of man, whose reason enslaves his desires, and who resembles the city in speech, happy? Would the forceful rule of almost his whole soul, albeit by his most decent part, deprive him too of happiness? Like the wretched tyrannic city, he is enslaved to a small part of himself, and slavery in any form may be incompatible with happiness.[9] After Socrates argues that the tyrant is wretched, we expect him to speak of the happiness of the just man, but Socrates is oddly silent (see 580a–c). The just man wins this first round of the contest only because his opponent has come forth and proved inadequate. He has, so to speak, not had to appear. Nor does Socrates argue in the second round of the contest that the man who enslaves his desires is happier than the unrestricted tyrant. There the well-ordered and just man who appears happier than the tyrant will be not the harsh ruler of desire but the lover of learning.

For his second proof that the just man is happier than the unjust man, Socrates returns to the notion of the tripartite soul. Socrates introduced this conception of the soul earlier to show that the soul resembles the tripartite city. Socrates presented the good condition of this soul, paralleling that of the city, as the rule of reason, allied with spiritedness, over desire. Desire was thus depreciated as the soul's lowest element, which needed to be held in check. When Socrates now returns to the tripartite soul, however, he claims that each of the soul's three parts has its characteristic desires and pleasures (580d). The highest part of the soul loves learning; the spirited part is "victory loving and honor loving;" and the lowest part's "pleasure and love is of gain" (581a–b). Socrates thus locates desires throughout the different parts of the soul. Desires open the soul to external objects and make a man aware of his own incompleteness. This account of the soul accords to desire a much higher status than Socrates' earlier account of the soul. Reason's major role is fulfilling its own desire to learn, rather than allying itself with spiritedness to rule desire. Various desires rule in men's souls and determine the kind of men they are. Men moved primarily by the part of the soul which loves learning are themselves lovers of learning; those moved primarily by the other parts of the soul are lovers of victory or honor and lovers of gain (581c). The soul of Book IV is self-contained: it takes its character from the relationship among its internal parts. The soul Socrates now describes is incomplete: it takes its character from its relations to external objects of desire. Just as the psychology Socrates presented earlier conformed to the requirements of the city, this new psychology is more consistent with the erotic activity of Socrates' political philosophy.[10]

Having derived these three types of human beings from the different desires in the soul, Socrates lets them contest. Each claims that his pleasures are the greatest and that he is therefore the happiest of men. The lover of learning, who is now identified with the just man, wins: because he has experienced the pleasures of honor and gain, as well as his own, Socrates argues, he is the superior judge of pleasure. The argument in favor of the lover of learning, however, is questionable. In the first place, Socrates presents no evidence that the lover of learning experiences the pleasure of honor. Glaucon merely agrees that he is honored, observing that any man who achieves his goal is honored (582b–c). Glaucon, who himself honors achievement, may wish that all achievement were honored, and he may be thinking of the honor bestowed on the philosophers of the city in speech. But, rather than being honored in actual cities, lovers of learning, or philosophers, were often held in disrepute. Adeimantus earlier appealed to the common opinion, for example, that philosophers are useless and vicious (487b–d). And Socrates himself, far from being honored in Athens, was executed by the city. In the second place, Socrates' unquestioned assertion that lovers of learning have tasted the pleasures of gain is rendered doubtful by his own poverty—a poverty of which the company was reminded earlier in the evening (337d). It therefore does not seem likely that the lover of learning possess the experience necessary to judge the different ways of life.[11] As long as this is the case, his knowledge of the way of life most productive of happiness will be incomplete. Men need a comprehensive experience in order to know fully, the argument suggests, but such an experience is unavailable to them.

Socrates' third argument that the just man is happiest is based on the distinction between body and soul and the different kinds of pleasures possible for each. Most experiences of pleasure, Socrates argues, are merely reliefs from pain. The pleasure of eating, for example, is relief from the pain of hunger. There are other pleasures, however, "that don't come out of pains" (584b). Socrates leads us to expect that the soul's pleasures are not mixed with pains. Such pleasures would appeal to a man like Glaucon, yearning as he does for goods without concomitant evils. Socrates nevertheless confuses the distinction between the pleasures of the soul and those of the body by claiming that the soul's pleasures fill the soul's emptiness, just as bodily pleasures satisfy the body's hunger (585a–b). The soul thus suffers like the body. In various ways, man is in pain and in need of things outside himself for fulfillment. The pleasures without pains that Glaucon seeks, Socrates implies, are unavailable to him.[12]

Socrates continues to emphasize the incompleteness of man when he argues that the soul's filling is more pleasant than the body's. Because what fills the soul "participate[s] more in full being" than what fills the body, the soul's satisfaction is greater and more pleasant than that of the body (585d–e). Socrates speaks of being as a matter of degree. This way of looking at being, however, is not consistent with his earlier account of the world, in which there was a strict division between being and becoming. Moreover, being is changeless, and, as Annas points out, "It is hard to see how being changeless could be a matter of degree."[13] Socrates' current way of speaking of being is consistent with the incomplete and complex soul his arguments are now revealing. The soul is in need of "opinion, knowledge, intelligence, and, in sum, all virtue," just as the body needs "food, drink, seasoning, and nourishment in general" (585b–c). Man is drawn to a variety of objects that satisfy him in different, if not contradictory, ways. Socrates has come very far indeed from the closed and spirited soul that defends its own and that is hostile to change.

Socrates ends his refutation of the man who says the unjust life is most pleasant "by molding an image of the soul in speech" (588b). Composed of disparate and even contradictory elements, the soul in this image resembles the monsters of Greek mythology (588c). Socrates constructs it out of "a single idea for a many-colored, many-headed beast that has a ring of heads of tame and savage beasts, . . . another single idea for a lion, and a single one for a human being" (588c–d). He then joins together these ideas so that "an image of one—that of human being" appears on the outside. "To the man who's not able to see what's inside," Socrates says, "but sees only the outer shell, it looks like one animal, a human being" (588d–e).

Socrates is providing Glaucon a glimpse inside of man, as if he had a magic ring that permitted him to penetrate the appearances to the reality beneath. In founding the city in speech, Socrates had given Glaucon another vision of a reality underlying the appearances—the simple ideas which, unlike their appearances, did not share in their opposites. But now Socrates shows him something that is closer to what Glaucon had originally suspected underlay the appearances. Rather than find an idea of beauty, he now finds a complex beast of disparate parts, some of them certainly more ugly than beautiful. This glimpse behind the appearances reveals complexity rather than simplicity— man is part human being, part lion, and part a conglomeration of tame and savage beasts. His soul does not resemble the soul that parallels the city in speech, where all the elements "sing the same chant" and are "of the same mind" (432a). Suffering more internal conflict than the soul that is well-ordered like the city in speech, this soul is a soul in pain—a soul that the rounds of the agon between the just and unjust man more and more explicitly reveal.

The unjust soul cannot be happy, Socrates concludes, because in it the many-headed beast runs riot. Socrates again leaves to implication the happiness of the just man, the human being "in control," "nourishing and cultivating the tame heads while hindering the growth of the savage ones" and "making the lion's nature an ally" (589a–b). Justice again moves in the direction of simplicity, making man less complex—"hindering the growth" of elements that cause conflict or discord. The many-headed beast within must be controlled. Man must become political. He must have a regime within himself—a regime supported by the laws of a city (590e), even if the city exists only in speech (592a–b). Socrates' image thus shows, not only man's complexity, but his need to impose order on that complexity. Spiritedness is necessary for human life in order to avoid disintegration and chaos. Following the desires belonging to the highest part of the soul is insufficient, perhaps because those desires cannot be completely satisfied, as the last rounds of the agon imply.

The three contests in which justice appears as superior to injustice, as well as Socrates' image of the soul, acknowledge both man's complexity, his dependence, and his need for rule or order. This view of man sheds light on the perfect justice of the city in speech. What we see is complex. In the first place, the new vision of the soul that Socrates presents in the agon suggests that man is necessarily incomplete. Socrates thus shows us what the city in speech denies. In the second place, Socrates' portrayal of man's misery, such as the painful desires that exist at all levels of his soul, or the servility of the tyrant addicted to the grossest physical pleasures, explains and justifies man's attempt to escape from such miseries. That attempt, taken to its conclusion, is the city in speech. However, this justification of the city in speech and its justice is finally ambiguous. For although the city provides the structure that makes life secure, it is based on a lie, albeit a noble one. The city pretends that man is simple enough that he can live merely as a citizen. It pretends that it is the whole that satisfies or completes man. By insisting that it fulfills man's eros, it destroys man's eros. Man's tendency toward the city in speech must be corrected by Socrates' political philosophy. However mindful of the need for politics and sympathetic to the benefits politics provides for men, Socrates' philosophizing reveals man's incompleteness and his complexity.

The just man who triumphs in the agon Socrates presents both rules his "many-headed beast" and is aware of his own incompleteness. Justice is to be found, not in the simple idea demanded by Glaucon, but in giving its due to the complexity of man—to both man's need for control and to his desires or yearnings. Those accomplishments of the city in speech that are defensible, as well as the human potentialities which the city suppresses, must be taken into account. Justice, the *Republic* thus teaches, lies in the difficult balance between spiritedness and eros.

When Socrates molds an image of man, he engages in poetry. His image suggests man's need for ordering or politics, as well as the difficulties and costs of an ordering that entails suppression of parts of the human soul. It is a poetry more supportive of political life than the poetry banned from the city in speech but also more complex than the poetry which that city allows. Some form of such a poetry might be useful, or even necessary, to express the insights of a political philosophy aware of this complexity. Socrates concludes his defense of justice in the *Republic* by reopening the question of poetry's value, asking how poetry can become acceptable, not to the city, as he had earlier, but to philosophy (607b). Socrates seems to be preparing the way for a defense of Plato's dialogues—poetry that defends philosophy at the same time it acknowledges man's need for political community.

Socrates' New Criticism of Poetry

Having looked at the passions of men that the city in speech tries to suppress and at the incompleteness of the human soul that it tries to deny, Socrates criticizes the poetry that supports the city. He speaks not from the perspective of the city, as he had earlier, but from that of his own philosophy. Far from being too complex, far from producing "double men" in a world where simplicity is the standard, the now censured poets bind men to simple and partial perspectives which they present as comprehensive or complete. By criticizing them, Socrates suggests that the comprehensive knowledge or completeness men long for is unavailable. We are left with only partial knowledge. The alternative to political-poetic insistence on completeness is Socrates' political philosophy which reveals the limits of man's understanding, just as it reveals the complexity and incompleteness of man's soul.

Socrates begins his criticism of poetry by setting forth a theory of three kinds of objects and three kinds of makers responsible for them. There is one idea, Socrates says, "for each of the particular 'manys' to which we apply the same name" (596a). For example, there is one idea of a table or of a chair. Imitating these ideas, the artisans or craftsmen make the tables and chairs that we use (596c). And it is by looking to the artifacts made by the craftsmen that the painter draws the tables and chairs in his pictures. Moreover, just as the painting is produced by a painter, and the artifact by a craftsman, so the idea is produced by a god. Socrates concludes that there are three kinds of couches: "one that is in nature which, we would say, I suppose, a god produced," "one that the carpenter produced," and "one that the painter produced" (597b).[14]

Although the painter imitates the couch made by the craftsman, he does not reproduce it "such as it is," Socrates says, but only such "as it looks" (598a). The couch looks one way if it is observed from the side and another way if it is observed from the front, although it does not itself become different when it is observed from different perspectives (598a). But the work of a painter can produce only a single perspective. As a simple reproduction of a complex object, it is a distortion. Imitation "lays hold of a certain small part of each thing," but it does not indicate or even know of its partial character (598b). The imitator presents his partial knowledge as if it were complete. And since the part masquerades as the whole, "it itself is only a phantom" (598b–c).

Socrates' attack on the painter is intended to pave the way for his attack on the epic and dramatic poet, especially the tragedian. This latter attack is more difficult to make. Even if a painter ordinarily paints a couch from a single perspective, it is not as clear that the dramatist presents a similarly simplistic view of human life. He does offer different perspectives by depicting a variety of characters, for example. Poetry seems to show a complexity in life; for it often leaves us with more than one possible explanation for motives and events and more than one way to evaluate them. Indeed, Socrates' earlier criticism of poetry acknowledged its complexity, for it was primarily its complexity that made it so objectionable. Given these difficulties, it is not surprising that Socrates prepares his transition from the painter to the dramatic and epic poet by giving a slightly more complex example of what painters do and showing how his criticism still applies. The painter, he says, "will paint for us a shoemaker, a carpenter, and the other craftsmen, although he doesn't understand the arts of any one of them" (598b–c). And yet he deceives foolish human beings into thinking that he "knows all the crafts and everything else that single men severally know" (598c). The painter knows the different arts he depicts no more than he presents all the different perspectives from which a couch may be viewed. His vision may appear complex, but he is, in fact, presenting a single perspective. In painting the artisans, as in painting the couch, painters present their own partial perspective as if it were the true one. While they seek to have a complete knowledge, some way of grasping all the things that individual craftsmen know, they grasp only phantoms. Complete knowledge evades them. As in Socrates' search for wisdom among the leading men in Athens (*Apol.*, 21c–23b), there appear to be only two alternatives: the artisan's knowledge of his single craft, or a vision of phantoms that pretends to be knowledge of the whole.

Just as the painter portrays a variety of crafts without understanding them, Socrates argues, tragedians and their leader Homer pretend to possess a knowledge that they do not have. They likewise deceive men, saying that they "know all arts and all things human that have to do with virtue and vice and the divine things too" (598d–e). Socrates argues against this opinion by claiming that, if poets did have such knowledge, they would not write poetry. If a man "were in truth a knower of these things he also imitates," Socrates tells Glaucon, "he would be far more serious about the deeds than the imitations and would try to leave many fair deeds behind as memorials of himself" (599b). Socrates thus insists that the poet's claim to knowledge must be substantiated by his deeds rather than by his words.

Socrates and Glaucon cannot find any cities that claim Homer as their lawgiver, any wars well-fought with his advice, any inventions in the arts attributed to him, or any companions he educated in virtue (599e–600e). From this, Socrates concludes that Homer could not have known the truth about what he wrote. His argument implies that, if knowledge exists, it must have a visible or tangible effect in the particular arts and actions of life. If knowledge can express itself in deeds, the universal can be related to the particular. But the *Republic* has shown a city where the universal replaces the particular and a decline of that city into individual selfishness, a condition that leaves the particulars as isolated units. The city in speech tries to be changeless, and therefore without action, while the deeds of men in the degenerate regimes are not directed by knowledge. Socrates' insistence that knowledge be manifest in deeds indicates his wish that the dichotomies of the *Republic* could be bridged. Words must express themselves in action if man is to achieve the completeness he desires.

After reaching an apparent conclusion to his criticism of the poet, Socrates claims that they must not leave the issues being discussed "half-said," but must "try to see [the situation] adequately" (601c). Unlike poets who take a single perspective in their productions, Socrates can take a second look. In particular, he looks again at the manner in which the poet is thrice removed from the truth, and he revises the theory. Rather than poetic imitator, craftsman, and god, Socrates speaks of poetic imitator, craftsman, and the user of the craftsman's product. In this new formulation, the craftsman looks not to the idea, the god's product, but to the user, who knows the purpose of the craftsman's product and is therefore able to direct him. It is the user who knows the good and the bad points of what he uses, Socrates says, and the craftsman follows his instructions without fully understanding what he does. Thus "even the maker [the smith and the leathercutter] does not understand [how the reins and the bit must be], only he who knows how to use them, the horsemen" (601c). The craftsman "trusts"; the user "knows" (601d–602a).

In the original theory of the three makers, the god who made the ideas has the complete knowledge lacked by the craftsmen. By replacing the god with the user, Socrates replaces the complete knowledge possessed by the god with the limited knowledge possessed by the user. Whereas there was one god who made all the ideas, there is no one user, who knows the good and bad points of each artifact and who can instruct all the artisans in their individual crafts. Just as the smith and the leathercutter are guided by the horseman, and the flute maker by the man who can play the flute (601c–e), so are other artisans guided by other users. By replacing the god with the user as the knower to whom the craftsman is subordinate, Socrates calls into question the existence of any complete knowledge. There is only the knowledge of how a variety of artifacts are used, and it is divided among the different users.

According to this revised theory of ideas, the idea that a carpenter, for example, has of a chair is not static or unchanging; rather, it comes from the uses to which a chair is put or the purposes a chair serves. But men find a variety of uses for the products artisans produce; even something like a chair can be built in a variety of ways in order to serve different purposes. The theory of ideas that Socrates first set forth in Book X, as well as in the earlier books of the *Republic*, suggested a unity underlying all the "manys" in the world. The new theory, in contrast, suggests only variety or diversity, only the heterogeneity of nature, which in its variety is open to human adapation or purpose.

Socrates distinguishes himself from the city in speech, not only in revealing the heterogeneity of nature that it attempted to hide, but in showing more sympathy with the man who loses someone he loves. As we have seen, when Socrates restricted poetry in the city in speech,

he banned poetry that depicted good men grieving, for "a decent man
. . . wouldn't lament as though he had suffered something terrible"
(387d). But now Socrates suggests that it is impossible that such a
man not be grieved at all. Rather, he must "somehow be sensible in
the face of pain" (603e). Unlike the city in speech, Socrates acknowledges that there is a certain validity to grief. Grief makes a man aware
of his incompleteness and dependence on particular human beings
whose loss causes his pain. The poetry that shows men the strength
of their attachments lets men sense that they belong to a heterogeneous
world. The poetry from which grief in excised, in contrast, weakens
men's sense of their attachment to others so that they can become
members of a homogeneous city.

When Socrates claims that a man should be sensible in the face
of his pain, however, he recognizes that poetry can go too far in
attaching men to their own. When a decent man loses someone he
loves, Socrates explains, he will be torn between his grief and the
counsels of reason and law, which make a man calm in misfortune
(604b–c). Men necessarily lose what they love insofar as they love
what is mortal, but poetry makes this loss unbearable by presenting
its pain. Consequently, poetry strengthens men's attachment to their
own and increases their hostility to whatever threatens it. Tragedy,
Socrates seems to be saying, might bind men so tightly to their particular attachments and limited world that they would try to preserve
them at all costs, even to the point of denying the inevitability of
change or that life is worth living when change occurs. And in attaching a man to his own limited connections, tragedy can attach a man
to the limited world of his city. In other words, rather than leading
to an acceptance of life's incompleteness, dependence, and mortality,
tragedy may produce an unshakable determination to preserve the
status quo; it can lead to the very poetry that supports the city in
speech.

In this final criticism of poetry, Socrates has attacked the poet
as an imitator who produces phantoms rather than the truth and as
a man who corrupts decent men by making them unable to accept
the necessities of life. In these two ways, poetry binds men to their
partial perspectives. In the first place, it deceives men into believing
that their partial vision is complete, that their own perspective is
conclusive rather than only one among many. In the second place,
poetry arouses passions that strengthen men's feelings that the particular things that they love are the greatest, perhaps the only, goods.

Poetry does not necessarily open men up to their numerous possibilities or provide different perspectives, as it had appeared to do when Socrates first censored poetry in the city. Indeed, poetry all too easily leads to and supports the city in speech. Had Socrates not returned to the issue of poetry in Book X, he would have left the case against poetry "half-said."

As do Socrates' account of the decline of regimes and the agon between the just and unjust men, Socrates' criticism of poetry in Book X implicitly criticizes the city in speech. Socrates has argued that the poet falsely claims to possess a knowledge of the arts, human virtue, and the divine. Lacking this comprehensive knowledge, ignorant of the whole he thinks he understands, he actually universalizes a part. Like the poet, the city in speech claims to possess a comprehensive knowledge of the arts, human virtue, and the divine. Just as poetry binds men to its limited and partial perspectives by deceiving them into believing they are complete, the city binds its citizens to itself and its own perspective, teaching them to believe that it is not merely their nurse and mother but their complete good. In its imposition of unity, in its cutting men off from their diverse possibilities, the city, like poetry itself, hides the heterogeneity of nature.

Poetry and the Reconciliation of the **Republic**'s Dichotomies

In spite of his condemnation of poetry, Socrates hopes that poetry has an argument to make in its defense. For, after all, even he is attracted by its charms (607c). He therefore offers poetry's protectors a chance "to speak an argument without meter on its behalf, showing that it's not only pleasant but beneficial to regimes and human life" (607d). But how might poetry be defended against Socrates' criticisms?

When poetry is charged with limiting a man to partial perspectives, especially that of his city, Socrates' earlier criticism of poetry for making man aware of a variety of perspectives seems to constitute a defense. Poetry holds two dangers—dangers to which human nature is prone and which Plato reveals in the *Republic*. The first is that man might lose himself in random diversity, a chaos without any apparent meaning or order, a seeming infinity of possibility without achievement. This danger constitutes the truth of Socrates' first criticism of poetry. It is illustrated by the complex poet, who imitates all things, without distinguishing between the human and the subhuman, and who is exiled from the city. It is a danger to which the democratic man succumbs and which the city in speech tries to remove. The second danger is that of partial perspectives restricting human potential. This danger is illustrated by the city in speech and constitutes the truth of Socrates' second criticism of poetry. Poetry can be defended against Socrates' criticisms if each of these dangers could be corrected by the other.

Socrates' two criticisms of poetry, however, although they come from opposite directions, do not cancel each other out. The conflict between the city and philosophy that the *Republic* reveals stands in the way of a successful balancing of these tendencies. The city requires poetry to strengthen man's attachment to itself and his hostility to whatever threatens his city, whereas philosophy requires poetry to broaden man's perspective by arousing his longing for what he does not possess. The city is spirited; philosophy is erotic. Poetry's potential complexity would not be as dangerous to a man's city if his city could accommodate itself to variety and change. But the *Republic* teaches that cities are threatened by such complexity. Poetry's ability to strengthen a man's attachments to his city, on the other hand, would not be as dangerous to philosophy, if man's investigation of nature, especially human nature, were not endangered by his acceptance of the perspective of his community. Again, the *Republic* teaches that philosophy is threatened by the closed character of the city. Socrates' wish for a defense of poetry is nothing less than a wish for a solution to the problem presented in the *Republic*, for a resolution of the conflict between the city and philosophy.

Socrates nevertheless concludes the *Republic* with an example of poetry of his own—the myth of Er. This myth is often considered an illustration of the proper kind of poetry and therefore an implicit defense of poetry.[15] And the myth of Er does teach that men's particular lives are both necessary and also related to a larger whole, eternity itself. Man is both a limited being, the myth shows, and one whose life goes beyond any of its particular manifestations. In other ways as well, the myth unites the goods that the rest of the *Republic* leaves simply as alternatives.

In the first place, the cosmos itself is made up of distinct parts—interlocking whorls, each of a different color and brightness, and each turning at a different speed (616c–617b). "Above, on each of its circles, is perched a Siren, accompanying its revolution, uttering a single sound, one note; from all eight is produced the accord of a single harmony" (617b). This music of the spheres differs from the song of the communistic city, where all classes "sing the same chant together" as to who should rule and be ruled (432a). There the citizens have "unanimity" or "the same mind" (*homonoia*) (432a). They all, in other words, sing the same note. The music of the spheres, which is part of the myth, in contrast, is that of a single harmony formed out of the voices of many Sirens, each singing her own note. On the other hand, the cosmos does produce a single harmony, unlike the random or chaotic voices that struggle in the political sphere when the city in speech degenerates.

The three daughters of Necessity, the Fates, sing of what has been, of what is, and of what will be (617c). They tell of time and its passage. The souls' choices of their own lives, however, influence the future. Patterns of different kinds of lives are spread before the souls, and, as they draw lots, they choose the lives they will lead when they take on mortal forms (617d–e). The life of a man therefore depends both on chance, the throwing of the lots, and the choice that he makes. This union of souls with particular earthly lives stands in contrast to the unions of men and women in the city in speech, which may appear to the participants to be entirely the work of chance but which are in fact wholly controlled by the philosopher-kings. In Socrates' description of the decline of regimes, in contrast, there is no control or choice at all. Men appear in the grip of necessity—their uncontrollable passions that lead them into greater and greater degeneration. No statesmanship promotes change for the better or even moderates the speed of the decline. The situation there stands at the opposite pole from the city in speech. The myth of Er corrects both, teaching the possibility of control, as well as the limits of control.

The souls in the myth choose from "all sorts" of lives—"lives of all animals, and, in particular, all the varieties of human lives" (618a). The patterns of lives that are presented to them recall the patterns of lives that are supposed to be found in democracy. But there no choice is ever made, no possibility foreclosed. At the opposite extreme is the city in speech, where men are limited to only one possibility, the single art they are said to possess by nature. The situation in the myth combines the variety and freedom found in democracy with the restriction to a single life placed upon men in the city in speech. The combination necessitates choice: men choose a single possibility out of the many available to them, but their choice is irrevocable (620e).

Because souls must make this choice, Socrates says, men must seek that study which gives them "the capacity and the knowledge to distinguish the good and the bad life" (618b–c). The habit of virtue is insufficient for this task, for, in the choice of lives, the greatest tyranny is chosen by "one of those who had come from heaven, having lived in an orderly regime in his former life, participating in virtue by habit, without philosophy" (619c–d). Although virtuous habits are not sufficient preparation to choose well, the knowledge that is necessary is a knowledge that eventuates in choosing and living. Since it is a knowledge of the different types of human soul, it is more akin to the knowledge sought by Socrates through his conversations with men than the mathematical knowledge of the city's philosophers. Nor is the situation Socrates presents in the myth like that in the decline of regimes, where there is no possibility that knowledge can affect the play of passions that control life. In the myth, knowledge informs choice and action.

The myth therefore appears to join what the *Republic* has presented as irreconcilable—the whole and the parts, control and chance, openness to a variety of lives and restriction to limited possibilities, and knowledge and action. But these reconciliations, we should remember, occur in a myth. Moreover, Socrates' presentation of the myth makes man's situation all the more puzzling. He argues that the soul is immortal just before telling the myth, and the myth presupposes the conclusion of that argument. The argument revolves around the idea that something is destroyed only by its own evil, so that if the soul's evil, injustice, does not destroy it, the evil of something else, the disease and finally death of the body, surely cannot do so. This argument presupposes that the soul and the body are distinct, so that the corruption of one does not affect the other.[16] But if the soul is immortal, as Socrates says, it is simple: it is "not easy" for something "composed out of many things" and therefore "full of much variety, dissimilarity, and quarrel with itself," to be eternal (611b). But can a simple thing exist in "community with body," with something so unlike itself? Socrates' argument for the immortality of the soul raises the question of the way in which man is or can be a whole—a question the *Republic* leaves unanswered, just as it leaves in mythical form the reconciliation of the dichotomies it has explored.

The question of the relation between the soul and the body, or the eternal and the temporal, raised by this argument preceding the myth, plagues the myth as well. In the myth, the soul endures a continuous series of earthly deaths and rebirths, each separated by a thousand year journey of reward or punishment. The soul constantly, as it were, unites itself with body, almost as if the simple desired the complex, or the eternal desired the temporal. Those incurably wicked, however, are not allowed to return to earth by being reborn in a body. When they approach the end of their journey, a roaring sound is heard and they are dragged back. Socrates' single example of a man not permitted to return to the earth is Ardiaeus the Great, a tyrant who "killed his old father and elder brother" (615c), a man whose crime, like Oedipus', strikes at his temporal existence. Of all the fears in the afterlife which souls suffer, "more extreme than any other was the fear that each man experienced lest the sound came as he went up, and when it was silent, each went up with the greatest delight" (616a).[17] The greatest fear is of not being able to regain a body and a particular temporal existence. The soul's longing for a body and therefore for a partial or limited life and perspective is the perplexing counterpart to man's longing for the eternal. Man remains torn between his partial perspectives and his ability to see them as partial. But will he ever be able to account for himself as the being who is so torn, to show that his limited perspectives do not disqualify him from the completeness he longs for?

Socratic poetry in the myth of Er tries to reconcile the wholeness man longs for—the wholeness sought by the city in speech—with the diversity that Socrates' own questioning philosophy brings to light. It therefore attempts to meet Socrates' two criticisms of poetry, to present a perspective complex enough to be acceptable to both the city and philosophy. In trying to unite the dichotomies of the Republic, Socrates' poetry expresses his wish for answers. And yet, as we have seen, his poetry throws doubt on the very answers it presents. The tensions of the Republic are resolved only in myth, and the myth raises perplexing questions about the relation between the body and the soul. Its implicit questions render it dangerous to politics. Although Socratic poetry may meet the Republic's philosophic criticism of poetry, it cannot meet its political one. Socrates' two criticisms of poetry reflect the duality at the heart of the Republic.

The Unresolved Quarrel between Aristophanes and Plato

Aristophanes presented philosophy, in the person of Socrates, as gaping at the phenomena in the heavens. He criticized it for abstracting itself from the concrete realities of life and thus ignoring man's limitations. Without a sense of those realities and limitations, men are apt to think that they can attain an absolute freedom, resulting in endeavors that have unjust and tragic consequences. According to this comic poet, philosophy is both a culmination of such aspirations and an activity that encourages them. He consequently sought to moderate this dangerous tendency by presenting it as laughable. The *Republic* shows that philosophy, again represented by Socrates, is aware of the dangers of man's search for absolute perfection and his denial of limitation. Moreover, Plato maintains that the dangerous desires that Aristophanes defines as philosophical or intellectual belong to political life itself. In the *Republic*, we see how the passion for justice and the attempt to found a perfectly good political community have the undesirable consequences that Aristophanes attributed to philosophy. It is not philosophy as such, and certainly not Socratic philosophy, that leads to the abstractions of the thinkery, rather it is the mathematically oriented philosophy that serves men's political passions by virtue of those very abstractions.

In contrast to that philosophy, which rules the city in speech, Socratic philosophy, Plato thought, could correct man's desire for perfect and abstract justice and his refusal to accept his limitations. For Socrates explores the complexity of the soul and therewith the elements that render impossible the perfect and permanent structures men seek. While Aristophanes ridicules this passion for absolutes in the hope of moderating it, Socrates tries to understand its source; he teaches that knowledge of man's incompleteness is superior to laughter as a means of combatting that passion. Not only is knowledge better able to accomplish this purpose, but it fulfills man's highest potential; it is the achievement of human excellence, an excellence Aristophanes discourages by ridicule.

Unlike Socratic science in the *Clouds,* Socrates' political philosophy explores the nature of man. It discovers the tensions and complexities in human life and man's attempt to overcome them. Man vacillates between accepting his complexity and denying it, between an awareness of his necessary incompleteness and action that gives order, structure, or wholeness to his life. Plato illustrates the latter by the city which Socrates and his interlocutors found in speech and which forms the center of the *Republic.* That city is an attempt to provide definitive answers to the questions of the goodness of justice and the best regime. More fundamental to the *Republic,* as it is to Socrates' political philosophy, however, is the *aporia* that throws doubt on the ultimate validity of the order that man imposes. We have seen this side of the *Republic* in the *aporetic* dialogue of Book I, as well as in the return to the Socratic perspective in the last three books of the *Republic*. In these books, Socrates indicates the human complexity that makes unity impossible, even undesirable. The *Republic* presents the opposed tendencies of man. We learn that man is torn, for example, between his desire for wholeness and his necessary incompleteness, between his desire for community and his irreducible particularity, between his spiritedness and his eros.

The community that Socrates forms with his interlocutors, however, does conjoin these opposed tendencies, offering community and common purpose and also allowing diversity. The community is held together by Socrates, who clearly presides over the conversations in which he takes part, guiding the discussion and giving it order and coherence. Socrates resembles the spirited guardian of the city in speech, in that he maintains the order of a community. Yet Socrates' rule is never absolute, for the opinions and the concerns of his interlocutors also influence the conversation. The Socratic dialogue is anchored in the distinct characters of his interlocutors, whose differences contribute to the comprehensiveness of the discussion. Socrates' *eros* not only discriminates, but it gives the particular characters of men their due. The Socratic community is a heterogeneous one, which comes closer than the politics described in the *Republic*, whether the city in speech or the degenerative regimes, to satisfying the demands of *both* Glaucon and Adeimantus.[18]

The *Republic*'s account of politics—the city in speech and its decline—gives us no reason to hope that this Socratic community ever could be a model for a political one. Moreover, the community ruled by Socrates is devoted to an exploration of the difficulties inherent in politics. Far from providing any positive guide for political action, Socrates' political philosophy, and the *Republic*, leave man at a loss or in a state of *aporia*. Political action leads to the suppressions characteristic of the city in speech, but without political action man's political life is degrading and finally brutal. Plato describes no decent politics in the *Republic* to which men can give their attention and loyalty. The best way of life for man is not political; rather, it is the philosophic examination of the dichotomies that make life and action so problematic.[19] For Aristophanes, Socratic political philosophy is not an adequate response to his criticism of Socrates. Even this philosophy is too abstract. If it leaves men in a state of *aporia*, it leaves them "in the clouds." It may be that it is for this reason that, in his portrayal of Socrates, Aristophanes did not distinguish between a pre-Socratic Socrates who investigated nature and the political philosopher who investigated moral and political questions. From his point of view, both natural philosophy and political philosophy separate men from their families, their political communities, and, in general, from the concrete or "earthly" contexts in which they must live.[20]

Because the *Republic* offers knowledge of the perils of political action rather than knowledge useful to guide politics,[21] Aristophanes would find it unsatisfactory. As long as knowledge yields no more fruit than this, he might ask, why is knowledge better for men than the forgetting that comedy is intended to encourage? Although knowing may be a human excellence, so too he might say is acting, and it is through acting in concert with others, in families and political communities, that men can best achieve happiness. If acting leads to the tragic consequences Plato depicts, the answer is not a knowledge that discourages action but a laughter that allows men to act because it moderates those tragic consequences. Aristophanes, after all, wants men to forget, not the tragic consequences of their actions, but the aspirations that lead to tragedy. For Socrates and Plato, this latter forgetting, even more than the former, constitutes a denial of humanity. The best human life, they would argue, lies in the pursuit of knowledge. Man can avoid the tragedy of reaching for an unattainable perfection by understanding its dangers. However, it is better to pursue even that dangerous aspiration for perfection than to rest with the blindness and self-satisfaction that, from Plato's point of view, is promoted by Aristophanes' comedy. The *Republic* does present the city in speech, in spite of its extremes, as a nobler achievement than the gross hedonism of the tyrannical life. The quarrel between Aristophanes' comedy and Plato's political philosophy remains unresolved.

Aristotle addresses the question of the relation between thought and politics through his own political science, which shows that philosophy can guide action. His political science therefore constitutes an answer to the question that divided Aristophanes and Plato. Aristotle maintains that man can acquire knowledge that results in action and that the most effective action is informed by thought. This can be true only if the most important dichotomies left by Plato can be brought into some sort of political balance or harmony. This is the achievement of Aristotle's political science. It shows that unity allows for diversity, that nature allows human choice, and that political communities are open to change promoted by the independent parts of which they are composed. These aspects of Aristotle's political science become obvious from an examination of Book II of his *Politics*, where he criticizes Socrates and his understanding of politics. Aristotle teaches men that through their choices and actions they can prevent their political life from slipping into the extreme unity of the city in speech or the degeneration that follows its demise. Although Aristotle does not deny that there is a tension between philosophy and politics, or thought and action, he believes that the tension can produce a beneficial alliance for both. His major political works are therefore treatises that give practical advice about politics rather than dialogues that are fundamentally *aporetic*.

Part III

Political Science: Aristotle's Achievement (Book II of the *Politics*)

Introduction

Aristotle agrees with Plato's primary response to Aristophanes—that philosophy should concern itself with human life. Aristotle claims in the *Ethics*, for example, that he is presenting a "philosophy about human affairs" (*NE*, 1181b15–16). Like Socrates and Plato, Aristotle speaks of the potentials and limitations of men, the meaning of justice, the relation between justice and the other good things men desire (e.g., *NE*, 1155a22–32), and even the conflict between philosophy and the city (e.g., *NE*, 1177a12–1179a31; *Pol.*, 1323a14–1325b33). He agrees that the problems that Plato's Socrates explores are the fundamental ones that men face. Platonic political philosophy thus forms the background and provides the questions for Aristotle's political thought.

In spite of the important similarities between Aristotle's thought and Plato's, and in spite of Aristotle's great indebtedness to Plato, Aristotle presents his political science as a correction of Plato's political philosophy.[1] Although he accepts the problems as Plato presents them, he offers answers that Plato did not give. Aristotle's concept of political science itself is his unique contribution. The word for political science is *politikē*, which can also mean political action.[2] Aristotle uses it to mean both. It is both knowledge of politics and an activity that produces better political communities. It aims at both understanding

153

and action. The end, Aristotle says, is not merely "to contemplate" and "to know," but "to act" (NE, 1179b1–2). Politikē therefore can also be translated as "statesmanship."[3]

Aristotle therefore unites thought and politics in a way Plato did not. The Republic, as we have seen, teaches that philosophy, at its best, contemplates the tensions and dichotomies that make action difficult and that politics either moves toward the unity of the city in speech or dissipates into chaos. In contrast, Aristotle teaches that philosophy is best made aware of the complexities and limitations of human life by applying itself to action (see, e.g., 1264a6) and that politics can be turned aside from its dangerous extremes when it is directed by philosophy (see, e.g., 1282b21 ff.). Whereas Socrates founded political philosophy by undertaking a philosophic examination of human affairs, Aristotle founded political science by directing philosophy to political action.

Although a complete understanding of Aristotle's political science requires a full examination of Aristotle's practical works, an investigation of Book II of the Politics indicates the direction his political science takes. In Book II, Aristotle examines the proposals made by other political thinkers about the best way to organize political communities, as well as the best political arrangements that have existed. By showing that the best proposals made and the best regimes existing are defective, Aristotle establishes the grounds of his own political science: the grounds on which he criticizes the thoughts and regimes of the past and present are those on which his own political science rests.

Although Aristotle discusses the proposals of other thinkers, he criticizes Plato's Republic in greatest detail. Book II of the Politics therefore contains Aristotle's response to Socrates. His criticisms of Socrates, as we shall see, in some ways resemble those of Aristophanes. By criticizing Socrates, Aristotle addresses the questions at issue between Aristophanes and Plato concerning the problem of Socrates and the character of philosophy. Aristotle's political science, which directs philosophy to political practice, constitutes an implicit defense of philosophy against Aristophanes' criticism and of politics against Plato's.

Aristotle criticizes the city in speech primarily for its excessive unity, for not recognizing the independence of families or the value of particular relationships between individuals. Socrates and Plato would agree that these are defects of the city in speech. But they would argue that these defects grow out of the city itself. Aristotle, in contrast, presents a different view of politics, claiming that a city is composed of dissimilar elements. A city, according to Aristotle, not only allows but even requires the existence of families and particular relationships. Aristotle thus criticizes Plato not primarily for failing to appreciate diversity, as it might appear, but for failing to see that politics is able to incorporate diversity and, in fact, must do so. From Aristotle's point of view, then, Socrates and Plato did not fully understand this potential of politics. Aristotle consequently attributes the excessive unity of the *Republic*'s city not to any inherent tendency of politics but to Socrates' and Plato's failure to understand political life.

Aristotle discusses political proposals made by Phaleas and Hippodamus, as well as those of Socrates and Plato. All the proposals, including those of Socrates and Plato, Aristotle says, were made by men who have not participated in politics themselves (1273b28–30). They are the proposals of an abstract reason, which is not anchored or rooted in action or practice. By pointing out the mistakes that such a reason makes, Aristotle indicates that he shares Aristophanes' belief that thought can undermine political life. In the second part of Book II, Aristotle criticizes the regimes that have the best reputations of those that exist in his time or that have existed in the past. He thus organizes Book II around the theme of thought and action—what men have thought about politics and what has happened. The best actual regimes, Aristotle shows, are defective in various ways; they lack, for example, cohesiveness or unity, stability, and sufficiently noble ends. They are defective because they have not been properly guided by political science or statesmanship. They are the products of chance, rather than of choice.[4] They need to be guided by thought—the kind of thought that avoids the dangers Aristotle has just attributed to the thought of his predecessors. Although Aristotle admits that philosophy can lead to dangerous abstractions, he nevertheless proposes that a philosophy "about human affairs" should guide political life. His disagreement with Aristophanes is thus more fundamental than his agreement with him.

Aristotle's treatment of these actual regimes complements his treatment of the political proposals that have been made. He criticizes past reasoning about politics because it has not recognized sufficiently the need to accommodate itself to the particular conditions that exist in the world. He criticizes the good actual regimes, on the other hand, because they have not been sufficiently directed by thought. Aristotle appropriately ends Book II with a brief list of legislators and the contributions that they have made. Legislators unite thought and action—the elements that have remained disjoined in the past thought and action that Aristotle has examined.

Book II of the *Politics* therefore addresses the question of the relation between thought and action, the question which forms the core of the quarrel between Plato and Aristophanes. Book II illustrates Aristotle's disagreement with Plato in two ways. The first is his explicit criticism of the *Republic*, in which he maintains that Plato did not understand the nature of the political community. His disagreement with Plato, however, is implicit throughout Book II in his discussion of other political proposals and actual regimes. His criticisms indicate that philosophy and politics have potentials not sufficiently developed in the past—potentials that Plato did not recognize. Necessary to their development is a cooperation between philosophy and politics. As long as it was believed that an inevitable conflict between them existed, however, their cooperation was less likely. Aristophanes and Plato both presented such a conflict, although they disagreed about its form and meaning. Their debate thus stood in the way of the founding of political science, which was Aristotle's chosen task.

I shall examine Aristotle's criticisms of past thoughts about politics, his discussion of the actual regimes reputed best, and his list of legislators at the end of Book II. Aristotle undertakes this investigation of what men have thought and done in the past, he says, so that he can establish the need for something "different" (1260b34). Because Aristotle's different political science corrects the defects of past political thought and action, Book II provides a good starting point for understanding its essentials.[5]

Aristotle's Criticism of Socrates and Plato

In the first part of Book II, Aristotle examines the best political proposals made by past thinkers. Although he discusses the ideas of Phaleas and Hippodamus, he is most concerned with Socrates' proposals in the *Republic*. His criticism focuses on the institution of communism, which he believes illustrates the mistaken assumptions the *Republic* makes about politics.

Aristotle begins by observing that Socrates' purpose in establishing communism is the unification of the city to the greatest extent possible. This excessive unity, Aristotle claims, is a mistaken goal, for it eliminates the distinctions among the particular beings that necessarily comprise any city. Contrary to Socrates, a city should not be homogeneous but is, of necessity, made up of diversity. To unify the city completely is to destroy it. As the city becomes more unified in Socrates' sense, it becomes more like an individual, for "the household is more of a unity than a city, and an individual more than a household" (1261a21). Aristotle implies that unity cannot be completely attained by an individual, let alone by a city. To the extent that a ruler unifies the city in Socrates' sense, he imposes an artificial unity upon it, constraining the growth of its parts and forcing them toward sameness.

What is the diversity of the city that Socrates denies? What are the city's parts? In Book I of the *Politics*, Aristotle finds the origin of the city in the association of human beings differing in kind: master and slave come together for the sake of security, man and woman come together for the sake of procreation. These relationships, as well as that between parents and children, comprise the household out of which the city develops (1252a26–31). The master is a man able to "foresee with his mind" what is to be done; the slave is a man analogous to the human body—strong enough to carry out what his master orders him to do. The city is based on the differences between mind and body, as well as the differences between men and women, who have characteristically different virtues (1260a20–31).[6]

In the *Republic*, in contrast, Socrates claims that the city develops not out of households or families but out of artisans, who associate in order to provide the necessities of life (*Rep.*, 369b ff.). Socrates bypasses the family and, by doing so, abstracts from the differences among human beings that stem from their bodies. As we have seen, in giving an account of the communism of women and children, Socrates claims that the physical differences between men and women are no more important than those between bald and long-haired men (*Rep.*, 454c; 455a–b). Just as Socrates ignores the physical differences between men and women, he ignores the physical resemblances between parents and their children. As Aristotle notices, the communism in the city in speech would not work if children and parents could recognize each other (1262a14–24). Its communism thus presupposes that children do not resemble their parents. The men who live under communism appear not to originate in the bodies of their parents, just as the city itself does not originate in families. Consistent with this development of the city out of artisans rather than families, the city's noble lie teaches that all its subjects were born and raised under the earth, their mother and nurse. Socrates does not, like Aristotle, make families the components of his city.

The natural distinctions that the *Republic* denies are limits on what men can do. Man's origins in the family, for example, should teach him that it is impossible for him to transcend altogether his particular, contingent existence. The natural diversity that Aristotle thinks politics should recognize and preserve thus acts as a restraint on man's tendency toward the abstractions that Aristophanes criticized. The diversity upon which Aristotle's politics is based, however, does not merely act as a limit or restraint. A man's particular contingent existence is the condition for his growth. The differences among men, most obvious in their bodies, become manifest in their characters as they mature through their exercise of speech and reason, their choices, and their relationships with others. What distinguishes men from one another, everything that makes them what they are, requires a certain freedom in order to develop. By denying natural diversity, the *Republic*'s city not only removes men from nature's limits, but also forecloses to them nature's complex possibilities.[7] For Aristotle, nature is both more closed and more open than the *Republic*'s city admits.

Aristotle therefore criticizes the *Republic* for imposing distinctions on men which stifle growth and prevent development in a variety of directions. As he points out, no man is a shoemaker by nature (1260b2–3). Although men do better jobs when they have only one job to do, nature does not endow men with the capacity for only one particular job.[8] Nor does she always divide men into rulers and ruled. Although it would be better for cities if they had permanent rulers, this is not possible in a city of free and equal men. For them it is just to rule and be ruled in turn (1261a32–b6). The distinctions that do exist in the city in speech, the differences among artisans and the division into classes, are not the natural differences that Aristotle is seeking as a guide to political life.[9] They both fail to teach men their natural limits, as distinctions based on body would do, and also stunt the development of a men's natural capacities, since they limit men to a single task. Moreover, the distinctions of the *Republic*'s city separate men from one another by teaching that men, inasmuch as they possess only one art or belong to only one class, are radically unlike others in the city. From Aristotle's point of view, these radical distinctions make political community impossible.[10] While the *Republic's* communism assumes too great an identity among men, its artificial class structure assumes too great a disparity among them. Both mistakes deny the complexity of human nature and the relationships with which Aristotle's political science is concerned.

Aristotle calls the situation in which men rule and are ruled in turn—the situation he contrasts with the rule in the *Republic's* city—by the name of "political rule" (1259b1–7, 1261a31–b6; 1287a17–18). It is the kind of authority which is most appropriate to political life and which characterizes political life at its best. Aristotle distinguishes political rule from the despotic rule of a master over his slaves and even from the rule of a father over his children. Political rule is rule among equals—men who, although they may not be absolutely equal, are never as unequal as masters and slaves or fathers and children.[11] It is because political rule occurs among men who are more or less equal that it is just that ruler and ruled rule in turn. The political ruler, or the statesman, then, acknowledges the independence of his subjects, since he rules them only "in turn." The phrase Aristotle uses may be translated also as "in part." While Aristotle may mean that the statesman actually yields his ruling office to others who will take their turns as statesmen,[12] his concept of political rule does not necessitate that rulers and subjects exchange positions. To rule and be ruled in turn may mean that rulers recognize their subjects' independence. Thus, while he rules them, he is also ruled by them—his rule is only partial, or "in part." He is limited by his subjects' desires and opinions, which he must take into account in his choices and actions. The ruled are independent of statesmen in a way that a slave is not independent of his master or a child (as long as he is a child) of his father.[13] Because of the independence of the men in the city, the statesman cannot, and indeed should not, exercise complete control over the city's affairs. If political rule occurs in a city, that city is composed of a variety of human beings, whose choices, actions, and opinions contribute to its political life. Just as the *Republic's* city does not recognize the independence of the city's parts, no political rule is to be found there.[14]

Socrates is mistaken not only in believing that the greatest possible unity should be the city's goal, according to Aristotle, but also in supposing that such unity is possible. Communism is not a good means to unity. If men say "mine" of the same things, they will fight one another to possess them. On the other hand, if men could really mean "mine as well as everyone else's" when they say "mine," as Socrates hopes, men will not care for the things that they call their own. "Men care most for their private things, and less for the common ones" (1261b33–35). Communism has deprived men of everything that is exclusively their own. Aristotle prefers the way "it is now in cities": the same person is called son by one man, nephew by another, and designated by different names according to a variety of relationships, whether of blood, of marriage, or of political fellowships (1262a9–14). A man is known through the variety of particular relationships that he has, some existing by kinship, others by choice.

Aristotle emphasizes the sacred ties men have to their parents: if men do not know their parents, as would be the case in the *Republic*'s city, they will not be able to guard against crimes against them (1262a28–32). From the point of view of the city, however, since all older citizens are regarded as parents, filial piety would protect all of them from crimes. Aristotle's objection assumes the importance of natural connections, while the *Republic*'s communism ignores the fact that what binds men to one another is more than the artificial ties created by the city.

Just as the city in the *Republic* ignores men's connections to their parents, the friendship it tries to produce through communism destroys men's separate identities. It resembles the friendship, Aristotle says, that Plato has Aristophanes describe in the *Symposium* in which lovers desire to become one. "In such a relation," according to Aristotle, "both or at least one must be destroyed," for by becoming one they cease to exist as two discrete individuals (1262b13–14). Aristotle gives another model for friendship when he discusses communism of property. Instead of common possession of property, he recommends that the legislator encourage the common use of property by inclining citizens to friendship (1263a39–40). Friends will choose to use their property in common while its ownership remains private. Possessing something of one's own makes an inexpressible difference in the pleasure one derives from it, Aristotle says (1263a41–42). Moreover, to please and help friends, visitors, and comrades is very pleasant, but this can take place only when men have private property (1263b5–7). Friends have something of their own which they are able to share with friends. Therefore, the separate identity of the individual is not lost, for friends use in common what each possesses privately. Like the citizens of the city Aristotle describes, friends form heterogeneous wholes.

Private property makes possible not only friendship but the virtues of moderation and liberality (1263b8–13). Moderation is the proper restraint toward what is not one's own, while liberality is the proper use of one's own in relation to others. The practice of these virtues therefore assumes a distinction between one's own and what belongs to others. With moderation, a man is free from the compulsion to take something from another in order to make it his own. With liberality, a man gives away something of his own; he does not have to keep everything in order to satisfy basic needs.[15] Like friendship itself, a man's practice of these virtues manifests his freedom. Freedom does not come through destroying the limitations that pertain to man as a particular being, but through the self-restraint that acknowledges what belongs to others and the liberality that properly bestows what is one's own.

Aristotle next argues that, had communism been a good device, it would have been discovered in the past (1264a2–4). He implies that the city in speech does not sufficiently take into account what has happened in the world. In prescribing its institutions, Socrates does not build on what has occurred in the past; rather, he reasons about what is good in abstraction from what has come into being. He acts as if reason were free from experience. Aristotle's next point is that the worth of Socrates' proposals would become evident if we could see his regime being formed "in deed" (1264a6). Socrates should have tested his thought by directing it toward action.

When one tries to see Socrates' city in action, one sees the disruptive force of the city's parts, which, after all, it must contain. Socrates, in his drive toward unity, has paid little attention to them, but, according to Aristotle, they threaten to break the city apart. The military class, "spirited and warlike men," will not tolerate being ruled by others (1264b9). And the members of the lowest class in the *Republic*'s city "are likely to be more difficult and full of conceit than the helots and the serfs and the slaves in some cities" (1264a34–35). Socrates has not said whether communism will apply to them. If it does, nothing will distinguish them from the upper classes. Why, then, should they submit to being ruled? If communism does not apply to them, the city will be two cities, antagonistic to each other because they have very little in common (1264a14–17). The city in the *Republic* does not satisfy men's pride or their desire to share in governing themselves. It seems to provide only the bare necessities. Socrates has tried to form a whole, ignoring the tensions that make wholeness problematic.

There are therefore two sides to Aristotle's criticism of Socrates' proposals in the *Republic*. First, Socrates encounters no natural limits when he arranges the city: he ignores the family, the physical resemblances between parents and offspring, and the irreducible diversity out of which the city is composed. Similarly, there is no political rule in the *Republic*'s city, for political rule encounters natural limits in the independence of the ruled. On the other hand, when Socrates arranges the city, he imposes an artificial unity on human beings, constraining the development through which men attain freedom. He goes too far in unifying the city; he limits men to one art; he deprives them of the independence implied in self-government; in general, he takes from them "their own," or their capacity to exercise in their relationships and through their activities the virtues that free them from the compulsions of their bodies. As Aristotle says, communism makes moderation and liberality impossible. Socrates' institution of communism shows that he both neglected natural limits and prevented men from transcending natural limits.

Aristotle prefers the regime in the *Laws* to the one in the *Republic* because it attempts to bring various classes into the regime without assimilating them to one another and because it permits the existence of families and private property. But it does not give sufficient scope to the elements of which it is composed. It doesn't allow for monarchy, for example, and the democratic element is weakened by the regime's inclination toward oligarchy (1266a5–8). It therefore fails to properly incorporate the parts into the regime. Moreover, it does not deal adequately with the problems generated by families and the private ownership of property. Specifically, the legislator has fixed the number of estates, presumably because the division of land into smaller units would lead to poverty and eventual revolution. But he has left the birthrate uncontrolled, assuming that the size of the population will remain stable (1265a4–b2). In assuming that there will be no population growth, the legislator of the *Laws* seems unaware of the extent of men's desire to have children and to support them by giving them a share in their estates. Not providing for the younger sons of property owners, he is preparing a regime of rebellious men. Men will have little loyalty to a regime that impoverishes them by forbidding them a share of their father's property. In trying to avoid revolution by fixing the number of estates, he has therefore made revolution more likely. Although he allows private property and families, he acts as if he did not have to contend with them, as if they did not really exist. The *Laws*, as Aristotle says, moves by degrees back to the *Republic* (1265a2–5). Perhaps it is for this reason that Aristotle attributes the political proposals in the *Laws* to Socrates (1265a10).

Aristotle thus criticizes Socrates for presenting a politics that insufficiently allows for the private dimensions of human life. According to Aristotle, Socrates' political thought does not deal sufficiently with the problems private life necessarily poses for politics nor does his thought incorporate into politics the benefits man's private life could provide. Like Adeimantus in the *Republic,* Aristotle claims that the communistic city in speech does not make its guardians happy. He does not accept Socrates' answer to Adeimantus—that the city is a whole that can be happy even though none of its parts are. The happiness of a city, Aristotle says, is not like a number, which could be even although all of its parts are odd. A city can be said to be happy only if all, or most, or at least some of its parts are happy (1264b16–23). Although man is a political animal and therefore dependent on the city for his happiness, he should not be entirely assimilated into the city, as in the *Republic.*[16] Socrates presents a politics that does not recognize the independence of the parts that compose the political community.

Aristotle's criticism of the *Republic* does not mention the institution of philosopher-kings. His silence raises the question of whether he found nothing to criticize in this institution.[17] Aristotle's objection to the *Republic* for not allowing political rule, however, is an implicit objection to the *Republic*'s philosopher-kings, who rule the members of the city as masters do slaves. Moreover, Aristotle's criticism of the *Republic*'s communism makes further criticism of its philosophy redundant. As I have argued, the mathematically educated philosophers, who love simple ideas and regard the complex and changing beings of experience as imperfect reflections of the ideas, are the appropriate rulers for a communistic city that conceives of unity as its greatest good and reduces its members to simple men defined entirely by their relation to the city. To criticize the *Republic*'s communism in the name of diversity is to criticize its philosophy in the name of heterogeneity.[18] Indeed, Aristotle did make this very criticism of the *Republic*'s philosophy in Book I of his *Nicomachean Ethics* in arguing against Plato's ideas of the good (*NE*, 1096a11–1097a14). Because Aristotle does not identify philosophy with mathematics, he finds no philosophy in the *Republic*'s city (1263b40).

When Aristotle criticizes the *Republic* in his *Politics*, he is objecting to Socrates' description of politics rather than to his philosophic activities. It is a criticism of his words rather than of his deeds.[19] Unlike the city in speech, Socrates does recognize the irreducible differences among individuals. He tries to treat each man in accordance with his distinctive character, potentials, and desires. Plato also recognizes the differences among men when he composes dialogues between different human beings. However, Socrates and Plato saw too great a disproportion between politics and their own philosophic activities to suppose that cities could imitate philosophy in recognizing the independence of men and in allowing the diversity and change that their independence implies. Through politics, they thought, men seek permanence, simplicity, and certainty. Aristotle claims, in contrast, that cities are composed of diversity. When he criticizes Phaleas and Hippodamus, who also made proposals for politics, he argues that cities must accommodate themselves to men's private passions, especially their passion for distinction, as well as to the changes in the city's life that arise out of such passions.

The Other Regimes in Speech

Aristotle turns from Plato to other thinkers who have made proposals that are "nearer to what has been established" (1266a33). Phaleas advocates that the size of men's estates be equal and permanent to avoid strife over inequality. But civil strife, Aristotle says, is caused by inequality of honors, as well as by inequality of property. Phaleas has not given the men who desire honor and preeminence a place in his regime. His scheme to equalize property is a less extreme version of Socratic communism, but it has the same tendencies. It might seem to allow for individuality by permitting private property, but what is possessed by each is identical to what is possessed by the others. Equality leads to homogenization. But men want to be honored for what is uniquely theirs. The threat to a regime comes, not simply from men who want to be included in the regime, but from men who want a position in the regime that they believe their merit deserves. The greatest crimes, Aristotle says, are committed, not by those seeking to avoid cold and hunger, but by those who desire "more than the necessities" (1267a6–7). Those who desire more than the necessities must either control themselves through moderation or turn to philosophy. Phaleas provides for only men's desire for the necessities (1266a37ff.) or the desires that are common to all men, rather than the desires that differentiate men from one another. In arriving at what is universal to man, his thought has reduced men to the lowest common denominator, their physical needs.

The last of the private men who have put forward views about regimes is Hippodamus. Before discussing his political proposals, Aristotle uncharacteristically gives a description of Hippodamus' person. His "love of honor" makes him peculiar, or, literally, "out of place" (*atopos*). He lets his hair grow, wears expensive ornaments, and cheap, warm clothing in both summer and winter (1267b25–28). There seems to be no single principle on the basis of which he distinguishes himself, for he distinguishes himself in contradictory ways—wearing both expensive ornaments and cheap clothes. Since he makes himself manifest in contradictory ways, he seems to lack any integrity. Perhaps this is why he seeks an arbitrary means of resisting change, wearing the same warm clothes through all seasons. Just as he acts "out of place," he also acts as if he were "out of time." He acts as if he did not have to change with the seasons of the year and divorces himself from the changing natural world around him.

Although he resists the changes of nature, he does try to learn about "the whole of nature" (1267b29). He finds a principle which he applies uniformly to a variety of things, making many of his proposals in terms of threes: he divides the land into three parts, establishes three divisions in the law, and separates the people into three classes (1267b30–39). Just as he does not adapt himself to the changing seasons by a change in clothing, so too he does not adapt his arrangements to the particular things with which he deals. Finding no natural boundaries he respects, whether between nature's seasons or between human beings and their productions, he treats different things as if they were the same. Hippodamus' street planning reveals the same mistake, eliminating the differences among cities, just as his mathematical principle ignores the differences among classes of things (1267b30–39; 1330b22–32). Not surprisingly, the "abstract" Hippodamus does not know what goes on in the world. Believing that he is making a novel proposal, he suggests that the children of men who die in war be given public support. However, such a law, Aristotle drily observes, exists in Athens and in other cities (1268a6–10).

Hippodamus also recommends that those who discover something beneficial for cities be honored (1268a7–8). This proposal raises the broader question of innovation in laws: should cities change their ancestral laws on the ground that some other law is better (1268b26–32)? Just as he orders the different things in the city according to a uniform principle, and places private houses along symmetrical streets, Hippodamus thinks that reason alone can control political development or change.

Hippodamus follows Socrates and Phaleas in regarding rationality rather than tradition as the basis of community. In his rational schemes, he encounters no natural limits, recognizing no irreducible diversity in the elements that compose a community. The city in the *Republic* ignores the body, as well as the variety of ways in which men express their individuality. Since it found no natural distinctions among men, it created distinctions when they benefitted the city. Phaleas also ignores the distinctions among men in advocating an equality in the size of estates. Hippodamus gives reason even more power in ordering political life. Political communities can be completely rational, he assumes, constantly changing their laws as better ones are discovered. Rationality rules human affairs. The logic of the *Republic* leads to Hippodamus' proposal for continuous change.

Men who favor change in laws, Aristotle says, could argue that, since the other sciences and arts have been improved by change, politics also could be improved (1268b34–38). Aristotle answers that there is a difference between politics and the other sciences and arts. Unlike the arts, laws compel obedience through custom or habit, so that to replace the existing laws lightly with new ones is to weaken the authority of the law (1269a20–25). Aristotle is saying that people obey laws, not simply because they reason about the laws' goodness, but also because the laws are their own laws which they have acquired through habit, just as their ancestors acquired them. In treating politics as if it were no different from the other arts, Hippodamus ignores the role of ancestral custom, just as, in general, he assimilates political life to a simple, rational order. He again ignores the particular: the ancestral, which means literally, "what belongs to one's fathers" (*to patrion*), is particular to a people, what is a people's "own." Aristotle's defense of the family and private property against Socrates is now broadened into a defense of the ancestral against Hippodamus.

Aristotle's argument against Hippodamus, however, is qualified. Although Aristotle argues against those who do not distinguish politics from the arts, he brings up several other arguments in support of Hippodamus' position regarding change which he does not subsequently refute.[20] One of them he states as follows: laws must be written in universal terms, but actions deal with particular situations (1269a11–12). Aristotle explains this more fully elsewhere: laws "speak in universal terms that do not hold universally, but only for the most part" due to "the infinite number of cases" that occur (*Rhet.*, I. XIII.13). Laws will therefore fail to do justice to all the cases that arise under them. Some situations are unique and may be classified under a universal category only with some distortion. Aristotle therefore proposes the concept of equity—a kind of justice whereby men suspend the law in order to do justice in the cases that do not fall under the universal rule (*NE*, 1137a31–1138a4; *Rhet.*, I.XIII.12–19). Equity, Aristotle says, is superior to the justice embodied in the law (*NE*, 1137b8–11).[21]

Aristotle deemphasizes the defect of the law when discussing Hippodamus' proposal by referring to the defect only briefly and then quickly moving to another point. But this means that Aristotle does not defend the law against this criticism. The defect therefore stands, especially since Aristotle mentions it in his own name in other works. The fact that laws cannot apply in all cases suggests the necessity of change. Although in the *Ethics* and the *Rhetoric* Aristotle proposes that laws be corrected by equity, which suspends the law in particular cases, rather than by a continual change in the law, there is a thin line between suspending the law and changing it. As novel cases arise and equity is applied, men will formulate new and better rules that take the novel cases into account. Although no universal formulation can take all possible situations into account, because there are infinitely novel situations, laws might nevertheless comprehend a larger number of situations over time. This would mean that the law, and therefore the regime behind the law, is subject to a constant process of slow change. The law would be constantly adapted in light of the particular situations that arise through men's actions (1269a11–12).

Another of the arguments is favor of changing the laws that Aristotle does not answer is that the ancient laws are "too simple and barbaric." This argument, Aristotle says, comes from looking at "what happens" (literally, at "the deeds") (1268b38–69a8). But when he argues against Hippodamus' proposal, Aristotle does not mention "what happens." He does turn to what happens, however, when he discusses the actual regimes in the next section of Book II. There he observes that the Spartan regime, built upon Cretan principles, has a more perfect finish than the Cretan one. On the basis of this observation he states a general principle: "most of the old things are less fully articulated than the newer ones" (1271b24–25). When Aristotle finally turns from the thoughts that men have about politics, to what happens, he finds support for the desirability of change.

Although Aristotle is aware that laws may need modifying in particular cases and that change may be desirable improvement, his criticism of Hippodamus still stands. Hippodamus ignores the ancestral and the limitations that deeds place upon reason. Change is good when human intelligence refines what is given, more fully articulates it, or brings out in speech and deed the possibilities inherent in what has come into being (see 1264a3–5). The abstract rationality underlying Hippodamus' proposal has been the primary object of Aristotle's criticism throughout his discussion of past political thinkers. That rationality is most manifest in the politics of the city in speech, especially in its communism, and in its mathematically educated philosophers.

Of the three thinkers Aristotle criticizes, he spends the most time arguing against Socrates and the *Republic*. Socrates is superior to men like Phaleas and Hippodamus, for he recognizes the dangers of the rationality of the city he founds in speech and tries to correct them through his own political philosophy.[22] But Socrates does not make his reservations against the city in speech explicit, and the *Republic*'s political proposals are more accessible to readers than its qualifications of them through Socrates' deeds. Aristotle's criticism of the *Republic* counters its potentially dangerous influence on men. Men might be impressed with the arrangements of the city in speech, in spite of how extreme they are. More likely, however, the kind of reasoning about politics that underlies that city might become accepted. Men would come to think about politics as if cities were not limited by their past, their material conditions, or other cities whose affairs impinge on their own. Phaleas' proposal for equality of property illustrates this manner of thinking, as do the numerous proposals of Hippodamus. Because these proposals are based on the *Republic*'s assumptions about politics, Aristotle's arguments against them implicitly criticize the *Republic*. Aristotle continues his implicit criticism of the *Republic* when he discusses the regimes that actually exist, the regimes "in deed" rather than "in speech," since Socrates does not engage in such a discussion.

Unlike the abstract rationality of the *Republic,* Aristotle's own political thought will take its bearings from what happens, or from deeds.

The Regimes in Deed

Aristotle discusses three regimes with good reputations, Sparta, Crete, and Carthage. Each of the three allows different groups to participate in government in different ways. Whatever stability they possess comes from their inclusion of different groups in the regime. The democratic Ephorate of Sparta, for example, "holds the regime together, since the people are calm because they share in the greatest office" (1270b18–20). The most stable regimes seem to be those which allow the greatest number to participate, since those who share in rule are "friendly to the regime" (1268a25) and wish it to remain as it is (1270b21–23).[23] Moreover, a regime's openness to variety allows it to incorporate merit or excellence. Carthage, the last of the actual regimes Aristotle discusses, mixes an aristocratic element with its democratic and oligarchic ones (1272b36).

Because these regimes are mixtures of different elements, ranging from democracy to monarchy, small changes in one part of the regime may incline the balance in one direction or the other. Sparta, for example, has moved from an aristocracy to democracy because the democratic Ephorate grew in power (1270b13–18). Although a regime may be stable because its many parts are friendly to it, it may also fluctuate because it contains so many active parts—parts that, no doubt, would like to increase their power. Any regime will fluctuate in this way, since a regime, to endure, must to some extent incorporate a variety of groups. The most repressive tyranny, which tries to exclude all but the tyrant from rule, not only runs the risk of revolution, but it is "least a regime" (1293b30). The regime that mixes oligarchy and democracy Aristotle calls simply regime or polity (1293b34–35), for it most clearly includes the diversity that characterizes regimes.

Regimes which change randomly due to the interaction of their diverse parts seem to lack direction and wholeness. Regimes need statesmen to guide the interaction of their parts and to direct change. Without such guidance, the conflicting parts of a regime try to direct political affairs in their own interests. The good of the whole city is left to chance. When Aristotle discusses the regimes that have the best reputations, he indicates the large extent to which men have not hitherto given overall direction to their political life. The best of the three actual regimes is Carthage, since it incorporates an aristocratic element—elections are made on the basis of merit, as well as wealth (1273a26–31)—and since it is free from civil strife (1272b30–33). These advantages of Carthage, however, seem to be the work of chance rather than any conscious plan. Aristotle mentions no legendary foun-der of Carthage, as he does of the other two regimes he discusses. The Carthaginian regime does not appear to be the product of a man who arranged or ordered it. When Aristotle mentions the lawgiver in his discussion of Carthage, he criticizes him for neglecting expedients which would have discouraged the city's oligarchic tendencies (1273b5–14). Carthage, in effect, has not had the care of a lawgiver. Because its aristocratic element is not protected by a lawgiver, it is extremely weak. Although the Carthaginians honor virtue, they believe that it is the wealthy who possess it. A poor man, they think, lacks the leisure to rule well (1273a23–25). "It is a bad thing," Aristotle says, "for the greatest offices to be for sale" (1273a38). Moreover, Carthage's free-dom from civil strife is not due to the efforts of its statesmen. The Carthaginians chance to have colonies to which a part of its population emigrates from time to time (1273b18–24). This enables the city to remove its poorer population, which might foment rebellion against the wealthy. But a city's domestic stability, Aristotle observes, ought to be due to the legislator rather than chance. If a "mischance" occurs, the multitude might revolt, and the laws would have no remedy (1273b21–24).

Sparta and Crete, in contrast to Carthage, were founded and given single direction by legislators. Their good qualities, nevertheless, may be the product of chance. For example, Aristotle leaves open whether the democratic Ephorate, which holds the regime together, is "due to the lawgiver or to chance" (1270b19–20). Crete is superior to Sparta in that its slave population is not rebellious. Although Aristotle first attributed this to Crete's granting its slaves certain priv-ileges (1264a20–23), he later indicates that Crete's location and the contingencies of its foreign affairs account for this difference between Crete and Sparta.[24] Its advantage over Sparta is therefore due to chance rather than plan. Moreover, Aristotle sheds doubt on the existence of Crete's founder, Minos. After mentioning him at the beginning of his discussion of Crete, he silently drops him from his account of Cretan history.[25]

When Aristotle examines the best actual regimes, he shows the limits within which thought must operate. Since cities are composed of diverse elements, regimes will change over time. Man cannot stop change. Moreover, to some extent change is caused by factors beyond man's control. As we have seen, Aristotle stresses the role of chance in the development of actual regimes. However, his emphasis on chance does not merely indicate the limits of statesmanship, it also constitutes a critique of past statesmanship. Chance has controlled human events partly because men have failed to direct them through their thought and foresight.

Aristotle's political science aims at minimizing the influence of chance over human affairs by teaching men how to preserve and improve their regimes. He gives accounts, for example, of different kinds of oligarchies and democracies and shows how each may be made more stable and more just by incorporating elements of the other (1291b14–1293a34; 1316b30–1321b3). In fact, the least extreme oligarchy hardly differs from the least extreme democracy (1293a11–21; 1292b25–35). Statesmanship, for Aristotle, consists of understanding the elements of which regimes are composed and knowing how to shift the relations among the elements in order to improve the regime. One regime shades imperceptibly into another, as elements are ordered in different ways. There are infinite variations. Aristotle introduces the notion of a mixed regime, the "polity," a rule of many which includes a role for the rich, as well as the poor (1279a31–39; 1293b38–b20).[26] If correctly organized, men may think this regime a democracy or an oligarchy, depending on which of its parts they see as the most important (1294b13–18).[27] By incorporating different elements into a regime—such as numbers, wealth, and even excellence of character—statesmen may form communities "out of diversities."

If statesmanship provides no order or cohesiveness, regimes fluctuate randomly in one direction or the other, as different groups gain an upper hand. When he discussed the regimes in speech, Aristotle showed how thought, divorced from action, leads to repressive homogeneity. Now, in discussing the actual regimes, he shows how action, uninformed by thought or statesmanship, leads to anarchic diversity. If thought were limited by the demands of action, its "abstracting" tendencies would be corrected, for, as Aristotle says, action concerns particulars (1269a11–12; *NE*, 1141b14–23; 1143a33–34). If political action were guided by thought toward an end or goal, the particular entities of the city would find a place in a whole—a city unified by the common purpose with which the legislator endows it. When men form a city while preserving its diverse elements, thought and action correct each other: action corrects the homogenizing tendencies of thought, and thought corrects the anarchic tendencies of unreflective action.

The List of Legislators

Aristotle ends Book II by listing lawgivers who "have put forward views about regimes" (1273b27). Unlike the men discussed at the beginning of Book II, who "have lived their entire lives in private," these men "have shared in political actions" (1273b28–32). It is fitting that Aristotle conclude by referring to lawgivers. They are the bridge between thought and actual regimes, since they found regimes and establish laws in accordance with their conceptions of what is good and possible. They complete thought by embodying it in what they find in the world, and they complete what they find in the world by arranging it in accordance with their thoughts. In the list of legislators some of the major themes of Book II converge.

Solon, Aristotle tells us, established "the ancestral democracy" of Athens, by "a good mixture of the regime." In particular, he derived the courts from all the citizens, while he preserved the Council of the Areopagus as an oligarchic element and the elective offices as an aristocratic one (1273b34–74a4). Although Aristotle attributes to Solon only one change in Athenian institutions and mentions other institutions that he preserved, he calls Solon the founder of a regime. Other statesmen, moreover, also made changes in Athenian institutions. Pericles and Ephialtes, Aristotle recounts, curtailed the power of the Council of the Areopagus, and Pericles began paying men to serve on the juries (1274a6–11). Thus Athens has come "by stages" to the present democracy, although this was not the "choice" of Solon (1274a13). A series of statesmen, each making a small change in what existed at the time, brought about a change in the regime. Is Pericles a founder less than Solon? When does a small change signify a larger one? The line between changing a law and changing a regime may not always be easy to draw. After indicating how a regime changes through the actions of successive statesmen as they modify laws and institutions, Aristotle refers to the role of chance in the formation of the present Athenian democracy: the power of the people grew as a result of its role in the Greek victory in the Persian War (1274a13–16). Foreign affairs perhaps unavoidably intrude upon domestic ones. Aristotle again acknowledges the limits to statesmanship, as well as its possibilities.

Aristotle next mentions two legislators, one of whom, Charondas, is said to be a student of the other, Zaleucus. Men trace further connections: Zaleucus, as well as Lycurgus, are said to be students of Thales (1274a22–30). Aristotle raises the question of whether legislators have been taught or whether they have acquired their skill by chance. And if legislation is teachable, is the teacher a legislator himself, like Zaleucus, who is said to have taught Charondas, or a philosopher, like Thales, who is said to have taught Zaleucus and Lycurgus? Is Aristotle looking to the past for a model for his own activity—for a philosopher who instructed others in legislation?[28] But Aristotle cannot take Thales for his model, for those who try to bring together Thales and Zaleucus and Lycurgus ignore the fact that these men lived at different times (1274a30). Although Aristotle is a philosophic teacher of statesmen, he finds no precedent for his activity.

Another tale, which Aristotle does not deny, connects the legislator Philolaos with a man name Diocles. The Olympic victor Diocles left his native Corinth for Thebes when he discovered his mother's unnatural passion for him. His lover Philolaos followed him there and became Thebes' lawgiver. Philolaos and Diocles, Aristotle tells us, are buried side by side, but, while Diocles' tomb faces away from Corinth because of his hatred of his suffering, Philolaos' tomb faces his native city (1274a31–b5). Diocles, who reminds us of Oedipus, since he journeyed from Corinth to Thebes when an incestuous relationship with his mother threatened, also tries to deny his origins, as symbolized by the location of his tomb. Perhaps Aristotle is suggesting that the proper legislator for a city is not Oedipus, the man who tried to rule by mind alone,[29] but the man who, although he loved a man like Oedipus, did not follow him in denying his origins. Although Philolaos' love carried him beyond his origins, to Thebes, the location of his tomb acknowledges his origins.

Philolaos' recognition both of man's connection to his own and of his ability to partially transcend that connection is illustrated by the legislation that is "peculiarly" his (literally, that is "private" to him). Aristotle tells us that Philolaos arranged the adoption of children so that the number of estates was preserved. Preserving the number of estates is desirable, we remember from Aristotle's discussion of the

Laws, so that the land will not be divided into smaller and smaller portions. Such divisions would eventually produce a poverty-stricken and discontented population. Unlike the legislator in the Laws, whom Aristotle criticized, Philolaos tries to provide for the children who will not inherit their parents' estates. His adoption law meets this concern. Aristotle does not give us the details of how the law worked. But, insofar as the law involves adoption, it promotes an expansion of love of one's own, whereby men make their own what is not naturally so. Philolaos' scheme might seem to resemble the Republic's communism, where men are also supposed to love the children of others as their own. But under Philolaos' law, a single couple, not a whole community, adopts a child, who comes to belong to them alone. Adoption extends love of one's own. Communism, in contrast, destroys men's sense that something is their own to the exclusion of others. Philolaos seeks to lessen the political dangers of the unrestricted satisfaction of love of one's own—the desire sustaining the household—without destroying the household. He stops far short of trying to extirpate that desire altogether, as the Republic's communism tries to do.

These lawgivers whom Aristotle mentions are obviously defective. The Athenian statesmen, for example, made only a few changes in the institutions and the result was not in all cases intended. Important changes were due to chance. Those reputed to be teachers of statesmen have not in fact taught, for too much time has separated the lives of these teachers from those reputed to be their students. Aristotle gives few details about Philolaos' legislation, and he does not say whether it succeeded or failed. These men cannot simply be models for Aristotle. But their attempts to influence regimes and the influence they did have indicate the possibility that thought shapes politics. Aristotle mentions these legislators not merely to show their limits—limits which he himself is aware of—but as evidence that statesmanship is possible. Aristotle is following in a line of statesmen, although he is improving on their work. Aristotle's statesmanship—in writing the Ethics and the Politics—corrects the activities of those legislators he mentions, while it imitates them in what is worthy of imitation.

Athenian statesmanship, for example, teaches that the small, but significant, changes legislators make can result in the change of a regime. From his knowledge of the times of Zaleucus, Charondas, and Lycurgus, Aristotle understands the need of finding a means to teach that carries his influence beyond his mortal existence. Finally, in Philolaos, he finds someone who both acknowledges and transcends his origins in his own life, as well as someone whose legislation encourages an expansion of love of one's own. In this, Philolaos may be a model for Aristotle. Aristotle's political science asks men to extend their love of their own to their city and their fellow citizens. Only such an extension could make political community possible. And yet for Aristotle, as for Philolaos, the family remains an integral part of the political community. It both serves as a reminder to men of their origins and limits and also nurtures the love of their own that men must extend to the larger community.

The legislator not only helps to elevate men to political existence but he moves himself beyond a merely private existence through his political activity. As lawgiver, his private thoughts become publicly enacted and enforced when they are adopted by others. When Aristotle lists the legislators, he mentions what is "private" or "unique" to each. By remembering the legislators' own innovations in laws, Aristotle is, in effect, honoring them for their political discoveries. He is following a version of Hippodamus' controversial proposal. The new things a man discovers and introduces to others make him worth remembering, and it is these discoveries that are most truly his own or private. This is Aristotle's last word on the private in Book II. What is most a man's own is the product of his mind, although it is something that can be embodied and shared. In this sense Aristotle concludes Book II by honoring thought.

Aristotle's Political Science as a Response to Plato

In his *Ethics*, Aristotle claims that "the young are not proper students of political science, for they are inexperienced in the actions of life, and the reasonings in [political science] come from these" (*NE*, 1095a2–4). Aristotle here distinguishes his political teaching from Socrates', which is typically addressed to the young, as in the *Republic*. In the *Republic*, Socrates did not describe the just city while Cephalus was present. A man with Cephalus' experience might understand and appreciate Aristotle's politics better than a young man who has not yet participated in "the actions of life." "Nor does it make a difference whether [men] are young in years or young in character," Aristotle says (*NE*, 1095a7–8). A man of mature character, seasoned by the actions of life, knows from experience life's complexities and limitations. Unlike the *Republic*'s city, the city formed by Aristotle's political science will acknowledge these complexities and limitations.

Aristotle therefore is seeking addressees who recognize the impossibility of perfect political solutions. He is seeking such addressees, not because they are most likely to be turned away from political life to something higher, but because such men of mature character will make the best political leaders.[30] Aristotle's politics urges statesmen to work with what is given, arranging the different parts of the community and improving the relations among them without destroying their differences. Aristotle teaches not only the numerous ways statesmen can do this but also the nobility of the task. His intention in the *Politics* is to correct what might be the effect of the *Republic*—discouraging men from participating in political life.

Aristotle makes political life attractive to men by explaining the way in which it fulfills man's nature. Because the city encompasses all other associations and their ends, its end, Aristotle says, is the supreme good (1252a1–6). Cities come into existence for the sake of life; they continue to exist for the sake of the good life (1252b29–30). Aristotle indicates the good life that the city makes possible when he explains that man is a political animal. He argues that man is political by nature because he alone of the animals possesses reason or speech. Speech indicates not merely pleasure and pain, which other animals indicate through mere voice, but the good and the bad, the just and the unjust. Since a city is a partnership in these things, man's speech or reason indicates that he is naturally suited to political life (1253a15–18).[31] At its best, politics involves communal action based on reasonable discussion of the alternatives possible at the time. The good life at which politics aims, then, is men's coming to understand, through discussion with others, the good and the just and making decisions and undertaking actions in light of that knowledge.[32] Implied in this view of the good life is man's need for others—both for coming to know the good and the just and for carrying out the measures suggested by that knowledge. When men fulfill their nature as political animals, they are engaging in political rule. They must rule and be ruled in turn, that is, they must contribute to political knowledge and action, just as their own knowledge and action must include the contributions of others. Political rule, which characterizes political life, is consequently an ongoing process.

Aristotle's view of the rationality of politics, however, does not imply that men are not motivated by passion and interest. Men must reason about what is beneficial to them and persuade others that what they want is just and good for the city. Men's selfishness leads them to considerations of justice, just as their attempt to preserve their lives by living in cities makes possible their attaining a good life. Political life is noble because of its ability to elevate men.

The politics of the *Republic*'s city in speech allows no room for the elevation of men through their discussion of the benefits and justice of what they desire. There we find no reasonable discussion of alternatives undertaken by a group of dissimilar individuals, each of whom makes distinctive contributions. Rather, in the city of the *Republic*, philosopher-kings impose general concepts upon the community, without taking individual opinions, desires, and choices into account. Indeed, rulers treat their subjects as slates that they should wipe clean (501a). There is no political rule in the *Republic*'s city; rulers are not ruled "in turn" or "in part" by those they rule. Nor does any equity recognize unique cases that arise; all particulars are forced into general categories. Political rule, like equity, ensures that individual cases are not reduced to a universal rule. Both therefore recognize diversity. But diversity implies change. The city in the *Republic* tries to be static or changeless. Such are the necessities of politics, the requirements of community, as Socrates presents them. Without such rigidity, chaos would ensue, as we saw in the decline of the city.

Just as Aristotle argues that the excessive unity of the city in speech in unnecessary to politics, so too does he argue that politics need not degenerate into excessive chaos. He claims that regimes do not necessarily decline in the single downward direction that Socrates describes. After explaining the complex causes of revolution in cities, he criticizes Socrates for his simplistic presentation of revolution. According to Socrates, revolutions change aristocracies to timocracies, timocracies to oligarchies, oligarchies to democracies, and democracies to tyrannies. Aristotle objects that a regime can change into any number of different forms; a democracy, for example, can change into an oligarchy or a monarchy, as well as a tyranny. Consequently, revolutions are not always for the worse, but also "occur the other way about" (1316a21–25). Even more important than the possibility that revolutions produce superior regimes is the possibility that regimes can be improved in less violent ways. Statesmen can produce small but significant changes by rearranging the parts of a regime. One regime merges almost unnoticeably into another, as Aristotle's description of polity indicates. The more parts a statesman can include in a regime, the greater harmony and stability he will achieve. A greater number of men will want to preserve the regime, for they have some influence in it. Moreover, the greater the number of men the statesman brings into the regime, as long as he does not deprive others of their proper place in order to do so, the greater is the regime's justice.

Aristotle can teach that politics is noble in a way that Plato cannot, because he shows that politics can combine many of the goods the *Republic* presented as conflicting. The city, Aristotle says in objection to the excessive unity of the *Republic*'s city, is a heterogeneous whole (1261a24). Although it is definitely a community—its members to a greater or lesser degree share a view of justice and nobility (1280a26–81a8), the city is made of a variety of human beings and groups who differ from one another. Unity or community, does not require uniformity. Nor need diversity give rise to degeneration and chaos, as in the decline of the city in speech, if statesmen direct the regime's potentially conflicting parts so that their actions do not subvert the regime. Rather than argue that regimes necessarily degenerate into inferior forms, as Socrates does in the *Republic*, Aristotle teaches statesmen how to preserve regimes and even how to guide them into superior forms. Aristotle's political science thus combines the unity or community that men seek to an excessive degree in the city in speech with the play of diversity that characterizes that city's decline. Because Aristotle combines the two, the unity of his community does not suppress man's private life, nor does its diversity lead to uncontrolled havoc. Aristotle thus denies that politics necessarily leads to the two extreme alternatives Socrates presents in the *Republic*. They can be avoided by adoption of Aristotle's political science or statesmanship.

Plato's Socrates, as we have seen, also avoids the two extremes to which he thought man's politics was inclined. Aristotle thus shows how a political community can do what Socrates did in his own philosophic life. Indeed, one can understand Aristotle's city at its best as an imitation of Socrates. Socrates' philosophic life, like Aristotle's city, aims at the supreme good for man, or the good life. That life, like the life of Aristotle's city at its best, consists of reasonable discussion among dissimilar human beings about what is beneficial and just for them. Like the men in the city as Aristotle sees them, the discussants in a Socratic conversation are motivated by passion and interest, but they are led to give reasons for the positions to which their passions and interests incline them. In the best case, they modify their positions as a result of other considerations that their discussion with one another brings to light. So also does Socrates listen to the opinions of others, and his arguments take their contributions into account. It is as if he exercises political rule as Aristotle conceives it, for he rules and is ruled in turn. He modifies his argument in light of the particular individuals with whom he converses, treating each of them differently. Socrates' treatment of others therefore is reminiscent of Aristotle's concept of equity. Socrates modifies his arguments in light of the individuals with whom he speaks, and he tries to treat each as he deserves, just as the man who practices equity modifies his general rule in light of the individual cases to which he applies it. Socrates makes the distinctions among men that the city in speech does not make.[33]

Moreover, because his conversations involve others who have independent opinions and interests which they often try to promote, Socrates cannot entirely direct the outcome.[34] His discussions might involve surprises. Like Aristotle's city, Socrates' way of life is open to change. His knowledge is partial, constantly modified by new considerations that arise when he converses with different individuals. Socrates even imagines that he might learn more about justice, for example, after death, if he has the opportunity to talk to the heroes of the past about their experiences (*Apol.*, 41a–b). Like political rule, Socrates' philosophizing is an endless affair, modified continually by the particular individuals and circumstances he encounters. By contrasting the life of Socrates with the rule of the philosopher-kings, Plato did distinguish different kinds of rule or authority. Aristotle's criticism of Plato, then, is that he did not make that distinction politically relevant, that is, he did not see the extent to which the city could imitate Socrates. Aristotle does not present as great a dichotomy between philosophy and the city as does Plato. The effect of Aristotle's political science is not only the elevation of politics but the inclusion of philosophy in the city.[35] Far from constituting a threat to the city's unity, the philosopher can share in political life by advising statesmen. Aristotle's *Ethics* and *Politics* are models of philosophic politics.

Plato, in contrast, believes that knowledge, being partial, cannot be a direct guide for politics, which requires definitive or certain knowledge. Politics therefore treats as absolute or unqualified knowledge that is not so. It simplifies what is complex for the sake of security. Ultimately, it suppresses individuality and change. Politics, for Plato, is based on a lie. At best, Socrates' understanding of incompleteness could be an indirect, or even negative, guide for political action, for it could teach men the dangers of politics, diminish their expectations, and perhaps even turn them away from political life. For Aristotle, however, partial knowledge can guide action, especially since action itself is incomplete and limited (*Pol.*, 1269a11–12; *NE*, 1141b14–23; 1143a33–34). Politics, especially when guided by Aristotle or by statesmen educated by Aristotle, can remain aware of its own limits. Aristotle's concepts of political rule and equity serve this end. Consequently, for Aristotle, knowledge can legitimately inform action; politics need not be based on a lie.

By suggesting that the city to some extent can imitate Socrates' way of life, Aristotle, in effect, changes the character of Socratic political philosophy. He does so by bringing political philosophy into touch with action. The highest way of life is no longer patiently exploring the fundamental alternatives and arriving at a partial understanding of them; rather it is *politikē*, which means both political science or knowledge and political activity. It is a union of philosophy and political practice that is illustrated by Aristotle's political science and that could be imitated by statesmen in their cities.

Aristotle unites philosophy and politics in his political science so that each compensates for the defects of the other. He tries to curb the dangerous propensities of philosophy toward abstract thought— which Aristophanes emphasized and Aristotle acknowledges in his criticism of Socrates' understanding of politics—by binding thought to the necessities of action. Because action involves particulars (*Pol.*, 1269a11–12; *NE*, 1141b14–23; 1143a33–34), thought will not bypass or deny such things as a man's love of his own, family life, or political tradition. From Aristophanes' point of view, then, Aristotle gives a more adequate defense of philosophy than Plato did. On the other hand, if political action could be influenced by thought—through the guidance of statesmen—political communities would be open to philosophy. From Plato's point of view, Aristotle provides a more adequate defense of politics than Aristophanes did. Aristotle's political community incorporates the diversity which Socrates' political philosophy recognizes but which Socrates did not make politically efficacious. It resembles less the communistic city of the *Republic* than the community formed by Socrates and his interolocutors, in which the independence of each is preserved as they pursue a common goal. Just as Aristotle denies that theory must be divorced from practice, as Aristophanes thought, he also denies that a political community can take philosophy in hand only by destroying it (cf. *Rep.*, 497d).

Afterword

Ancients and Moderns:
Another Debate

$\mathbf{A}$ristotle's political science is based on the view that man is a political animal. Man develops his full potential only by participating in a community in which he pursues with others what is advantageous and just. He may initially participate in a community in order to foster his individual goals, but his interactions with others, who are also seeking their own goals, compel him to use his abilities as a rational and speaking being. He consequently changes or grows through his relationships with others. Man is not a self-contained whole who is merely protected through his membership in civil society. He is an incomplete being who becomes more complete through political activity. Although Aristotle teaches that man is a part of a whole, he nevertheless insists that the good of the community cannot be understood apart from the good of its members. The common good is a complex goal, which recognizes the desires and opinions of the individuals composing the community. The community is not homogeneous; man cannot be reduced to his citizenship. While man is a part of a whole, he is also more than a part of a whole.

Because Aristotle views man as both a communal and a private being, his political science is a complex attempt to reconcile individuality and community. These two sides of Aristotle's political science can be seen, for example, in his criticism of Phaleas for neglecting man's desire for honor and preeminence, on the one hand, and in his criticism of Hippodamus for trying to give that very desire too great a place in the city, on the other. By proposing that estates be equalized, Phaleas tried to impose an intolerable equality on men, acting as if a

181

man's passion for distinction could be ignored for the sake of a communal good. Hippodamus, in contrast, encouraged that passion when he proposed that those who made beneficial political discoveries be honored by their communities. Because his proposal placed no restraints on constant change in a community's institutions and laws, Aristotle claims it neglected the needs of the community and the role of ancestral custom in men's obedience to the law and loyalty to the regime. Aristotle distinguishes himself from both these men by means of his political science: his political science allows change and individual achievement by encouraging statesmen to improve their regimes, at the same time that it respects the role of regimes in providing continuity for the lives of their members (see, for example, 1289a2–4).

The two sides of Aristotle's political science can be seen also in his criticisms of the *Republic's* communism. To what extent, he asks, must men hold things in common in a political community? Without any sharing, there would be no community, he notes (1260b35–40), but the total sharing that Socrates proposes in the *Republic* suppresses the diversity necessary for political life (1261a22–24). With respect to property, Aristotle advocates private ownership and common use, but the common use must arise out of friendship rather than from institutions such as communism (1263a34–39). To deprive men of property of their own makes friendship impossible, for men without property have nothing to share with friends. Aristotle's position against common ownership of property provides a model for what he thinks the political community can be: while men possess things of their own, they choose to share them with others toward whom they have friendly feelings.[1] It is the special task of the legislator, Aristotle says, to promote friendship (1263a39–40).

Aristotle's statement that man is a political animal thus does not deny that there is a private element to human life. In fact, it is only because a man has something of his own to contribute to politics that it is good for the community that he participate in its ongoing search for the advantageous and the just. To assimilate men to one another under the category of homogeneous citizenship makes political rule superfluous. Identical citizens need not rule "in turn" or "in part," for they have nothing of their own to add to the community. For Aristotle, the political community is a heterogeneous whole. Because the political community is a heterogeneous whole, Aristotle can find a place within it for philosophy, not merely as one element along side the

many others necessary for community, but also as the human capacity
to see the possible relations between the diverse elements of the community and the different orders that might be formed out of them
(see, for example, 1279b13 ff. and 1280a7–81a10). By demonstrating
this capacity of theory—showing that it is anchored in man's particular
associations and relationships and necessary to their harmonious flour-
ishing within a political community—Aristotle defends theory against
Aristophanes' criticism. By demonstrating that the political community does not require despotic rule but is open to this kind of ordering,
Aristotle defends politics against Plato's criticism.

Even if Aristotle's political science constitutes a successful defense
of philosophy against Aristophanes' criticism and of politics against
Plato's, it does not satisfy modern political thinkers. When they object
to the political thought of antiquity, they make no exception for
Aristotle. Machiavelli, for example, objects to the imaginary republics
and principalites of the past that turn men's attention toward ideals
that cannot be realized and away from men's actual behavior. The
political thought of the past, from his point of view, ill equips men
to live in this world.[2] Hobbes, similarly, claims that the ancients aim
too high in that they hold up to men an imaginary Summum Bonum
and make them unfit to enjoy the low but solid pleasures available to
them.[3] In inveighing against imaginary principalities and the concept
of a Summum Bonum, modern political philosophers echo Aristophanes' complaint against the abstractions of theory that remove men
from the demands, as well as the pleasures, of human existence. To
them, ancient political theory, whether it describes cities based on a
perfect justice, such as Plato's *Republic,* or cities in which men share
speech about the advantageous and the just, such as Aristotle's *Politics,*
was, like Aristophanes' Socrates, "up in the clouds." And, like Strepsiades, these modern thinkers remind men of their bodies and the
limitations their bodies place upon them. Hobbes' political science
resembles Aristophanes' comedy in that it attacks the ethereal in the
name of earthly political life.

From Hobbes' point of view, the Socratic political philosophy
presented by Plato is as ethereal as political communities aiming at
justice and the good life. Socrates' exploration of tensions, such as
that between the community and the individual, or the whole and
the parts, does not permit him to establish a political science. His
philosophizing is not sufficiently useful to man. Not only echoing

Aristophanes in his complaint against the abstractions of theory, Hobbes also resembles Aristotle in his concern that theory have a direct bearing on practice. Like Aristotle, he proposes a political science intended to effect this very thing. But Hobbes rejects community in the Aristotelian sense as one of those imaginary goods, like the ideal principalities of the ancients or the Summum Bonum. By grounding his political science on man's desire for self-preservation and limiting the end of politics to the protection of life, Hobbes asserts that men are not parts of a whole. To the contrary he views men as self-contained wholes, which political life protects, rather than as beings completed by their political activities. Only when their pride is held in check by their fear of an absolute sovereign can men escape the deadly conflict resulting from their selfish or apolitical natures. Only thus can men find the security necessity for life and comfortable living.[4] In this conception of government, liberal regimes find their origin. Instead of promoting friendship or community as political ends, rulers, imitating Hobbes' political science, are supposed to administer to the personal or private needs of men. Even when living in political society, men are not to be citizens in the ancient sense. They remain fundamentally private individuals.

Later modern thinkers find Hobbes' rejection of community for the sake of peace inadequate. They nevertheless accept one fundamental premise of Hobbes—the apolitical character of man. While denying that men are naturally directed toward community, they propose that men might attain community through the will or history or some combination of the two. Rousseau teaches, for example, that men might become citizens, as opposed to private individuals, by an act of the will whereby they will exactly what any other man would will if he considered only the whole and himself only insofar as he is a member of the whole. The man who wills the general will thus overcomes his particular interests and desires, or all the attributes that belong to him as a particular being, in order to act simply as citizen. As citizens, men are not distinct from one another, for their wills are identical. Their community is total.[5]

According to the modern understanding of history, man's nature is indeterminate, or at least flexible enough, to permit radical development or change.[6] Once this notion is introduced into political thought, it becomes possible to view history as progressive or purposive, directed toward an end or goal. That end or goal is conceived as a social arrangement that not only satisfies the human need for community neglected by early modern thinkers such as Hobbes but also secures preservation of life more certainly than Hobbes' political science, precisely because the community at the end of history is supposed to be universal. But the place of the individual in this "universal cosmopolitan condition," is ambiguous, to say the least.[7] If a man follows Kant's categorical imperative, he, like Rousseau's citizen, "abstract[s] from the personal differences of rational beings, and likewise from all the content of [his] private ends."[8] Similarly, for Marx, man must evolve beyond the stage of "an isolated monad withdrawn into himself": when man has "in his everyday life, his individual work, and his individual relationship, become a *species-being*, . . . only then is human emancipation complete" (emphasis in original).[9]

To simplify, whereas early moderns try to secure individualism at the expense of community, later moderns try to secure community at the expense of individualism. And just as in early modernity, so also in later modernity, philosophy or theory becomes active in the achievement of this end. Kant's theories of history, for example, are intended to encourage men to work for historical progress,[10] just as Marx's theories provide men with models of philosophic activity intended to change the world, rather than merely contemplate it.[11] Political science can now promote radical political change. But now there are no restraints on this union of thought and action provided by the irreducible elements of the community, as in Aristotle's political science, or even that of Hobbes, for, in the thought of later modernity, individuals become lost in the common or universal end.

The ancient thinkers whom we have examined would have had grave reservations about these modern alternatives. Although Aristophanes attempted to remind the Socratics of those things on which Hobbes based his political science, he also presented the predominance of the passions and self-interest in politics as the victory of the Unjust Speech and the demise of decent political life (*Clouds*, 1068–1104). Because Hobbes describes justice as a means of securing life and comfortable living, and therefore a means of serving the passions,[12] he would have seemed to Aristophanes to present the Unjust Speech disguised as justice. With Hobbes, as well as with the Socratics and the Unjust Speech of the *Clouds*, reason liberates men from the traditions and standards of the community and administers to their self-interest and private pleasures. Should Aristophanes have admired Hobbes for his clever disguise of injustice, he also would have considered him to be as dangerous as the Socratics he mocked in the

Clouds. On the other hand, Aristophanes would have had little more sympathy for the later moderns. Although, like them, he fought for community against the self-interested actions recommended by the Unjust Speech, he would have recognized no allies in men who undermined the particular associations in which he thought men might find happiness. Like the Socratics of the *Clouds,* the later moderns use reason to discover universals and thus lure men away from their concrete, particular lives. Far from healing men, like Aristophanes' Zeus, so that they can turn to "the deeds of life," they promote deeds to bring about a condition, the end of history, in which there is no action or change. If they try to bring men down from the thinkery in order to act, the action they recommend, Aristophanes would have thought, is the erection of a thinkery for all men.

Plato would have sympathized with the modern attempt to move beyond the endless conflict he presented between man's desire for political community and his inability to live within such a community. He is certainly sympathetic to Glaucon's desire for unity and wholeness, as he is to Adeimantus' awareness of the private, irreducible character of men. Nevertheless, he thinks that it is both unphilosophic and politically dangerous to deny either of these two sides of man. Such a denial not only blinds men to the truth about themselves but it is also fraught with the potential for tyranny, whether the tyranny of one man or of the community itself. He therefore tries to show in the *Republic* the power and legitimacy of both man's desire to be part of a community and his desire to have things of his own, even if the tension between these desires means that tragedy is at the core of politics. Modernity attempts to deny this tragedy by rewriting the *Republic.* Hobbes rewrote the *Republic,* denying the legitimacy of those desires culminating in the city in speech and bringing reason to the service of securing the stability of the inferior regimes of Books VIII and IX. The later moderns rewrote the *Republic,* denying the legitimacy of those desires calling into question the city in speech. If early moderns rewrote the *Republic* without Glaucon, the later moderns rewrote it without Adeimantus.

Aristotle resembles the moderns in that he also objects to the endless exploration of the tensions within man that constitutes Socratic philosophy. Like the moderns, Aristotle establishes a political science. Nevertheless, his reservations against the moderns would have been even greater than Plato's. The early moderns could establish a political science because they deny that men are parts of a whole;

later moderns could do so because they deny that men are more than parts of a whole. It is Aristotle's achievement to establish a political science that does justice to both these truths. Indeed, his political science demonstrates that political communities require diversity, that families are the indispensable supports for cities, and that man's highest and most enduring individual achievements are political ones, as well.

Aristotle's political science is superior to the major modern alternatives precisely because it offers a perspective from which the partial truths embodied in modern thought can be understood and reconciled. Because early moderns emphasize individuality, and later moderns community, they stand in unrelieved opposition to each other. Each offers a vision of human life that fails to do justice to the complexity of human nature. The one envisions an individualism to which community is only a means, the other a community into which no private considerations or personal distinctions intrude. Unlike these modern alternatives, Aristotle's political science provides a theory that can explain and inform political life, at the same time that it accepts the elements central to modern thought. To accept an Aristotelian perspective is not to return to the ancient city. It is to affirm both the principle of individualism found in early modern thought and also the sense of a common—and a higher—human nature found in the thought of the later moderns. Aristotle's political science suggests a basis for reconciling the poles of modern political thought.

Notes

Introduction

1. Citations to primary sources will appear in parentheses in the text. With one exception, citations to Plato are to the edition by John Burnet and translations from the Greek are my own. The exception is the *Republic*, for which I relied on the translation of Allan Bloom, with minor changes where my emphasis differs from his. For a Greek text of the *Republic*, I consulted the edition of James Adam.

2. Specifically, Aristotle argues that in the *Republic* Socrates converts the polis into an individual by imposing excessive unity upon it. As it "becomes increasingly unified it will no longer be a *polis*" (1261a15–20). The Greek word *polis* may be translated "city," if it is understood by city an independent political community. The problems with translating city as "state" are pointed out by Harry Jaffa, "Aristotle," *History of Political Philosophy*, ed. Leo Strauss and Joseph Cropsey (Chicago: Rand McNally and Company, 1963), p. 65. Polis might best be translated simply as "political community." Although the word usually refers to a relatively small political community, such as Athens or Sparta, it is not clear how large a political community the word might encompass. Aristotle argues that a political community, beyond a certain size, will no longer be a political community (*Pol.*, 1326a36–b6), for its size is related to its function (*ergon*, the work that is proper to it) (1326a10–17). But the "function" of a city, its proper work, is one of the issues that divides Greek political thinkers. (References to Aristotle's *Politics* are to the edition of W. L. Newman, and those to his *Nicomachean Ethics* are to the edition of Ingraham Bywater. Translations from the Greek are my own.)

3. The word *theoria* in Greek is etmylogically related to "seeing" and commonly means observation or contemplation. The word was used for spectators at athletic contests, as opposed to those who took part in them. Thus

theoria is commonly used in opposition to practice or action (praxis). In the *Nicomachean Ethics*, for example, Aristotle notes that "the theoretical or contemplative life" (*theoretikos bios*) is presented as an alternative to political life (*politikos bios*) in the popular literature. He associates men of action (*hoi praktikoi*) with political life (*NE*, 1095b17–25; see also *Pol.*, 1324a29–32 and 1324a40). The relation between theory and practice, and therefore the meanings of theory and practice, however, are far from clear. Aristotle certainly suggests that the two ways of life are not mutually exclusive, not only by pointing to the activity involved in contemplation (*Pol.*, 1325b16–31), but also by presenting his political science, which aims at action (e.g., *NE*, 1094a18; 1095a6; 1099b29–32; 1103b26–31; 1179a35–b4), as a kind of *theoria* (e.g., *Pol.*, 1288b21, 28, and 37). Similarly, for Plato, *theoria* may be used of contemplation of unchanging being (see *Phdr.*, 247c and *Rep.*, 486a), but by examining political questions Socrates engages in a theorizing of his own (e.g., *Rep.*, 372e)—a theorizing that was meant to have an effect on men's actions (e.g., *Rep.*, 344e). I am using "theory" in the broad sense of "thinking" or "thought," in a way that does not presuppose an answer to the question of the relation between theory and practice.

4. The *Clouds*, of course, is a comedy, but comedy does not preclude serious reflection on philosophic and political issues. For interesting discussions of the serious ideas behind the *Clouds*, see Martha Nussbaum, "Aristophanes and Socrates on Learning Practical Wisdom," *Yale Classical Studies*, 26, *Aristophanes: Essays in Interpretation* (Cambridge, Mass.: Cambridge University Press, 1980), pp. 43–97; Charles Segal, "Aristophanes' Cloud-Chorus," *Arethusa*, 2 (1969), pp. 143–61; and Leo Strauss, *Socrates and Aristophanes* (New York: Basic Books, 1966), pp. 9–54.

5. These principles of textual interpretation of Plato are explained and defended by Leo Strauss, *The City and Man* (Chicago: Rand McNally and Company, 1964), pp. 50–62; Stanley Rosen, *Plato's Symposium* (New Haven: Yale University Press, 1968), pp. xi–xxxiv; and Jacob Klein, *A Commentary on Plato's Meno* (Chapel Hill: The University of North Carolina Press, 1968), pp. 3–31.

6. Examples of interpretations of other Platonic dialogues as defenses of Socrates against Aristophanes' criticisms include Thomas L. Pangle's interpretation of the *Theages* in "Socrates and the Problem of Political Science Education," *Political Theory*, 13 (February, 1985), pp. 112–137; and Thomas G. West's introduction to *Four Texts on Socrates: Plato's Euthyphro Apology, and Crito and Aristophanes' Clouds* (Ithaca: Cornell University Press, 1984), pp. 36–37. Xenophon's Socratic dialogues can also be read as a defense of Socrates against Aristophanes' charges. See Leo Strauss, *Socrates and Aristophanes*, p. 314, and *Xenophon's Socratic Discourse: An Interpretation of the*

Oeconomicus (Ithaca: Cornell University Press, 1970), p. 112 and pp. 163–64.

7. See also Allan Bloom, "Interpretive Essay," *The Republic of Plato* (New York: Basic Books, Inc., 1968), pp. 308, 337, 387, 416, and "Response to Hall," *Political Theory* 5 (August, 1977), p. 323; and Paul Friedlander, *Plato,* Vol. 3, *The Dialogues: Second and Third Periods,* trans. Hans Meyerhoff (Princeton: Princeton University Press, 1969), pp. 108–109.

8. Martha Nussbaum also observes an affinity between Aristotle and Aristophanes and raises the question whether Aristotle meets the challenge which the *Clouds* poses. Since Aristophanes is both critical of the Just Speech's irrationality and sympathetic to its appeal to tradition and custom, she argues, Aristotle's view that both reason and habituation have a place in moral education seems to answer Aristophanes' concern ("Aristophanes and Socrates on Learning Practical Wisdom," p. 89). Her account of the relation between Aristotle and Aristophanes parallels my own, which focuses on the *Politics* rather than the *Ethics,* but which emphasizes Aristotle's reliance on both reason and custom as supports for the political community. Nussbaum concludes, however, that Aristotle's view would be finally rejected by Aristophanes, who is closer to Plato in his cynicism about the selfishness of the ordinary man (pp. 96–97).

9. For lists of "some striking discrepancies between the Platonic Socrates and the figure in the *Clouds,*" see Nussbaum, "Aristophanes and Socrates on Learning Practical Wisdom," pp. 45–46; and Strauss, *Socrates and Aristophanes,* p. 314.

10. My interpretation of the city described in the *Republic* and the philosophers who rule it takes issue with most major interpretations, inasmuch as I contend that through Socrates' depiction of that city and its philosophers Plato meant to point out the dangers inherent in politics rather than the desirable potentials that politics holds for men. Both scholars who present a sympathetic account of the *Republic*'s city (see, for example, Paul Friedlander, *Plato,* Vol. 3, *The Dialogues: Second and Third Periods,* pp. 63–144; and Dale Hall, "The Republic and the 'Limits of Politics,' " *Political Theory,* 5 [August, 1977], pp. 293–313) and those who criticize it as antipolitical (see Sheldon S. Wolin, *Politics and Vision* [Boston: Little, Brown, and Company, 1960], pp. 28–68; and also Hannah Arendt, *The Human Condition* [Garden City, New York: Doubleday and Company, 1959], especially pp. 197–206) or even totalitarian (see Karl R. Popper, *The Open Society and Its Enemies,* Vol. I [London: Routledge and Kegan Paul, 1945]) find no discrepancy between what Socrates describes in the *Republic* and Plato's own views. Indeed, scholars who distinguish between Plato's early "Socratic" dialogues and later ones

in which he develops his own position hold that in the *Republic* Plato uses Socrates as a mere mouthpiece for his own thoughts and that the city and philosophy described there are Platonic and not Socratic. (See, for example, Paul Friedlander.) Taking this assumption about Plato's development for granted, Nussbaum makes the interesting argument that the views propounded in the *Republic* constitute Plato's own implicit criticism of Socrates on largely Aristophanean grounds, "Aristophanes and Socrates on Learning Practical Wisdom," pp. 86–87. Even the Straussian school (especially Leo Strauss, *The City and Man*; and Allan Bloom, "Interpretive Essay," and "Response to Hall,") which offers a complex and subtle reading of Plato, maintains that Plato is sympathetic to the just city and its philosophic rulers. Although Bloom, for example, argues contrary to other interpretations that the city in the *Republic* is intended to be against nature and consequently impossible to realize, he nevertheless maintains that "all of Western man's aspirations to justice and the good life are given expression and fulfillment in Socrates' proposals for a city," ("Interpretive Essay," p. 410). Moreover, he describes the philosopher whom Socrates designates as ruler as "the highest kind of individual," (p. 415). Underlying my disagreement with Bloom, I believe, is a fundamentally different understanding of what is desirable for men, both politically and philosophically.

11. I share this distinction between Socrates and the philosophers described in the *Republic* with those scholars who find a development in Plato's thought—seen in early dialogues that are faithful to the historical Socrates and later ones, including the *Republic*, in which, they contend, Plato presents his own views rather than Socrates'. (See previous note.) My own interpretation, however, is based neither on assumptions about Plato's development nor on any radical distinction between Plato and Socrates. Not only early Platonic dialogues but also the *Republic* itself, I argue, teach us about Socratic philosophizing, which Plato, even at this so-called later stage, holds up as a model for men. The city and the philosophy Socrates describes in the *Republic* is not only not Socratic, as the "development" theory maintains, but it is also not Platonic. Rather, they illustrate a view of the dangers of politics that both Socrates and Plato share. In denying that theories about Plato's development help us to understand the *Republic*, I follow the approach of Strauss and Bloom. However, those theories are useful in emphasizing how "un-Socratic" the politics and philosophy described in the *Republic* are and thus provide a corrective to accounts such as Bloom's that do not distinguish between Socrates and the philosophers he places in the city. Bloom writes, for example, that by the end of Book VII "a city has been formed in speech of which Socrates is a member" (p. 413).

12. This is ultimately true of the *Laws* as well. See Thomas L. Pangle, "Interpretive Essay," *The Laws of Plato*, trans. with notes and an interpretive

essay by Thomas L. Pangle (New York: Basic Books, Inc., 1980), pp. 508–10, and especially, p. 441.

Part I. Aristophanes' Laughter (The Clouds)

1. Henri Bergson describes the social function of laughter. Men laugh, according to Bergson, at "what inclines to swerve from the common centre round which society gravitates," at "sign[s] of an eccentricity." "By the fear which it inspires, [laughter] restrains eccentricity." "Laughter, then, does not belong to the province of esthetics alone, since unconsciously (and even immorally in many particular instances) it pursues a utilitarian aim of general improvement." Bergson, "Laughter," in *Comedy*, ed. Wylie Sypher (Garden City, New York: Doubleday and Company, Inc., 1956), p. 73.

2. One senses that Aristophanes sympathizes with his Socrates. As Cedric H. Whitman notices, "The caricature of Socrates differs from that of Cleon in that it lacks hatred," *Aristophanes and the Comic Hero* (Cambridge, Massachusetts: Harvard University Press, 1964), p. 142.

3. Unless otherwise stated, references in parentheses in Part I are to Aristophanes' *Clouds*. I have used Dover's edition and translations are my own.

4. Charles Segal gives several examples of how the language and the action of the *Clouds* imitate tragedy, especially with respect to the role of the chorus. He notes the Clouds' "paratragic solemnity [at line 755] which prepares for the doom of a hero," "the archaic pattern of rash confidence before disaster" found in Strepsiades' boasts, and the Clouds' "Aeschylean formula" at 1457–61 that catastrophe befalls evil men so that they learn to fear the gods, "Aristophanes' Cloud-Chorus," p. 153. The ending of the play thus seems like "the *peripeteia* of a tragedy," p. 154.

5. Strepsiades wishes that he "would have struck out [his] eye with a stone" before he had incurred his debts (24). An ambiguity in Greek allows one to read Strepsiades' line as if he wishes that the horse had been blinded before the debts had been incurred. Such a reading, however, misses Strepsiades' tendency to find tragic overtones in his situation. In this instance, he reminds the reader of Oedipus' self-mutilation. William James Hickie is an example of someone who has Strepsiades refer to the horse's blinding rather to his own in *The Comedies of Aristophanes*, (London: Bell and Daldy, 1871), p. 118. My reading follows that of K. J. Dover, *Clouds* (Oxford: Clarendon Press, 1968), note on line 24, p. 96, as well as that of William Arrowsmith, *The Clouds* (New York: The New American Library Inc., 1962), p. 18.

6. Strepsiades says that "a love-of-horse disease" (*hipperon*) consumed his property (74). Aristophanes has probably coined this word, for it occurs only here in extant Greek literature. The word combines the word "horse" (*hippos*) and the suffix *eros*, which indicates a disease in such words as *ikteros*, jaundice, and *huderos*, dropsy. But the suffix *eros* sounds like *erōs*, the word for love. The horse disease is a horse love. Strepsiades thus has an intimation that Phidippides is moved by some perversion of *eros*.

7. Aristophanes mocks the "pale," "unearthly" hue of the Socratics when one of them tells Strepsiades that they are not permitted to spend too much time in the open air (198–99). After Phidippides finally attends the Socratic school, Strepsiades believes that his son's education has been a success by the pale complexion with which he returns home (1171). See also 1112.

8. Socrates, suspended in the air, calls Strepsiades "ephemeral" (223), evidently excluding himself from such a category.

9. The student uses the verb "to sing" (*adein*) to refer to the gnat's humming (158)—a verb that suggests activities of music and poetry. Homer, for example, begins the *Iliad* by asking the goddess, or the Muse, "to sing" of the wrath of Achilles (*Iliad*, I, 1). The Socratics fail to distinguish the singing of the Muses from the noises made by gnats.

10. Moreover, by placing Socrates' students in such a position, Aristophanes implies that they are homosexuals. Perhaps he is suggesting that they deny their dependence on women out of their desire for self-sufficiency, just as they (as we shall soon see) forget about their need for food.

11. K. J. Dover points out that Socrates' theory of the mind's operation is similar to one actually propounded by Diogenes of Apollonia. See his comments, *Clouds*, note on line 230, p. 12.

12. The magnanimous man whom Aristotle describes in the *Ethics* also wants to have others indebted to him without his being indebted to them. He therefore remembers the favors he confers but forgets those which others have done for him (*NE*, 1124b12–15). He, too, tries to escape from necessity, desiring, for example, to possess beautiful but useless things (*NE*, 1125a11–13).

13. Critics have been puzzled as to how this theft provides food. Arrowsmith removes the difficulty in his translation by letting the student add, "He pawned the cloak; we ate the proceeds," *The Clouds*, note on lines 177–79, p. 124. However, the story of Socrates' providing food by stealing a cloak reveals how ineffective Socrates is in taking care of man's fundamental needs. Dover is correct in observing that Socrates imitates a cook, but he sprinkles

ashes rather than barley, "for instead of dinner, the students are to have a geometry lesson," note on line 177, p. 86. We should be reminded of the *Republic*, where a Socratic conversation about justice replaces a dinner. Plato's Socrates also finds a substitute for food, but it is a different kind of substitute. We shall see both similarities and differences between Aristophanes' portrayal of Socrates and Plato's.

14. In other ways as well, Strepsiades constantly reminds the Socratics of the physical dimensions of life. When Socrates summons the "divine" Clouds, Strepsiades is afraid of getting wet; he wants to fart in imitation of the Clouds' thundering; and he claims that he has to relieve himself (267; 294–295). In response to Strepsiades' physical references, Socrates tries to silence him, since Strepsiades is "mocking" the divinities and speaking words of bad omen (296).

15. Dover, *Clouds*, note on line 381.

16. Although Chaerophon is not identified by his father's name, he is identified by his deme (156). But even this identification does not serve to associate him with a particular place, for Chaerophon is called a "Sphettian," it is generally believed, not because he is from Sphettos but for the sake of a pun on the word *sphēx*, meaning "wasp." See Dover, *Clouds*, note on line 156, p. 114. If "Sphettian" is simply a pun and not a true reference to Chaerophon's deme, the Socratic way of identifying Chaerophon suggests that words can free a man from his origins: Chaerophon is a Sphettian because of a play on words rather than because of his birthplace.

17. Strepsiades calls attention to the war in the first few lines of the play. He curses the war, because it has made his slaves unruly (6–7). Apart from Strepsiades' references to the war when he looks at the map of the world, the *Clouds* seems to forget about the war. Its subject, man's desire to escape from limitation—a desire that leads to Aristophanes' Socrates—necessitates such a forgetting.

18. When Strepsiades first sees the Clouds, he believes they must be women, and not clouds, for "they have noses" (344). To have a nose is to have a particular shape. Aristophanes may be reminding the audience that Socrates is famous for his distinctive, if ugly, nose. Socrates is famous for his particular shape; his attempt to transcend his material being is doomed.

19. When Socrates prays for the Clouds to come, he invokes them in the traditional way by specifying several places where the divinities may be (270–273). The invocation usually indicates the piety of the man who prays, for he does not presume to know the whereabouts of the gods. (See, for example, Homer's *Iliad*, XVI, 514–15; and Aeschylus' *Eumenides*, 292–97.) Socrates, however, makes the traditional invocation amusing by elongating

it, for he gives five possible places the Clouds may be. The length of the list suggests an infinite number of possibilities. The Clouds have no particular haunts, just as they have no particular shapes.

20. Segal argues that Socrates' view of the Clouds as representatives of formless chaos and the amoral world of unjust rhetoric is mistaken. Rather, for Aristophanes, the Clouds "are connected with *physis* [nature], but not the *physis* of the unjust Argument" (Aristophanes' Cloud-Chorus," p. 156). The Clouds, associated with "joy, life, light of nature" and "fecunding moisture," represent a "healthy aspect of *physis*," pp. 154–56. Consequently, the Clouds, Segal argues, are appropriately allied with the Just Argument, pp. 150–52. Moreover, their statement that Strepsiades' fall is justified due to his evil ways is thoroughly in character, pp. 155–57. Segal's position, however, too easily connects vitality with moral order and neglects the full implications of the Clouds' formlessness. The Clouds are indifferent to the various forms they imitate. Their sympathy with the Just Speech is a sign not of their justice but of their willingness to take any side of an issue. They also encourage the Unjust Speech (1034–35). Insofar as they are formless, they are always changing (see 275 and 348). That Socrates cannot control them indicates, not their superior stance to life and morality, but their essential unreliability. Although chaos may initially suggest to a clever man an opportunity to control or manipulate, it may ultimately signify the impossibility of control.

21. Strepsiades reminds us of the materiality of the Clouds when he compares their thunder to his farting (293–94).

22. Whitman observes "the ambiguity of the clouds both as goddesses, indeed the only goddesses, and as natural phenomena, controlled by 'necessity,' that is physical laws" (*Aristophanes and the Comic Hero*, p. 139). Although Whitman notices "the wedding of the astronomic with the gastronomic," he does not fully explore the serious meaning underlying this comic absurdity. This "wedding" reflects the union of Socrates' ethereality with his study of material nature.

23. The divine Clouds are said to favor idle men, or, literally, men who perform no deeds (316). But the idle men include the poets, (literally, "those who make music," 334), who celebrate the Clouds in their verse (334–39). Socrates, in contrast, does not make anything.

24. The word *wise* (*sophos*) also has the connotation of clever. Whitman, however, does not think that the *Clouds* is one of Aristophanes' better comedies. The only extant version of the *Clouds* is a revision of an earlier play that did not win the prize. The original play, Whitman speculates, portrayed the victory of the comic hero—the triumph of the unjust speech and Strepsiades' escape from his debts. Such a play would have been unpopular, according to Whitman, because it would have been "all too sympathetic

to the new education," p. 136. In revising, Aristophanes attempted "to redress the moral balance," but "seems to have recognized that he could not moralize his play without ruining it, and given up the attempt," p. 137. Whitman therefore supposes that the extant *Clouds* is a misconceived revision that was abandoned before it was completed. His dislike of the *Clouds* stems from its failure to portray the "comic heroism" that he sees as essential to Aristophanes' comedy. That heroism necessitates a triumph of "the illimitable, libidinous *joie de vivre*," "an assertion, in one way or another, of boundlessness, a dethronement of limit, of reason, and even of the gods themselves," pp. 22 and 24; see also pp. 21–58. The fact remains, however, that Aristophanes called the play that most obviously falls short of Whitman's ideal his "wisest." In arguing that there is a happy assertion of boundlessness at the core of comedy, Whitman fails to give sufficient attention to the fact that this comic resolution presupposes that the impossible is, in fact, possible. (See Leo Strauss, *The City and Man*, p. 62.) Aristophanes shows that the triumph of "the illimitable, libidinous *joie de vivre*" takes place in a fantasy world. He thus allows his audiences to delight in comic triumph at the same time he leaves them with the impression that *joie de vivre* is attainable only in the comic theater. The *Clouds*, as the wisest of Aristophanes' comedies, makes explicit through its action that the desire for the illimitable and boundless cannot be satisfied.

25. One of the offenses listed is "shouting *iou iou*" (543), which is the lament with which Strepsiades began the play. As Hickie observes, "The Scholiast has very justly found fault with these boasts of our poet; and proved, from his own works, that he has been guilty of all the offenses against decency and good taste which he reprehends so freely in others," *The Comedies of Aristophanes*, note 5, p. 140.

26. Aristophanes mentions Hyperbolus for example, in the *Acharnians*, 846, and the *Peace*, 681. See Dover, *Clouds*, note on line 552, p. 170. Dover suggests that one of Aristophanes' rivals portrayed Hyperbolus' mother as a drunken old woman, note on line 555, p. 171.

27. "How will rhythms help me to obtain barley?" he asks (648).

28. Socrates gives several examples of how masculine names, when placed in the vocative, have the ending of a feminine nominative (686–91). Not surprisingly, he does not use his own name as an example or see that the change he is proposing will affect his own name as well as others.

29. "Nature" (*phusis*) is often used in opposition to *nomos*, meaning "convention," "custom," or "law." The Unjust Speech appeals to nature when he advises actions contrary to *nomos*, while the Just Speech's appeal to tradition is a defense of Athenian *nomos* (e.g., 961 ff.) Contrary to tradition,

which does not make such a clear distinction between nature and convention, the Unjust Speech takes the sophistic position that justice is merely conventional and injustice natural (see also *Rep.*, 359c; and *Gorg.*, 482e–484c). The exact meanings of *nomos* and *phusis*, however, are far from clear. Nature is often associated with necessity and refers to what cannot be otherwise, whereas conventions are established by men's agreements. Thus the Unjust Speech refers to "the necessities of nature" (1075). But the Unjust Speech obviously believes that man can, at least to some extent, resist those necessities, since he must persuade Phidippides to "indulge his nature" (1078). To follow nature, then, cannot be unqualifiedly necessary, as is indicated by the existence of conventions, if conventions are viewed as possibly "contrary to nature." Dover indicates this ambiguity in the use of nature when he comments on the Unjust Speech's references to nature: the necessity of nature "could mean the physical laws of the universe, . . . including the law of mortality . . . and the life of the body in general. . . . It could also be used as an excuse for illegal or immoral action," *Clouds*, note on line 1075, p. 227. His remarks suggest that nature includes what cannot be otherwise and also what allows human modification. The natural urges of men can be controlled for the sake of decency and morality. But is such control natural? This is one of the central questions of the *Republic*, which explores the question of whether justice exists by nature or merely by convention (359c; see also Aristotle, *NE*, 1134b18–35a5). In the former case, the conventions in support of justice would be in some sense natural, and the *nomos/phusis* distinction not absolute.

30. Dover, *Clouds*, note on line 977–78, pp. 216–17; Whitman, *Aristophanes and the Comic Hero*, p. 123.

31. Strepsiades is delighted when his son is returned to him, for he has "a refutative and argumentative look" (1172–73). Strepsiades exclaims with pleasure, "oh, oh, my child, oh, *iou, iou*" (1170). He here repeats the cry with which he opened the play, but there the cry was one of lament. His repetition of the scream here is therefore ominous. It forbodes the third time in which he utters the scream—when his son is beating him (1321)—an act that is reminiscent of Oedipus' patricide.

32. See Leo Strauss, *Socrates and Aristophanes*, p. 41.

33. Strauss argues that the incest between mother and son, which underlies mother-beating, cannot be made explicit in a comedy: "Father-beating may be laughable, but there are crimes that are not," *Socrates and Aristophanes*, p. 51.

34. On this apparent "moralism" of the Clouds, see note 20 of this chapter.

35. Strauss, *Socrates and Aristophanes*, p. 45.

36. After failing to obtain his son's assistance, Strepsiades asks one of his slaves to help him move against Socrates, saying, do what I ask "if you love your master" (1488). He echoes his earlier request to his son: go to school at the thinkery, "if you truly love me in your heart" (86–87). His final reliance on his slave underscores his inability to rely on his son.

Part II. *Political Philosophy: Plato's Response (The* Republic)

Introduction

1. Unless otherwise stated, references in parentheses in Part II are to Plato's *Republic*.

2. Leo Strauss argues that in fact "the only available presentation of the 'pre-Socratic' Socrates is that which we find in Aristophanes' *Clouds*," *Socrates and Aristophanes*, p. 4. This position does not explain why Aristophanes chose to criticize a "pre-Socratic" Socrates when a more mature Socrates had corrected his youthful mistakes (the *Clouds* was first performed in 423 B.C., when Socrates was over forty years old). Moreover, this position concerning the discrepancy between the Aristophanic and the Platonic Socrates suggests that Aristophanes might very well agree with Plato concerning the Socrates who engages in political philosophy. I take issue with this view in my conclusion to Chapter 4 when I return to the question of whether Plato's presentation of Socratic philosophy meets Aristophanes' concerns. At the end of his book, however, Strauss himself raises doubts about his early assertion that Aristophanes' *Clouds* portrays a simply "pre-Socratic" Socrates: it is almost impossible, Strauss concludes, "to say whether the profound differences between the Aristophanean Socrates and the Platonic-Xenophontic Socrates must not be traced to a profound change in Socrates himself," *Socrates and Aristophanes*, p. 314.

3. As Allan Bloom says, the *Republic* "is the first book which brings philosophy 'down into the cities'; and we watch in it the foundation of political science," "Interpretive Essay," p. 310 (cf. Strauss, *The City and Man*, p. 21). Although it might be argued that Plato's *Laws* is Plato's classic work of political philosophy, Socrates is absent from that work. It is, therefore, not the primary source for understanding Socratic political philosophy, which, I argue, constitutes Plato's response to Aristophanes and his defense of philosophy to the city. Contrary to those interpretations that suggest that the *Laws'* Athenian Stranger is an image of Socrates, the philosophic advisor to political communities that Socrates would have become had he left Athens

(Leo Strauss, "What is Political Philosophy?" *What is Political Philosophy?* [Greenwood Press: Westport, Connecticut, 1973], p. 33; and Pangle, "Interpretive Essay," *The Laws of Plato*, p. 379), I argue that the Athenian Stranger has more in common with the *Republic's* philosopher-kings than with Socrates. See my review of Pangle's *The Laws of Plato* in *Ancient Philosophy*, 4 (Fall, 1984), pp. 237–40.

4. See my comparison of the philosopher-kings to Socrates in "The *Republic's* Two Alternatives: Philosopher-Kings and Socrates," in *Political Theory*, 12 (May, 1984), pp. 252–274.

5. As if in answer to the *Clouds*, Plato has Socrates identify most of the characters of the *Republic* by their patronymics (327a–c, and 328b). In the case of the foreigner Thrasymachus, however, Socrates does not use the patronymic, thus suggesting the distance of Thrasymachus from his origins (328b).

6. Although the city in speech is composed of three distinct classes, it treats each member of a class only as a member of a class, rather than as a distinct individual.

Part II

Chapter 1. Plato's Introduction to Political Philosophy (Book I of the Republic*)*

1. The word *poros* means a passage or an opening, especially a means of crossing a river. *Aporia* is, literally, a condition that is without passage.

2. An *aporetic* dialogue lacks a natural stopping point because it does not reach a conclusion. The discussion in the *Lysis*, for example, ends, although its participants have not discovered what a friend is, when Lysis' and Menexenus' tutors come and order the boys to go home (*Lysis*, 223a–b). The *Theaetetus* ends, although Theaetetus has not said what knowledge is, when Socrates says that he has to leave to answer the suit which Meletus has brought against him (*Th.*, 210d). Similarly, at the end of the *Meno*, Socrates proclaims that "it is the hour for me to go somewhere" (*Meno*, 100b).

3. Paul Friedlander, for example, believes that "the main body of aporetic dialogues" are those of Plato's earliest period, in which he was most influenced by Socrates. He discusses them in *Plato*, Vol. 2, *The Dialogues: First Period*, trans. Hans Meyerhoff (New York: Random House, Inc., 1964),

pp. 5–116. See also Julia Annas, *An Introduction to Plato's Republic* (Oxford: Oxford University Press, 1981), pp. 3–4.

4. Paul Friedlander even treats Book I as a separate dialogue with the title of *Thrasymachus*. He cites the scholarly discussion of *Thrasymachus* in *Plato*, Vol. 2, *The Dialogues: The First Period*, p. 305.

5. Friedlander, *Plato*, Vol. 2, *The Dialogues: The First Period*, pp. 50–66. See also Richard Lewis Nettleship, *Lectures on the Republic of Plato*, 2d ed., (London: Macmillan, 1901), p. 14; and Annas, *An Introduction to Plato's Republic*, pp. 16–17.

6. See also Strauss, *The City and Man*, p. 138.

7. See also Strauss, *The City and Man*, p. 106.

8. Nettleship, *Lectures on the Republic of Plato*, p. 15.

9. As Arnold Toynbee observes, the Piraeus is "the oldest social melting-pot of the Greek world," *A Study of History*, abridged edition (New York: Dell Publishing Company, 1946), p. 479, quoted by Friedlander, *Plato*, Vol. 2, *The Dialogues: First Period*, p. 51.

10. Bloom, "Interpretive Essay," p. 331.

11. Friedlander, *Plato*, Vol. 2, *The Dialogues: First Period*, p. 51.

12. In his funeral oration in Thucydides' *History of the Peloponnesian War*, Pericles presents Athens' openness to novelty as its virtue and strength, II, 37–41. The context of his oration and the subsequent events (for example, the reaction of Athenians to the plague), however, suggest that Thucydides was aware of Athens' moral and political weakness. See also Xenophon, *Hellenica*; and George Wilhelm Hegel, *The Philosophy of History*, trans. J. Sibree (New York: Dover Publications, Inc., 1956), pp. 76–77.

13. Hegel makes a similar point, *The Philosophy of History*, pp. 76–77. For Hegel, the disjunction between thought and activity is true for all historical cultures. Consider his statement in the *Philosophy of Right*, trans. T. M. Knox (London: Oxford University Press, 1967): "The owl of Minerva spreads its wings only with the falling of dusk," p. 13. It is unclear, however, whether for Hegel this remains true at the end of history.

14. See also Bloom, "Interpretive Essay," p. 312; and Strauss, *City and Man*, p. 64. Neither Bloom nor Strauss places sufficient emphasis on the extent to which Socrates' "consent" is forced rather than chosen. Since "rule" in the opening scene is a reflection of rule in the *Republic*'s city, emphasis on the "compromise" of this scene obscures the tyrannical character of rule in that city.

15. As Socrates says in the *Phaedrus*, he prefers to spend time with the people in the city, rather than with the beauties of nature outside the city, because it is the people who are able to teach him (*Phdr.*, 230d). See also his account of his "second sailing," where he tries to learn through "arguments" or "speeches" in the *Phaedo* (99d ff.).

16. An interpretation of this scene as a compromise between force and consent, in contrast, suggests that the community formed by Socrates and his interlocutors is fundamentally similar to the city in speech: both are based on compromise, on a mixture of coercion and persuasion. See note 14.

17. Strauss, *The City and Man*, p. 66.

18. See, for example, Aeschylus, *Agamemnon*, 177.

19. Socrates even emphasizes to Cephalus that he is about to die: "You are now at just the time of life the poets call 'the threshold of old age,' " (328e). As Adam points out, "old age" is a descriptive genitive; that is, "old age" is itself the threshold by which we leave life and enter the afterlife. James Adam, *The Republic of Plato*, ed. with critical notes, commentary, and appendices 2 vols., 2d ed. (Cambridge, Mass.: Cambridge University Press, 1969), Vol. 1, note on 328e, p. 5.

20. See also Bloom, "Interpretive Essay," p. 314.

21. Bloom, "Interpretive Essay," p. 312.

22. For Polemarchus' lack of experience in comparison to Cephalus, see Nettleship, *Lectures on the Republic of Plato*, pp. 16–17.

23. Nettleship, *Lectures on the Republic of Plato*, pp. 19–20, and Bloom, "Interpretive Essay," p. 322.

24. Friedlander presents a different interpretation of Polemarchus' character. Rather than nobility and decency, he attributes to him a financial spirit and a petty vindictiveness, *Plato*, Vol. 2, *The Dialogues: First Period*, pp. 55–58. Closer to my own interpretation of Polemarchus are those of Bloom, "Interpretive Essay," p. 320, and Kenneth Dorter, "Socrates' Refutation of Thrasymachus and Treatment of Virtue," *Philosophy and Rhetoric*, 7 (1974), p. 27.

25. As he asked Socrates when Socrates wanted to return to Athens, "Could you really persuade [us], if we don't listen?" (327c).

26. For a different interpretation of the meaning of this argument on friendship, see Bloom, "Interpretive Essay," p. 324.

27. Bloom, "Interpretive Essay," p. 324, and Strauss, *The City and Man*, p. 73. Socrates himself did not abide by the precepts implied in this argument—he fought in the Athenian army (*Apol.*, 28e).

28. Both Bloom and Dorter recognize Thrasymachus' intellectual concerns but believe that they are merely in the service of the passions, "Interpretive Essay," p. 330–31, and "Socrates' Refutation of Thrasymachus," pp. 27–28.

29. For a different interpretation of the conflict implied in Socrates' distinction between a man's two arts and of Thrasymachus' failure to respond to that distinction, see Bloom, "Interpretive Essay," p. 332.

30. A blush is an involuntary physical manifestation of a psychological state. It indicates, at the very least, that a man has lost control. Thrasymachus blushes just at the moment when his lack of control of the argument is clear to himself and to everyone present. On Thrasymachus' blushing, see also Strauss, *The City and Man*, p. 74; and Bloom, "Interpretive Essay," p. 336. Thrasymachus must sense that Socrates has manipulated the argument unfairly but that he is powerless to catch Socrates' trick. The unjust man, according to Thrasymachus, does get the better of everyone and, therefore, is like the skilled artisan. The just man, in contrast, being a naive simpleton, can get the better of no one. He belongs in the camp of the ignorant and the unskilled, whereas the unjust man belongs among their opposites. Socrates reaches the opposite conclusion by substituting what men think ought to happen for what in Thrasymachus' view does happen (349b–c). Thrasymachus allows him to do this. He, after all, desires an ideal world almost as much as some of the other interlocutors.

31. Socrates' treatment of Thrasymachus in Book I stands in contrast to his treatment of the city he describes in the *Republic*. Whereas he "disunifies" Thrasymachus in order to tame him, he unifies the city as much as possible. Is the unified city as wild a beast as the unified Thrasymachus?

32. Socrates' analogy between the city and the individual foreshadows the one that he proposes in Book II in order to justify examining a city in the search for justice. The problems with the analogy in Book I are more immediately apparent than in the later analogy. For example, there is no reason to assume that an individual's justice, like that of a city, resides in an internal harmony rather than in his relations to other men. Socrates' argument requires that a human being be as self-contained as a city.

33. See, for example, Socrates' description of the doctrines of Melissus, Parmenides, and others in the *Theaetetus*, 180e. See also Aristotle's discussion of the Eleatics in *Metaphysics*, 986b10 ff.

Part II

Chapter 2. Justice in the City and the Soul (Books II–IV of the Republic)

1. Barker recognizes that these two different movements could stem from a dissatisfaction or a disgust with the world, and he correctly sees that such a disgust motivates the politics described in the *Republic*. But because he fails to locate the origin of the *Republic*'s city in the passions of Socrates' interlocutors, he attributes the disgust with the world and the attempt to remake it to Plato himself, *The Political Thought of Plato and Aristotle*, (New York: Dover Publications, 1959), p. 150.

2. Glaucon's story of the ancestor of Gyges is an adaptation of a story told by Herodotus, *History* I, 8–13. For a discussion of the changes which Glaucon made in Herodotus' story, see my "Glaucon's Adaptation of the Story of Gyges and Its Implications for Plato's Understanding of Politics," *Polity*, 17 (Fall, 1984), pp. 30–39. Parts of my discussion of Glaucon's character first appeared on pp. 31–33 and 36 of this article.

3. Herodotus, *History* I, 8.

4. Nettleship, *Lectures on the Republic of Plato*, pp. 58–59. Although Nettleship's observation is sound, he does not pursue its implications. He merely notes that Glaucon's "picture is overdrawn," and maintains that it is nevertheless a useful illustration of the fact that things are not always what they seem, p. 59. One should ask, however, why Glaucon separates so radically the appearances and reality and how this separation is developed in the *Republic*.

5. Adeimantus mentions "ruling offices and marriages and all the other things Glaucon a moment ago attributed to the man with a reputation for justice" (363a). He believes that Glaucon has treated these things adequately and dwells instead on those things he is most interested in. Bloom points out that when Adeimantus quotes Homer's list of the goods that came to the king who upholds justice, he drops the line that refers to the king's power over men (363b), *The Republic of Plato*, note 9, p. 447.

6. In contrasting Glaucon's toughness and Adeimantus' love of ease and pleasure, I am following the interpretations of Strauss, *The City and Man*, pp. 90–91; and Bloom, "Interpretive Essay," pp. 339–343. Neither of them, however, emphasizes Glaucon's desire for something simply good and his tendency to reject the world with its imperfections. And although they both note Adeimantus' love of ease and pleasure, they also attribute to him characteristics that seem to me to obscure the differences between him and Glaucon. Strauss, for example, implies that Adeimantus is less attracted to

poetry than Glaucon when he observes that "Glaucon's speech makes use of poetry; Adeimantus' speech is so to speak nothing but an indictment of poetry," p. 91. However, Glaucon's poetry—his polishing the just and unjust men, as Socrates says, like statues (361d)—is particularly unpoetic. Like the austere poetry Socrates gives to the guardians, Glaucon's poetry portrays simple forms, men who are only one thing, rather than the complex forms a poet typically dramatizes. Furthermore, although Adeimantus indicts poetry, he knows what poets say in great detail and takes it seriously. His attraction to poetry is consistent with his desire for private pleasures, which poets give to men by arousing their passions. Bloom corrects Strauss' view of Adeimantus when he writes that Adeimantus "is particularly addicted to poetry," p. 342, also see p. 359. Bloom nevertheless speaks of the austerity of Adeimantus, p. 360, especially, p. 413. In this context, Bloom calls Adeimantus a lover of Sparta, p. 413. Sparta, however, is not a place of poetry, private pleasures, and easy living. Nor is Adeimantus' contentment with the first city Socrates describes a sign of austerity. That city, as Glaucon says, is a city of pigs, with whom we do not usually associate austerity.

7. After Adeimantus' speech, Socrates "wonders" at the natures of Glaucon and Adeimantus, praises them for their speeches, and quotes a verse which refers to them as "Sons of Ariston, divine offspring of a famous man" (368a). Perhaps he wonders that two such different men come from the same source. The "good," literally, "the best" (*ariston*) produces opposite natures, with each possessing good qualities. Socrates may therefore be wondering at the complexity of the good—a complexity which the argument on behalf of justice will soon obscure.

8. At the outset of his account of the formation of the city, Socrates gives the impression that he is taking nature as a standard for political institutions. Contrary to the sophistic view of the opposition between nature and convention (see note 20 of Part I), Socrates presents the politics that he is describing and its conventions as if they are in accordance with nature. That Socrates' initial justification of the one-man, one-art formula is the "finer job" that this arrangement will produce, however, raises the question of whether Socrates is not presenting a view of nature required by political goals, rather than vice versa. The proceeding discussion provides evidence that this is the case. The *Republic* reestablishes the distinction between nature and convention but along lines quite different from the sophistic one.

9. Barker's observations concern the specialization of men into classes which occurs at a later stage of the *Republic*, but they apply to the specialization in arts as well. *The Political Thought of Plato and Aristotle*, p. 93.

10. "The various arts present in the first city, however diverse in skill or product, all serve bodily satisfaction and are practiced for money. Ultimately

they are the same; their practitioners are all included together in what will be called the wage-earning class," Bloom, "Interpretive Essay," p. 349.

11. See Bloom, "Interpretive Essay," p. 347, and Strauss, *The City and Man*, p. 97.

12. Seth Benardete, "Achilles and Hector: The Homeric Hero," Part I, "Style," in *The St. John's Review*, 36 (Spring, 1985), p. 48.

13. For a different interpretation of the conflict between Achilles and the city, see Bloom, "Interpretive Essay," pp. 354–55. Bloom argues that Achilles is dangerous because his love of his own hinders philosophy, whereas I argue that Achilles is dangerous because his love of his own makes him, like the philosopher, independent of the city. Bloom's understanding of the conflict between Achilles and the city is related to his view that the city is open to philosophy.

14. Although Bloom notes that Socrates' comparison of philosophers to dogs is "not serious," he finds it justified in the limited sense that the warriors' "love of the known extends their affections beyond themselves to the city; it partakes of the universalizing or cosmopolitan effect of philosophy," "Interpretive Essay," p. 351. I argue, in contrast, that it is not because the guardians are open that the comparison between them and philosophy is apt, but because the philosophers who are to rule the city are closed. The comparison may be more "serious" than it at first appears.

15. Even though the art of war might enable its possessors to take from others what they produce, it would acquire what others produce rather than produce anything itself. The education of the guardians, however, is meant to guarantee that they do not try to use their military art in such a way. Their art will be directed solely to maintaining the city against whatever threatens it. It is not to be used for acquiring more land or wealth for the city as a whole, as had seemed its original purpose. Socrates is now "purging" the men in the city of desires for relishes or luxuries (399e).

16. Barker makes a similar point with regard to women's place in the communistic city. If Plato "aims at emancipating women from the bondage of the household, it is only to subject them again to the service of the community at large," *The Political Thought of Plato and Aristotle*, p. 145.

17. For a different interpretation of the education's detachment from particular friends and relatives, see Bloom, "Interpretive Essay," pp. 356–358, esp. p. 358.

18. Because Adam sees no preparation for Socrates' reference to rulers, he finds it jarring. He does not understand how Socrates could be referring to the rulers of the city, since "they are not described until 412B." He suggests

that "the solution may be that the present section on truth is a later addition made by Plato after he had written his first account of the rulers in Book III," *Plato's Republic*, note on line 389c15, Vol. 1, p. 137. Adam does not mention that Socrates' definition of moderation, which immediately follows his reference to truthfulness, also mentions the rulers.

19. When Socrates specifies the two elements of moderation, he assimilates the guardians to "the multitude" (to *plēthos*) (389d–e).

20. Of course, one could suppose that self-mastery is a precondition or at least a concomitant of submission to authority. In this sense, the two "halves" of moderation can be reconciled.

21. Strauss, *The City and Man*, p. 100. Strauss argues that the parallel between the city and the individual requires the omission of justice, for the relation of the city to other cities cannot be understood in terms of justice, pp. 100–01.

22. This is true of both Polemarchus' definition of justice as helping friends and harming enemies and of Thrasymachus' definition of justice as the advantage of the stronger.

23. Nettleship is so impressed with the artificial environment of the *Republic*'s city that he suggests that Plato ascribes "to [art] a function . . . more important than perhaps any other philosopher has ascribed to it," *Lectures on the Republic of Plato*, p. 112. Barker observes that, in this description of the city, "the environment makes the soul," *The Political Thought of Plato and Aristotle*, p. 123.

24. Barker senses the animus against the natural in the institutions and principles of the *Republic*'s city. "There is a flight from the natural world in Plato," he writes, *The Political Thought of Plato and Aristotle*, p. 150. Barker does not understand, however, that this flight is not Plato's but belongs to man himself—a flight that Plato depicts as culminating in the artificiality of the city in speech.

25. Although Glaucon would not love someone "if there were some defect in [his] soul," if someone with a beautiful soul had "some bodily defect, he'd be patient and would willingly take delight in him" (402d–e).

26. The noble lie thus prepares the way for the image of the cave (514a–517c). That image also asks men to substitute an invisible and alien world for their ordinary experience and to devote their lives to it as their true home and source of their existence.

27. Strauss obscures the artificiality of the city's classes when he explains that, "The god did not however create the brothers unequal by arbitrary

decision, as it were choosing some for rule and others for subjection, he merely sanctioned a natural difference or put a stamp on it," *The City and Man*, pp. 102–03.

28. Strauss makes the opposite point about the relation between the ring of Gyges and communism: under communism, "there does not exist that approximation to the ring of Gyges which is the private home: . . . secrecy . . . is no longer possible,." *The City and Man*, p. 103. In effect, no one can become invisible, like the wearer of the ring. This observation should not suggest, however, that Glaucon will be dissatisfied by the arrangement. The ring is attractive to him, I have argued, not because it permits its wearer to hide from others but because it permits no one to hide from its wearer. In this latter sense, communism, rather than deprive everyone in the city of the ring of Gyges, gives such a ring to everyone.

29. According to Barker, "it is exactly this power of knowing ourselves as separate individuals which Plato really destroys, when he abolishes property; for property is a necessary basis of any conscious sense of an individual self," *The Political Thought of Plato and Aristotle*, p. 156.

30. Aristotle observes that the lower classes in the city in the *Republic* "are likely to be far more unmanageable and rebellious than the classes of helots, serfs, and slaves in some cities today," *Pol.*, 1264a34–36. Moreover, he points out that the "high-spirited and warlike men" in the silver class may be dissatisfied with their permanent exclusion from the rule which the golden class possesses, 1264b7–9.

31. Adam, *Plato's Republic*, Vol. I, note on lines 427e33–34, p. 225. Adam does note that Plato "not unfrequently extends the methods of mathematical reasoning beyond what we would consider their proper sphere," p. 225. Other commentators note the procedure without comment. See, for example, Barker, *The Political Thought of Plato and Aristotle*, pp. 115–116. Annas, however, discusses the ways in which Socrates' procedure is questionable, *An Introduction to Plato's Republic*, pp. 110 ff.

32. *Prot.*, 329c. See also *Lach.*, 199d, *Meno* 78d, *Gorg.*, 507b. Commentators typically assume that Socrates looks for these four virtues in the city because these four are "the cardinal virtues of the Greeks," Nettleship, *Lectures on the Republic of Plato*, p. 146; Barker, *The Political Thought of Plato and Aristotle*, p. 116. Annas, in contrast, recognizes that Socrates' omission of piety needs to be explained. Focusing on piety in the sense of conventional actions concerning the gods, she argues that Socrates leaves piety out of his list in accordance with his conception of virtue as an internal state of the soul rather than a certain kind of action, *An Introduction to Plato's Republic*, p. 111. Her explanation is insufficient, however, since it leads us to expect

that Socrates would include reverence or awe, an internal state of the soul, among the virtues of the city.

33. *Eusebeia*, piety or reverence, is also counted among the virtues in Greek literature. See Xenophon, *Mem.* IV. 6. 1–12, and Aeschylus, *Sept.* 610.

34. For the traditional link between piety and the family, see, for example, Sophocles, *Antigone*, 74 and 730–31. I discuss the incestuous character of the *Republic*'s communism in Ch. 3.

35. Cf. Bloom, "Interpretive Essay," p. 374, and Annas, *An Introduction to Plato's Republic*, p. 119.

36. Two related errors might blind one to the full extent of the depreciation of desire and the struggle against incompleteness that occurs in this soul that parallels the city. In the first place, one might identify the desires that Socrates is criticizing as hostile to reason with merely physical desires. That Socrates is not making this identification, in spite of his giving hunger and thirst as examples, is indicated clearly in his discussion of spiritedness, where the desire at issue is a desire to look at corpses. I shall discuss the relation between spiritedness and desire below. In the second place, one might erroneously attribute love or desire to the calculating part of the soul Socrates is describing here. Commenting on Socrates' tripartite division of the soul, Barker, for example, attributes two functions to the "element of reason," "for by it men both learn to know, and (because they have learned to know) are ready to love," *The Political Thought of Plato and Aristotle*, p. 104. Socrates does not, however, infer, as does Barker, that the calculating part of the soul is ready to love because it has learned to know. Moreover, although Socrates initially describes the rational element as the part by which we learn, he immediately emphasizes its function in opposing desire. As Socrates describes it, the reason that presides over this soul holds desires in check more than it moves toward any objects of its own. Nettleship makes a similar mistake, identifying the calculating part of the soul with the eroticism of the philosopher, *Lectures on the Republic of Plato*, p. 157. Annas, as well, notes that reason has two roles—not only to rule in the soul but also "to love and search for the truth in all its manifestations." She observes that this second role is "not much stressed in Book IV" without explaining why this is the case, *An Introduction to Plato's Republic*, p. 134.

37. He makes his agreement emphatic by swearing "by Zeus" when he affirms Socrates' statement (440b).

38. Just as Socrates must be going up from the Piraeus when the dialogue begins, for he "went down" (*katabainō*) (327a) in order to get there, Leontius

is "going up" (*anabainō*) from the Piraeus when he spots the corpses. In both cases, Socrates uses a compound of the verb "to go" (*bainō*).

Part II

Chapter 3. Communism and Philosophy (Books V–VII of the Republic)

1. See, for example, Arlene W. Saxonhouse, "Men, Women, War, and Politics: Family and Polis in Aristophanes and Euripides," *Political Theory*, 8 (February, 1980), 65–80.

2. See, for example, Apollo's argument in Aeschylus' *Eumenides*, 665–71.

3. Plato illustrates the dangers of the feminine love of her own by Diotima's speech in the *Symposium*. See my "Women in Western Political Thought," *The Political Science Reviewer*, 13 (1983), pp. 247–48.

4. This is true in spite of the fact that Socrates calls his discussion of women in Book V "a female drama" (451c). Strauss agrees that the city described in the *Republic* is, as he says, "altogether of male origin," *Socrates and Aristophanes*, p. 282. He argues that Socrates' communistic scheme is a correction of the one instituted by Praxagora in Aristophanes' *Assembly of Women*, a scheme obviously of female origin. Although Strauss refers to the failure of Praxagora's communism and therewith to "the failure of Woman, the limitation of Woman," he points there to no corresponding failure of Socratic communism, p. 281. Strauss consequently spares Man. Perhaps the ugliness that Strauss observes in Praxagora's communistic scheme is rooted in the selfishness that it serves and fosters, unlike that of the *Republic*, which aims at eliminating selfishness. In this sense, the communism of the *Assembly of Women* is more moderate than bold. But if "the ugliness of the *Assembly of Women* reflects the ugliness of moderation", as Strauss says (p. 281), the beauty of the *Republic* (527c) hides the ugliness of manliness. For further discussion of the relation between the *Assembly of Women* and the *Republic*, see Bloom, "Response to Hall," pp. 323–28.

5. Bloom argues that Socrates insists on the same education for men and women and thereby gives a vital place in the regime to women, in part because women have definite characteristics of their own to contribute to both the regime and the soul. He writes, for example, that "the female represents gentleness, and the complete soul must embrace both principles," "Interpretive Essay," p. 384. Although it may be true that the complete soul must embrace both principles, Bloom's account misses the defeminization of

women that occurs in the *Republic*. Socrates gives women an equal education, not because they have something of their own to contribute, but in order to make it less likely that they contribute anything of their own. Their gentle and moderating influence plays no role in the *Republic*'s city. Annas recognizes this fact and objects to it. She criticizes the *Republic* for not giving a rightful place to the feminine character Bloom describes, *An Introduction to the Republic*, p. 185. Arlene W. Saxonhouse, however, gives persuasive reasons why the nature of politics requires the "de-sexing" of the female. She provides an excellent discussion of the de-sexed female of the *Republic*'s fifth book in "The Philosopher and the Female in the Political Thought of Plato," *Political Theory*, 4 (May, 1976), pp. 196–203.

6. The word I am here translating as "classes" is the word *eidē*, commonly translated as "ideas" or "forms". *Eidos* refers to a general or class characteristic that defines the members of a class. All beautiful things, for example, belong to the class of beautiful things, or share in the same idea or form of beauty. Similarly, all men skilled in medicine belong to the class of doctors, or share in the same form. For further discussion of Socrates' use of *eidos*, see note 11 of this chapter.

7. For a different interpretation of why it is appropriate that the city be incestuous, see Bloom, "Interpretive Essay," p. 386–88.

8. Bloom presents a different interpretation of Socrates' relation to the city. He argues that Socrates is trying to construct a regime that is especially suited to him—"one in which philosophy does not have to be a private, hidden activity because it contradicts the authoritative prejudices," "Interpretive Essay", p. 387. But doesn't the city in speech have its own set of authoritative prejudices, such as the one-man, one-art formula, to say nothing of the noble lie? Although the philosophers of the city understand that the noble lie is a lie salutary for the city, and that the city's members are not descended from the same mother, do they also understand that its teaching about homogeneity and simplicity is untrue? This is a teaching that, I will argue, their own mathematical education makes them inclined to accept.

9. Commentators usually assume that Socrates is presenting his own understanding of love here and do not note anything untrue about it. See, for example, Friedlander, *Plato*, Vol. 3, *The Dialogues Second and Third Periods*, p. 106; and Nettleship, *Lectures on the Republic of Plato*, pp. 189–90. James Adam even gives Socrates himself as an example of a lover who loves all the members of a class. He cites Socrates' confession in the *Charmides* that "almost all [boys] at that age appear to me beautiful" (*Charm.*, 154b), *The Republic of Plato*, Vol. I, note on line 474d23, p. 333. But even apart from the "almost" with which Socrates qualifies his statement, the context of Socrates' confession makes it ironic. That context is a discussion of the superior beauty of

one boy in particular, Charmides, who is so beautiful that even the other beautiful boys are in love with him (*Charm.*, 154a–d). Bloom, who recognizes that Socrates' account of love is not true in the case of all men, appears to believe that it is accurate for the highest kind of love, "Interpretive Essay," pp. 392–94.

10. Socrates earlier mentioned that Glaucon was the lover of a boy with a pure soul and a defective body (402d–e)—a sign of Glaucon's rejection of appearances in a quest for some underlying perfection. However, Glaucon may have rejected even this boy. Socrates refers to a beloved which Glaucon "has *or had*" (emphasis mine) (402e).

11. Socrates uses "idea" to mean not merely something that exists in a man's mind but something that exists independently of man and that man can grasp. Socrates uses two different words to refer to an idea in this sense, *eidos* and *idea*, both etymologically related to the verb "to see." The passages cited in the text (479a and 476a) indicate that both words refer to ideas of properties, such as beauty and justice. Later, in Book X, when Socrates describes ideas of artifacts such as chairs and tables, ideas that he claims are made by the god, he again uses both these words to refer to these ideas (e.g., 596a–b and 597a). (On the differences between the ideas described in Book X and the ideas described in the middle books of the *Republic*, see note 14 of chapter 4.) Although Socrates uses both *eidē* and *ideai* to refer to ideas of both properties and artifacts, *eidos* has a broader application in the *Republic* than *idea*. In addition to referring to the ideas, *eidos* refers, for example, to physical forms (618a), forms in the soul (581e), the visible forms used by geometers (510d), as well as the classes into which dialectic separates its objects (454a).

12. My interpretation follows the traditional one—that Socrates is identifying the objects of opinion with the world perceived by the senses. Annas provides an interesting argument to the contrary, *An Introduction to Plato's Republic*, p. 210.

13. As Nettleship says, "the negation of being . . . is nothing, nonentity—not a mysterious something beyond what we know, but just *nothing*, of which we can say nothing and think nothing," *Lectures on the Republic of Plato*, p. 192.

14. For a good account of the manner of rule of the philosopher-kings, see Sheldon Wolin, *Politics and Vision*, pp. 38 ff. Wolin, however, assumes that Plato advocated such rule.

15. I explain the *Republic*'s "metaphysics" in terms of its politics, rather than its politics in terms of its metaphysics. In this, I differ from most scholars, both those who have reservations about the *Republic*'s metaphysics and those

who give sympathetic accounts of it. Among the former is Ernest Barker, who observes that the "relation of the Idea to particulars as conceived by Plato is parallel to that of the ruler to his people. There is a despotic unity, attained by the annihilation of the full individuality of each of the many particulars, and their subjection to the Idea," *The Political Thought of Plato and Aristotle,* p. 114, n. 1. Although Barker sees this similarity between the *Republic's* metaphysics and its politics, he explains what he regards as the *Republic's* political mistakes in light of its more theoretical ones. He does not see that the mistakes he attributes to Plato, in fact, follow from the requirements of the city. Other scholars more sympathetic to the *Republic's* metaphysics than Barker nevertheless follow Barker in explaining the politics in terms of the metaphysics. They argue that communism in the *Republic* is not a serious political proposal but a reflection of the necessarily universal character of philosophy. Because communism is impossible for a political community, which cannot tolerate such universality, the proposal for communism, they argue, indicates the limits of politics and the disjunction between politics and philosophy. See, for example, Strauss, *The City and Man,* p. 115; Bloom, "Interpretive Essay," pp. 394 and 409–10; and Arlene W. Saxonhouse, "Family, Polity, and Unity: Aristotle on Socrates' Community of Wives," *Polity,* 15, (Winter, 1982), pp. 213 and 218. Arendt comes closer to my own position, insofar as she explains Socrates' account of the good in the *Republic* as required by the politics described there. She argues that the account of the good is a transformation of Plato's doctrine of ideas to fit the *Republic's* political purpose—in the *Republic,* the ideas become "standards, measurements, and rules of behavior," *The Human Condition,* p. 202. She believes, however, that the Platonic ideas are not themselves political but escape political distortion when described as variations of the beautiful, p. 202. She thus ignores the broader connection between the ideas and rule in the communistic city.

16. As Friedlander observes, the *Republic* shows "that philosophy is an advance toward the world of order and eternal being, *in which there is no injustice and no wrong,*" (emphasis mine), *Plato,* Vol. 3, *The Dialogues Second and Third Periods,* p. 112. In explicating Socrates' description of the good, Annas says, "If goodness is fundamental for our understanding of the nature of things, then it must be fundamental in the nature of things, or else our understanding would not reflect the world as it is," *An Introduction to Plato's Republic,* p. 246. Wolin detects in the philosopher's impulse to rule "the motivation of an aesthetician" whose political art is "antithetical to the untidiness, dissymmetries, and moral ugliness of 'politics'," *Politics and Vision,* p. 46. Wolin's explanation of the philosopher's motivation, I would argue, applies to Glaucon, who craves the kind of perfection, both moral and aesthetic, found in the city in speech and its philosophy.

17. Jacob Klein provides a good account of this third segment of the divided line, *A Commentary on Plato's Meno*, (Chapel Hill: University of North Carolina Press, 1965), pp. 117–19.

18. As John Burnet explains, "the doctrine [of ideas] arose in connection with the study of mathematics, which had already reached the stage of making confident assertions about things which are never perceived by the senses." This way of looking at things "was extended so as to cover certain objects of moral and aesthetic importance which seemed to have a similar character to the mathematical 'forms' . . . ," *Platonism* (Berkeley: The University of California Press, 1928), pp. 42–43.

19. Nettleship, *Lectures on the Republic of Plato*, p. 251.

20. This is the usual understanding. Adam, for example, refers back to Socrates' earlier account of the ideas at 476a, in which visible objects participate, when he discusses the dialectic that operates on the highest segment of the divided line, *The Republic of Plato*, Vol. 2, note on line 511c14, p. 71, and Appendix to Book VII, "On Plato's Dialectic," p. 169.

21. In spite of his assumption that the ideas on the highest segment of the divided line are the ideas of such things as justice and beauty, Adam nevertheless maintains that there is a distinction between the objects of the two highest segments of the divided line, *The Republic of Plato*, Vol. 2, Appendix to Book VII, "On the Similes of the Line and the Cave," p. 157. Annas recognizes the difficulty. "[S]ince [the highest segment] contains Forms," she asks, "what does [the third segment] contain?" The explanation that mathematics studies objects that fall between eternal ideas and those of sense experience, she notes, is not consistent with the fact "that mathematicians talk about 'the square itself' and 'the diagonal itself' (surely Forms) as well as the stress throughout the central books on mathematics as the best introduction to the kind of thinking that recognizes Forms," *An Introduction to Plato's Republic*, p. 251. She suggests that the difference between the two highest segments of the line is one of method as regards the same objects, although she admits that if the two highest segments have the same objects "the scheme of the Line breaks down—the structure of the bottom part has no real analogy in the top part." The "insolubility" of the problem, she says, illustrates the difficulty of "using images to make a philosophical point," pp. 251–52. The confusion in the image seems to me, however, to illustrate Plato's point—that the city reduces philosophy to mathematics.

22. In the image of the cave, moreover, it is not clear that there is any connection between the objects seen by the prisoners, the shadows of artifacts, and the objects seen by the philosophers outside the cave. Annas observes, correctly I believe, the sharp division between the world inside and outside the cave, but she attributes it to Plato's "antipathy to the passive and acquiescent state of the unreflective," *An Introduction to Plato's Republic*,

p. 253. I argue, in contrast, that such a division reflects the disjunction between the ordinary lives of men and the philosophy the city requires for its philosophic rulers.

23. Annas, *An Introduction to Plato's Republic*, p. 259.

24. For a different account of the divided line and the image of the cave, see Bloom, who assumes that the man who proceeds upward is erotic, "Interpretive Essay," pp. 402–06, esp. p. 402. Strauss, in contrast, notes that the abstraction from eros that occurs in the *Republic* "is effective in the simile of the Cave in so far as that simile presents the ascent from the cave to the light of the sun as entirely compulsory," *The City and Man*, p. 128. Strauss, however, seems to note this fact in passing and does not make its implications explicit. Annas observes that "Plato sometimes (though not in the *Republic*) talks of the ascent to the Forms as being one of love and desire," *An Introduction to Plato's Republic*, p. 237. She does not, however, explain this fact about the *Republic*, although she recognizes its connection to the kind of knowledge implied in the cave image of which she provides an excellent discussion, pp. 252–69, esp. p. 259.
Later in Book VII, Socrates does refer to the education of the philosophers as playful rather than compulsory when he describes their learning the mathematical disciplines preparatory to dialectic as children. Because "no forced study abides in a soul," he warns, "don't use force in training the children in the studies, but rather play. In that way you can also better discern what each is naturally directed toward" (536e–537a). That Socrates suggests making a game of mathematics in order to see which children have a greater aptitude for it, however, does not contradict the compulsory aspect of the philosopher's ascent from the cave. As children, their learning may be playful, but, as the image of the cave indicates, their more strenuous education as adults is not. It is not even clear how free their childhood play is: their instruction, Socrates says, "must not be given the aspect of a compulsion to learn" (536d). Immediately after speaking of this mathematical play, Socrates reminds Glaucon that at the same age they are thus occupied, they "must be led to war on horseback as spectators; and if it's safe anywhere, they must be led up near and taste blood, like the puppies" (537a). Here is an example of the association of mathematics with war characteristic of Book VII. See n. 30 of this chapter.

25. Annas, *An Introduction to Plato's Republic*, p. 259. Annas gives an excellent discussion of this point. She contrasts the *Republic*'s image of the cave with Bertolucci's use of it in *The Conformist*, where the knowledge gained by the hero is self-knowledge, pp. 257–59.

26. Annas provides an interesting explanation of why the philosophers are willing to rule the city. "They go down because they realize that it is best—simply *best*, not best *for* any particular group of people. They know

what is really good, not good relative to the interests or situation of anyone. And it demands they return. . . . Their motivation is very abstract. They are not seeking their own happiness. Nor are they seeking that of others. They are simply doing what is impersonally best. . . . They take a wholly impersonal attitude to their own happiness, along with everybody else's, and this is because their judgements are made in light of the impersonal Good." *An Introduction to Plato's Republic*, p. 267. Similarly, Hall explains that philosophers rule the souls of others in the city because they do not distinguish others' souls and their own: "Given the nature of reason, . . . there is no ground for restricting its natural function of ruling to any one *psyche* rather than another. Even between its own *psyche* and others, the philosopher's reason can find no ground for differentiation," "The *Republic* and the Limits of Politics," pp. 307–08. See also Wolins's observation that the aim of the *Republic*'s social arrangements and educational institutions "was to create an elite which would rule not as ordinary men but as selfless instruments," *Politics and Vision*, p. 53.

27. Commentators typically believe that Socrates' presentation of the philosopher-kings' education is, in the words of H. B. Joseph, "what Plato thought that a philosophic—i.e. the highest—education should be," *Knowledge and the Good in Plato's Republic*, reprint of the 1948 edition (Westport, Connecticut: Oxford University Press, 1981), p. 1. John Burnet suggests that Socrates here gives the curriculum of the Academy itself, *Platonism*, pp. 101–02.

28. Even though the philosophers rule, as Socrates said, out of their obligation to the city who reared them, rather than out of any natural inclination, their rule is nevertheless natural to them, given the character of their education. On this point, I agree with Hall in his argument against Strauss's and Bloom's position that ruling is incompatible with the philosophic nature described in the *Republic*. Hall argues that "there is nothing more appropriate than that philosophers should rule, for that activity consists in modeling the moral and social whole according to the harmony of the forms," "The *Republic* and the Limits of Politics", p. 309. My distinction between Socrates and the philosopher-kings, however, brings me closer to Strauss and Bloom concerning Plato's final position on the incompatibility between philosophy and politics, although we explain that incompatibility in opposite terms.

29. Socrates does "call that man dialectical who grasps the being of each thing," in contrast to the man who is unable "to give an account of a thing to himself and another" (534b). But even here he does not say explicitly that the dialectician does give an account to others of the being of each thing. In any case, it remains true that others play no role in the dialectician's search for truth, although he may impart the results to them afterwards.

Annas tries to equate the study included in the philosophers' education in the *Republic* with the Socratic conversation. She is not deterred by the fact that the two understandings of dialectic "at first glance do not happily go together," *An Introduction to Plato's Republic*, p. 282.

30. Annas finds Socrates' associations of philosophy and war distasteful and attributes them to Plato's contempt for practice. His contempt is so great, she claims, that when he argues that the philosophers' studies are not useless, "as if uneasy about [their contemplative nature]," "practice is dragged in . . . in a degraded role," *An Introduction to Plato's Republic*, pp. 275–76. Bloom's position provides a defense against Annas' charge in that he argues that Plato does not claim the philosophers' most important studies are useful for war. References to their utility drop out, he points out, as the discussion proceeds, "Interpretive Essay," p. 408. Although it is true that Socrates and Glaucon explicitly mention war as an end of the studies of the philosopher only through the discussion of astronomy (527d), however, Socrates does continue to use terms with military connotations. When speaking of dialectic, the final study before the vision of the good, Socrates refers to the "journey" or "march" (*poreia*) that dialectic takes. For the use of *poreia* in a military sense, see Thucydides, 1.18; Xenophon, *Anabasis*, 5.6.11; and Xenophon, *Cyropaedia*, 8.6.18. The more important question, however, is whether the frequent references to war early in the discussion of the philosophers' education reveal the character of that education as a whole. All the studies are intended to turn the soul from becoming to being, and Bloom contrasts this end with all ends involving action in the city, such as war. But isn't such a turn akin to war, as suggested by Socrates' initial association of the two (525c)? Both destroy the particular, or the individual; both are destructive of life. Isn't the turn from becoming to being a preparation for the "action in the city" that the philosopher-king undertakes—elimination of the individual natures of the citizens?

31. Parts of my discussion of the *Republic*'s philosopher-kings first appeared in my "The *Republic*'s Two Alternatives: Philosopher-Kings and Socrates," *Political Theory*, 12 (May, 1984), on pp. 253–65.

32. By assimilating philosophy to mathematics, the city corrupts philosophy or "politicizes" it. In this, my interpretation agrees with that of Arlene W. Saxonhouse. Saxonhouse draws a parallel between the city's treatment of the philosopher and its treatment of women. "In both cases," she writes, "the needs of politics distort the needs of the individual," "The Philosopher and the Female in the Political Thought of Plato," p. 202. I attribute to the city, however, an even greater distortion of philosophy than Saxonhouse does. Saxonhouse locates the city's corruption of philosophy in the fact that the philosopher is compelled to rule, without extending this "politicization" to his education as well. Consequently, she believes that the

philosophers' "true nature" emerges after his introduction in Book V and that, until he is compelled to rule in Book VII, he "is allowed to pursue reality freed from the demands of the political community," p. 203. Socrates portrays the philosopher, she believes, as an erotic man, p. 203 ff. I have argued, in contrast, that the "eroticism" of the philosopher is one perverted to meet the requirements of the city and that the philosopher enters the world of politics from the moment he is introduced into the city. See Saxonhouse, p. 205.

Part II

Chapter 4. A Return to the Socratic Perspective (Books VIII–X of the Republic)

1. Oligarchies, for example, are not willing to pass legislation, Socrates says, to prevent the accumulation of wealth in a few hands, such as abolishing legal means for the recovery of debts or restricting the alienation of private property (556a–b). This is one of the few times Socrates mentions possible legislation in his account of the decline of the city, but he gives an example of legislation that is not undertaken.

2. It is for this reason, I believe, that we should not view Socrates' account of regimes in Books VIII and IX as "the outlines of a political science" that can guide political life, Bloom, "Interpretive Essay," p. 414. Bloom argues that by "categorizing political phenomena and understanding their causes," Socrates "provides guidance in political deliberation and choice," "Interpretive Essay," p. 414. But, as Socrates presents the degeneration from one regime to another, there is little room for deliberation and choice. Bloom himself recognizes this fact when he observes that "any changes in the present regime can only lead to a worse regime," p. 414.

3. For a different interpretation of why Adeimantus is the appropriate interlocutor for this discussion, see Bloom, "Interpretive Essay," p. 413; and Strauss, The City and Man, p. 133. Both argue that Adeimantus' austerity makes him likely to condemn the degeneration that Socrates depicts. Strauss mentions, for example, Adeimantus' admission that Socrates' description of democracy's freedom is actually his own dream (563d), p. 133. Strauss apparently interprets this passage to mean that Adeimantus is indignant at the ill effects of freedom. However, if a man's dreams reveal his desires (571b–572a), Adeimantus' dream about democracy's easygoing nature might indicate a similar characteristic in himself, rather than indignation. This interpretation would be consistent with Adeimantus' acceptance of the easygoing life of the city of pigs.

4. The emergence of inferior regimes out of the one possessing perfect goodness is surprising because Socrates had earlier claimed that its goodness became firmer and firmer over time—"the regime, once well started, will roll on like a circle in its growth. For sound rearing and education, when they are preserved, produce good natures; and sound natures, in their turn receiving such an education, grow up still better than those before them" (424a).

5. Bloom says that this is "one of the darkest passages in Plato's works," *The Republic of Plato*, note on 546d, p. 467. See Adam, *Plato's Republic*, Vol. I, pp. xlviii ff., for a discussion of different interpretations.

6. Strauss, *The City and Man*, p. 132; Annas, *An Introduction to Plato's Republic*, p. 301.

7. Socrates claims that democracy is likely to be judged beautiful by many, "like boys and women looking at many-colored things" (557c). The beauty that appeals to women, he suggests, differs from that which appeals to men. Consistent with the diversity that the various regimes, especially democracy, reveal, Socrates now drops the premise of the city in speech that men and women have the same natures. If women have a stronger sense of their own than men, as Greek tradition taught, they would know that all things cannot be reduced to the uniform principle that defines a regime. A regime that made no demands on the private, and that strictly speaking is not a regime at all, might strike women as especially beautiful, as it would a boy who still shared the perspective of the family. Just as everything peculiarly feminine was purged from the city in speech, in the democracy Socrates describes, the feminine is at home, and the masculine spiritedness that forms parts into wholes and finds beauty in simplicity plays little role.

8. Socrates says that in a democratic city, fathers try to be like sons, teachers fawn on students, and the old come down to the level of the young (562e–563a). Everyone becomes alike. Democrats, however, are not moved merely by a desire for equality but by a yearning for freedom. Trying to make themselves like sons, students, and youth, they want to resemble those for whom the most possibilities remain open. But, if all possibilities remain open, men do not do or become anything.

9. Barker's reservations about Socrates' presentation of the soul in Book IV apply here. Barker criticizes the view that the soul is "an eternal war between reason and desire." The "unity of the soul [for Socrates] is a unity not of reconciliation but of subjugation," *The Political Thought of Plato and Aristotle*, p. 113. The best condition is therefore only "a despotism of reason," p. 114. He "urge[s] against Plato . . . that man's mind is not primarily a war of elements which must be united by the triumph and supremacy of one, [but] that it is from the first a unity," p. 114. Barker, however, sees

no problem in maintaining the soul's unity. Nor does he consider the possibility that Socrates (and Plato) understands the despotic aspect of reason in the soul but see its necessity.

10. Commentators typically assimilate the two different accounts of the soul. Consequently, they do not have to explain the alternative understandings of the soul that the *Republic* presents. See note 36 of Ch. 2.

11. Annas, for different reasons, also questions whether the lover of learning has the experience necessary to judge the pleasures of the different ways of life, *An Introduction to Plato's Republic*, p. 310.

12. So much does Socrates lead us to expect that he is going to maintain that the philosopher's pleasures, those of the soul, are unmixed with pain, that commentators assume that this is indeed his final position. See Bloom, for example, "Interpretive Essay," p. 424.

13. Annas merely points out the peculiarity of Socrates' argument without explaining why Socrates refers to being in a way inconsistent with his earlier account, *An Introduction to Plato's Republic*, p. 44.

14. For a discussion of the discrepancies between Socrates' presentation of the Ideas in Book X and his earlier account, see Annas, *An Introduction to Plato's Republic*, pp. 227–32; W. D. Ross, *Plato's Theory of Ideas*, pp. 78–79; A. D. Woozly and R. C. Cross, *Plato's Republic: A Philosophical Examination of Plato's Doctrines*, 2 vols. (New York: St. Martin's Press, 1964), I, p. 147; H. F. Cherniss, "On Plato's Republic X," *American Journal of Philology*, 53 (1932), pp. 239–41; and especially, Charles Griswold, "The Ideas and the Criticism of Poetry in Plato's *Republic*, Book 10," *Journal of the History of Philosophy*, 19 (April, 1981), pp. 135–50.

15. Bloom, "Interpretive Essay," p. 427.

16. See Annas' objection to Socrates' argument, *An Introduction to Plato's Republic*, p. 345.

17. The souls' regaining a human form resembles the philosopher-kings' reentry into the cave of political life. Both move back to a limited, temporal existence. The souls, however, are eager to return. They desire a body as eagerly as philosopher-kings desire to escape their bodies. The myth therefore constitutes an implicit criticism of the philosopher-kings' desire to escape the world.

18. Like the Socratic community, the Platonic dialogue also constitutes a heterogeneous whole. Given the relative permanence of a written work, as opposed to an unrecorded Socratic conversation, as well as the greater control exercised by an author over his characters than by Socrates over his

interlocutors, the whole formed by a Platonic dialogue may be more "political" than the Socratic community. The Platonic dialogue gives greater weight to spiritedness than to eros when it balances the two, whereas the Socratic conversation gives greater weight to eros. These considerations, although they suggest that Plato is closer to Aristophanes than Socrates is, especially since Plato also has offspring (see *Clouds*, 530–32), do not imply that Plato offers a more political alternative in any ordinary sense or that the Platonic dialogue about the limits of political life would be any more acceptable to Aristophanes than Socrates' conversations about such things. For discussions of the differences between Socrates and Plato, that are based on Plato's writing in the face of Socrates' criticisms of writing in the *Phaedrus*, see my "The *Republic*'s Two Alternatives: Philosopher-Kings and Socrates," pp. 270–71; and Joseph Cropsey, "Plato's *Phaedrus* and Plato's Socrates," *Political Philosophy and the Issues of Politics* (Chicago: The University of Chicago Press, 1977), pp. 231–251.

19. Plato explores these dichotomies from a different perspective in the *Laws*. In that work, he portrays an old philosopher (an Athenian Stranger) giving advice to two men who are about to found a political community. The more fundamental purpose of that work is nevertheless not to give practical political advice but to explore the tension between philosophic and political virtue. As Pangle so aptly states, "From the beginning to the end of the *Laws*, we . . . never lose sight of the problem of the unity of virtue, or more generally of the problem of the *ideas*, of the one and the many, as exemplified in the preeminent *idea* of virtue, "Interpretive Essay," p. 388. Plato indicates that the *Laws* does not solve that problem through the closing drama of the dialogue. When the future founders invite the Athenian stranger to remain and take part in the actual founding, the stranger silently refuses to accept. According to Pangle, this ending suggests that the tension between the philosopher and the city, or between the different parts of virtue, has not been overccome, p. 509.

20. Nussbaum defends Aristophanes against those who claim that he presented an unfair portrait of Socrates. These critics argue that Aristophanes confused Socrates with natural philosophers and sophists of the time and that he did not take into account the moral and political aspects of Socrates' philosophizing. Nussbaum shows that the Socrates of the *Clouds* shares fundamental similarities with Plato's Socrates (at least of the early dialogues): for example, an intellectualism that undermines traditional moral values by demanding reasons but does not put anything in their place, and a method of teaching or conversing that brings out the contradictions in others' beliefs, "Aristophanes and Socrates on Learning Practical Wisdom," pp. 50–79. Nussbaum's argument explains the quandary posed by Strauss: how Nietzsche could use "Aristophanes' critique of the young Socrates as if it had been

meant as a critique of the Platonic Socrates," *Socrates and Aristophanes*, p. 8; see Nussbaum, p. 65.

21. Bloom also concludes that the *Republic* turns men away from political life, but for different reasons, "Interpretive Essay," p. 415.

Part III
Political Science: Aristotle's Achievement (Book II of the Politics)

1. Unless otherwise stated, references in parentheses in Part III are to Aristotle's *Politics*.

2. The word is an adjectival form that Aristotle uses as a noun. Its gender allows it to agree either with science or knowledge (*epistēmē*) or action (*praxis*).

3. See R. G. Mulgan, *Aristotle's Political Theory* (Oxford: Oxford University Press, 1977), p. 8.

4. Of course, some of their defects are a result of bad choices, that is, choices based on insufficient reflection or experience. The lack of thought or experience underlying such choices, from Aristotle's point of view, further indicates the domination of human affairs by chance.

5. There has been very little detailed criticism of Book II of the *Politics*. Exceptions are Arlene W. Saxonhouse, "Family, Polity, and Unity: Aristotle on Socrates' Community of Wives," *Polity*, 15, (Winter, 1982), pp. 202–19; Darrell Dobbs, "Aristotle's Anticommunism," *American Journal of Political Science*, 29 (February, 1985), pp. 29–46; and Martha Craven Nussbaum, "Shame, Separateness, and Political Unity: Aristotle's Criticism of Plato," *Essays on Aristotle's Ethics*, ed. Amelie O. Rorty (Berkeley, California: University of California Press, 1981.) All these authors, however, discuss only the beginning of Book II—Aristotle's criticism of Plato. In general, as Saxonhouse points out, "analyses of Aristotle's *Politics* largely ignore Book II," p. 209, n. 15.

6. Saxonhouse argues that "By preserving the family, Aristotle is also trying to preserve the diversity of elements which comprise the city, a diversity which includes the difference between the male and female bodies," "Family, Polity, and Unity: Aristotle on Socrates' Community of Wives and Children," p. 203.

7. See Aristotle's discussion of the different meanings of nature in the *Metaphysics* (1014b–15a). I discuss the complexity of Aristotle's understanding of nature in my analysis of Book I of the *Politics*, "The Good Life, Slavery,

and Acquisition: Aristotle's Introduction to Politics," *Interpretation*, 11, (May, 1983), pp. 171–83.

8. When discussing the different parts of the city in Book IV of the *Politics*, Aristotle contrasts the variety of occupations necessary in the city with the differences between the rich and the poor. While "the same persons could be warriors, farmers and artisans, and all lay claim even to virtue, and suppose themselves capable of ruling in most offices, it is impossible for the same persons to be both poor and wealthy" (1291b3–7). Aristotle, however, casts doubt on the absolute character of even this latter distinction in his analysis of the middle class polity. There, rule is in the hands of men who are moderately well off and who are therefore to some extent both poor and wealthy (1295b1–96a20).

9. Socrates himself suggests the artificial character of these distinctions. At least, he proposes the one-man, one-art formula as much on the ground of its efficiency as on the ground of its naturalness (*Rep.*, 370b). And the city's classes, which are necessary for its preservation, are fashioned by a god (*Rep.*, 415a).

10. Because these distinctions do exist in the *Republic's* city, some scholars conclude that Aristotle's criticism of that city's homogeneity is unfair. See, for example, W. D. Ross, *Aristotle* (London: Methuen, 1964), p. 244; Mulgan, *Aristotle's Political Theory*, p. 29. These distinctions, however, are less fundamental than the city's homogeneity. As Ernest Barker points out in defense of Aristotle's criticism of the *Republic's* city for its lack of diversity, the lower class disappears from view, and the other two classes lose their distinctness "in a uniform system of common life," *The Political Thought of Plato and Aristotle*, p. 403. Regardless of whether the institution of communism is limited to the upper classes of the city, the institution reveals the city's essential character.

11. Mulgan makes this same point and supports it by reference to Aristotle's statement in the *Ethics* that "political justice is found among men who are 'free and either proportionately or arithmetically equal' " (*NE*, 1134a26–28), *Aristotle's Political Theory*, p. 37. "If proportionate equality is allowed," he argues, "each person must merely have *some* share in ruling; this is still sufficient to distinguish 'political' from 'kingly' rule, for in kingly rule the subjects have no share in ruling at all," p. 37.

12. This is the usual interpretation of political rule. See Mulgan, for example, *Aristotle's Political Theory*, p. 36.

13. Although Aristotle says that the rule of a husband over his wife is political (1259a41), he claims that the husband rules his wife continuously (1259b9). If one subscribes to the common interpretation of political rule as

an alternation among ruler and ruled, this passage is inexplicable. My interpretation of political rule explains this passage. The husband's rule of his
wife acknowledges her independence and therefore the distinct contribution
she can make to his own rule. He is ruled "in turn" or "in part" by her. So
too does Aristotle claim that "the mind [or 'the part having reason'] rules the
appetites with a political and kingly rule" rather than a despotic one (1254b4–
8). It is proper that reason both lead and be led by the appetites. The appetites
limit what reason can do and also act as a guide. In the *Nicomachean Ethics*,
Aristotle defines choice as "appetitive reason" or "rational appetite" (*NE*,
1139b5–6). Man is moved, in the best case, by some kind of cooperation
between his reason and his appetites. The concept of reason's political rule
of the appetites is absent from the psychology in the *Republic*, as is the concept
of political rule in general.

14. Aristotle makes the point that Plato does not see the importance
of political rule in politics even more strongly at the beginning of Book I of
the *Politics*. There he speaks of those who mistakenly believe that the statesman, the king, the head of a family, and the master of a slave exercise the
same kind of rule; they consequently do not distinguish a large family from
a small city, unaware that these associations have different ends (1252a8–
14). Commentators agree that Aristotle is referring to Plato. Barker, for
example, cites the *Statesman*, where "domestic management and political
government . . . had been improperly confused by Plato," *The Political Thought
of Plato and Aristotle*, p. 357. It seems plausible, however, that Aristotle has
in mind the *Republic* as well. Not only do philosopher-kings rule subjects
who consider one another as family members, but they are related to them
as Aristotle describes the master's relation to his slave. In philosopher-kings,
the rational capacities are developed, but not in the subjects (cf. *Pol.*, 1252a32–
34), who are allowed no independent judgment. Nussbaum gives a good
account of the slavery implied in the unity of the city in speech. She describes
the philosopher's rule of the nonphilosophers in terms similar to Aristotle's
description of a master's rule of his slave, "Shame, Separateness, and Political
Unity: Aristotle's Criticism of Plato," p. 413.

15. In discussing liberality in the *Ethics*, Aristotle says that liberality
has more to do with giving than taking (*NE*, 1120a10–12). But giving, as
opposed to taking, suggests freedom from need.

16. In Books VII and VIII of the *Politics*, where Aristotle describes the
best regime, he does not introduce communism of property or of women and
children.

17. The question is raised by Saxonhouse, "Family, Polity and Unity:
Aristotle on Socrates' Community of Wives," p. 212, see also p. 219. Leo
Strauss argues that "Since the rule of philosophers is introduced not as an

ingredient of the just city but only as a means for its realization, Aristotle legitimately disregards the institution in his critical analysis of the *Republic*," *City and Man*, p. 122. I agree with Dobbs that Strauss' explanation is insufficient, for "whatever the initial cause on account of which Socrates *introduces* philosophers, he leaves little doubt that the philosopher-king is essential to the *intrinsic* perfection of the city" (emphases in original), "Aristotle's Anticommunism," p. 33.

18. Dobbs explains Aristotle's silence about the *Republic's* philosopher-king "as an implicit *denial* of the continuity [between the city of warriors and the city ruled by philosophers] that Socrates affirms." He argues that "Aristotle disregards the philosopher king precisely because, in his estimation, the communistic political arrangements Socrates endorses *preclude* the education of a philosopher" (emphases in original), "Aristotle's Anticommunism," p. 34. Dobbs' essay is extremely useful in raising the question of the place of philosophy in the city in speech and in suggesting that philosophy is incompatible with that city. Although I agree on this point, there are several fundamental differences between Dobbs' position and my own. Dobbs argues that the communistic city stands in the way of the universal perspective required by philosophy because its members are too attached to their own city. See, for example, p. 44. I argue, in contrast, that the communistic city, precisely because of its universality, is a hindrance to understanding the complexity that Socrates' philosophizing reveals. Moreover, while I agree that the communistic arrangements obstruct the pursuit of Socratic philosophy, I argue that those arrangements require the support of the mathematically oriented philosophy of the city's rulers. Dobbs does not make this distinction.

19. Aristotle describes Socrates' words as "unusual, clever, original, and searching," but incorrect (1265a10–12).

20. These arguments are not necessarily Hippodamus' own; in fact, the context suggests that they are Aristotle's. Since "we have mentioned [the broader question]," he writes, "it is better if we set out a few details about it" (1268b30–31).

21. Aristotle elaborates this problem inherent in law in other contexts, for example, when he discusses the arguments that favor the rule of good men over the rule of good laws. Unlike laws, men can take particular situations into account as they arise (1286a8–16). Although Aristotle ultimately prefers the rule of law as a restraint on the rule of men (e.g., 1286a17–24; 1287a33; 1287b4–8), he does propose the concept of equity.

22. Whereas Aristotle describes Hippodamus' eccentricities in ludicrous terms, he mentions no personal attributes of Socrates, except that his speeches are "sophisticated, original and penetrating" (1265a10–11). Socrates had

enough personal eccentricities to make personal ridicule of him easy (as indicated by the *Clouds*), had Aristotle desired to mock him as he did Hippodamus. But Aristotle obviously has more respect for Socrates.

23. As long as human beings are not blessed with a divine status or degraded below the level of humanity, they can participate *in some way* in a regime. Aristotle, however, finds that such exclusions from humanity, and hence from political life, are very few indeed. See my discussion in "Slavery, Acquisition and the Good Life: Aristotle's Introduction to Politics," pp. 171–83, especially pp. 175 and 181–83.

24. Crete's neighbors do not try to stir up the Cretan slaves to rebel because they too possess a slave class (1269a39–b3), and it is only recently that Crete has engaged in foreign wars (1272b20–23).

25. In first discussing Crete, Aristotle says that it "is naturally well-situated for the rule of Hellas," for it extends across the whole sea. Minos subjected some of the islands, and he colonized others. Finally he died attacking Sicily (1271b30–40). However, Aristotle's last word in his discussion of Crete is that the Cretans are not involved in foreign rule and only recently did foreign war come to the island (1272b20–23). Aristotle thus casts doubt on the deeds and even the existence of Minos.

26. Aristotle claims that polity is not noticed by those who enumerate the forms of government because it does not often occur. He mentions Plato as one of those who overlooked the existence of polity (1293a40–1293b1). Aristotle's description of polity is one of the unique features of his political science.

27. Aristotle uses Sparta as an example. Some call it a democracy because the sons of rich and poor are educated in the same way and because the people elect the Elders and share in the Ephorate—the two greatest offices of the city. Others call Sparta an oligarchy because offices are elected rather than distributed by lot and judgments of death and exile are in the hands of a few (1294b18–35). Men who enumerate regimes may have overlooked polity, then, not only because polities are rare but also because men have not identified them correctly, missing their complexity. See previous note.

28. In Book I of the *Politics*, Aristotle illustrates monopoly as a form of acquiring wealth with a story about Thales. When taunted with the uselessness of philosophy, Thales learned from astronomy that there would be a large olive crop, rented all the olive presses from others, and then rented them out on higher terms when the crop was harvested (1259a6–18). When Aristotle demonstrates the benefit of philosophy, in contrast, he does not try to become "the only seller," for his political science leaves room for the actions of statesmen who follow him.

29. Oedipus' claim to be ruler of Thebes is based solely on the work of his mind—answering the riddle of the Sphinx, rather than on any inheritance from his father.

30. Plato's *Laws* might seem to be a forerunner of Aristotle's political science in that its Athenian Stranger discusses politics with two old men who are about to found a political community. But whereas Aristotle addresses the old out of moderation, the Stranger addresses the old out of daring or manliness. He speaks to the old in order to overcome their typical characteristics, on which Aristotle relies. The Stranger's enterprise must overturn the old; as Pangle says, "the old and sacred habits must be uprooted," "Interpretive Essay," p. 439 (see also p. 383). Consequently, the Stranger tries to rejuvenate his interlocutors. The discussion of drinking parties in the first two books of the *Laws*, for example, is intended to have the same effect as wine—"a drug that heals the austerity of old age." "Its effect," the Stranger claims, "is that we are rejuvenated" (666b–c). (See Leo Strauss, *What is Political Philosophy?*, p. 31.) So too do "we elders," the Stranger says, "establish contests [in poetry] for those who can as much as possible restore us, through memory, to youthfulness" (657d). And at 752a, the Stranger admits that he must "overcome old age sufficiently."

31. Aristotle says that the family also is a partnership in these things. The family evidently possesses to some extent what becomes most fully manifest in the interactions of men in a city.

32. My explanation of the meaning of the good life at which politics aims is based on the early part of Book I. I do not mean to deny an explanation such as Ross's, which is compatible with mine. According to Ross, "Good life includes for Aristotle two things, moral and intellectual activity. The state offers a more adequate field than its predecessors [i.e., the family and the village] to moral activity, a more varied set of relations in which the virtues may be exercised. And it gives more scope for intellectual activity; . . . each mind is more fully stimulated by the impact of mind on mind," *Aristotle*, p. 238.

33. Gerald M. Mara's position on the Socratic way of life parallels my own, for he argues that Socrates' philosophizing demonstrates a compatibility between theory and practice that does not appear in the politics described in the *Republic*. He suggests that in the *Republic* Socrates tailors his account to Glaucon's needs. Moreover, Mara also sees that Socratic justice is "not obviously identical with the Socratic description of purely philosophic justice," "Constitution, Virtue, and Philosophy in Plato's *Statesman* and *Republic*," *Polity*, 13 (1980), p. 379. Mara attributes to Socrates the practice of *politikē*, "a kind of science that is particularly suited to the study of changing human things. *Politikē* is not equivalent to either *dianoia* or *pistis* on the

Republic's divided line," p. 381. I have reservations with Mara's position, however, to the extent that he draws his conception of *politikē* from Socrates' account of philosophy in the *Republic* rather than solely from Socrates' own deeds. (See especially Mara, "Politics and Action in Plato's *Republic*," *Western Political Quarterly*, 36, [December, 1983], pp. 606–09.) Moreover, it may be going too far to attribute *politikē* to Socrates, since Socrates' *politikē* is distinctly apolitical in the ordinary sense of the term. The full blown expression of the *politikē* that Mara attributes to Socrates, I would argue, can be found in Aristotle. Concerning Mara's observation that Aristotle saw a greater distance between theory and practice than did Plato, I would caution that Aristotle's deeds are as important for understanding his *politikē* as Socrates' deeds are for understanding his. Just as Socrates' political science is not equivalent to either *dianoia* or *pistis* on the divided line, neither is Aristotle's political science equivalent to either wisdom or prudence in Book VI of the *Nicomachean Ethics*. See John W. Danford's discussion of this point in *Wittgenstein and Political Philosophy* (Chicago: The University of Chicago Press, 1978), pp. 128–45.

34. A good example of this is the *Gorgias*. Not only does Socrates find it impossible to persuade Callicles of what he would like, but also at one point Callicles refuses to participate in the discussion. Socrates must answer his own questions (*Gorg.*, 505d–509c). Even who discusses with Socrates is often a result of the passions of his interlocutors as they break into the discussion (*Gorg.*, 461b; 481b–c).

35. Bloom makes the opposite point about Aristotle, arguing that, unlike the *Republic*, Aristotle excludes both the highest and the lowest, both the divine and the beastly in man, from the political community, "Interpretive Essay," p. 425, see also p. 415. Bloom's statement suggests that he accepts the traditional understanding that Aristotle regards an apolitical life of contemplation as the best and the happiest. See, for example, Werner Jaeger, *Aristotle: Fundamentals of the History of His Development* (Oxford: Oxford University Press, 1934), especially Appendix II, "On the Origin and Cycle of the Philosophical Ideal of Life," pp. 426–61. Consistent with Bloom's statement of the difference between the *Republic* and Aristotle's view of politics, Jaeger finds in Aristotle "an even purer representative of the theoretic life than Plato," p. 435. While a full defense of my statement that Aristotle's political science effects an inclusion of philosophy in the city requires an analyses of the *Nicomachean Ethics* that is beyond the scope of this book, I would emphasize the irony in Aristotle's presentation of wisdom in Book VI of the *Ethics* and of the superior happiness of the contemplative life in Book X. For a good discussion of the contradictions in Aristotle's argument for contemplation in Book X, see Joseph Cropsey, "Justice and Friendship in the

Nicomachean Ethics," *Political Philosophy and the Issues of Politics,* p. 254. Aristotle's arguments indicate the insufficiency of speeches or reasons (*logoi*) without deeds (*erga*).

Afterword
Ancients and Moderns: Another Debate

1. Aristotle calls "political friendship" *homonoia,* usually translated as "concord" or "likemindedness." It refers to a condition in which men share a judgment about the advantageous and the just (*NE,* 1167a22–b16). Although *homonoia* literally means "of the same mind," Aristotle makes clear that *homonoia* among citizens does not preclude their consideration of their personal or private advantage. Consider, for example, his recommendation for the division of land in his best regime for the sake of producing greater *homonoia* among the citizens (*Pol.,* 1330a16). As a complex mixture of public and private elements, Aristotle's *homonoia* differs from that of the city in speech (432a). For a good discussion of Aristotle's criticism of the *Republic's* communism as undermining the *homonoia* of a political community, see Dobbs, "Aristotle's Anticommunism," pp. 36–41.

2. Nicolo Machiavelli, *The Prince,* trans. Mark Musa (New York: St. Martin's Press, 1964). As Machiavelli writes, "a man who wishes to profess goodness at all times must fall to ruin among so many who are not good," p. 127.

3. Thomas Hobbes, *Leviathan* (New York: Collier Books, 1962), p. 80.

4. Hobbes, *Leviathan,* p. 102.

5. Jean-Jacques Rousseau, *On the Social Contract with Geneva Manuscript and Political Economy,* ed. Roger D. Masters and trans. Judith R. Masters (New York: St. Martin's Press, 1978), pp. 52–56; 59–64. Rousseau thus objects to Hobbes' notion of inalienable rights (*Leviathan,* p. 105): "Properly understood, all of these clauses [of the social contract] come down to a single one, namely the total alienation of each associate, with all his rights, to the whole community," *On the Social Contract,* p. 53.

6. Jean-Jacques Rousseau, "On the Origin and Foundations of Inequality," *The First and Second Discourses,* trans. Roger D. Masters and Judith R. Masters (New York: St. Martin's Press, 1964), pp. 114–15. Consider Rousseau's description of the task of the legislator in *On the Social Contract:* "One who dares to undertake the founding of a people should feel that he is capable of changing human nature, so to speak, of transforming each individual, who

by himself is a perfect and solitary whole, into a part of a larger whole from which this individual receives, in some sense, his life and being," p. 68.

7. The expression comes from Immanuel Kant, "Idea for a Universal History from a Cosmopolitan Point of View," trans. Lewis White Beck, in *On History*, ed. Lewis White Beck (Indianapolis: Bobbs-Merrill Company, ᴖInc., 1963), p. 23.

8. Immanuel Kant, *Fundamental Principles of the Metaphysics of Morals*, trans. Thomas K. Abbott (Indianapolis: Bobbs-Merrill Company, Inc., 1949), p. 51.

9. Karl Marx, "On the Jewish Question," in *Writings of the Young Marx on Philosophy and Society*, trans. and ed. Lloyd D. Easton and Kurt H. Guddat (Garden City, New York: Doubleday and Company, Inc., 1967), pp. 235–41. On the homogeneity of communism at the end of history, see Joseph Cropsey, "The Moral Basis of International Action," *Political Philosophy and the Issues of Politics*, pp. 182–83. See also Immanuel Kant, "Conjectural Beginning of Human History," trans. Emil L. Fackenhein, in *On History*, p. 60.

10. Kant, "Conjectural Beginning of Human History," pp. 66–68.

11. Karl Marx, "Theses on Feuerbach," in *Writings of the Young Marx on Philosophy and Society*, p. 402.

12. Hobbes derives justice, which he presents as one of the laws of nature, from the fundamental law of nature, which is to seek peace. Justice demands "that men perform their covenants made," or keep their agreements, "without which, covenants are in vain, and but empty words; and the right of all men to all things remaining, we are still in the condition of war," *Leviathan*, p. 113.

Selected Bibliography

I. Primary Works

Aristophanes. *Clouds.* Edited, with an introduction and commentary by K. J. Dover. Oxford: Clarendon Press, 1968.

Aristotle. *Ethica Nicomachea.* Edited by Ingraham Bywater. Scriptorium Classicorum Bibliotheca Oxoniensis. Oxford: Clarendon Press, 1894.

Aristotle. *The Politics of Aristotle.* Edited, with an introduction, two prefatory essays, and notes critical and explanatory, by W. L. Newman. 4 vols. Oxford: Clarendon Press, 1887–1902.

Plato. *Opera.* Edited by John Burnet. 5 vols. Scriptorium Classicorum Bibliotheca Oxoniensis. Oxford: Clarendon Press, 1900–1907.

Plato. *The Republic of Plato.* Edited with critical notes, commentary, and appendices by James Adam. 2d ed. 2 vols. Cambridge, Mass.: Cambridge University Press, 1963.

Plato. *The Republic of Plato.* Translated with notes and an interpretive essay by Allan Bloom. New York: Basic Books, 1968.

II. Secondary Works Frequently Cited

Annas, Julia. *An Introduction to Plato's Republic.* Oxford: Oxford University Press, 1981.

Barker, Ernest. *The Political Thought of Plato and Aristotle.* New York: Dover Publications, 1959.

Bloom, Allan. "Response to Hall." *Political Theory*, 5 (August, 1977). Pp. 316–330.

Cropsey, Joseph. *Political Philosophy and the Issues of Politics*. Chicago: The University of Chicago Press, 1977.

Friedlander, Paul. *Plato*. Vol. 2. *The Dialogues: First Period*. Translated by Hans Meyerhoff. New York: Random House, 1964.

————. *Plato*. Vol. 3. *The Dialogues: Second and Third Periods*. Translated by Hans Meyerhoff. Princeton: Princeton University Press, 1969.

Hall, Dale. "The *Republic* and the 'Limits of Politics.' " *Political Theory* 5 (August, 1977). Pp. 293–313.

Mulgan, R. G. *Aristotle's Political Theory*. Oxford: Oxford University Press, 1977.

Nettleship, Richard Lewis. *Lectures on the Republic of Plato*. 2d ed. London: Macmillan, 1901.

Nussbaum, Martha. "Aristophanes and Socrates on Learning Practical Wisdom," *Yale Classical Studies*. Vol. 26. *Aristophanes: Essays in Interpretation*. Cambridge, Mass.: Cambridge University Press, 1980. Pp. 43–97.

————. "Shame, Separateness, and Political Unity: Aristotle's Criticism of Plato." *Essays on Aristotle's Ethics*. Edited by Amelie O. Rorty. Berkeley, Calif.: University of California Press, 1981.

Saxonhouse, Arlene W. "Family, Polity, and Unity: Aristotle on Socrates' Community of Wives." *Polity*, 15 (Winter, 1982). Pp. 202–219.

————. "The Philosopher and the Female in the Political Thought of Plato." *Political Theory*, 4 (May, 1976). Pp. 195–212.

Strauss, Leo. *The City and Man*. Chicago: Rand McNally and Company, 1964.

————. *Socrates and Aristophanes*. New York: Basic Books, 1966.

Whitman, Cedric. *Aristophanes and the Comic Hero*. Cambridge, Mass.: Harvard University Press, 1964.

Wolin, Sheldon S. *Politics and Vision*. Boston: Little, Brown, and Company, 1960.

Index

Achilles, 70–73, 77, 107, 206n.13

Adam, James, 88, 189n.1, 202n.19, 206n.18, 208n.31, 211n.9, 214nn.20, 21

Adeimantus, 73, 110, 119, 127, 134, 163, 218n.3; contentment with the city of pigs, 67, 69, 74; in contrast to Glaucon, 58, 64–66, 69, 86, 88, 95, 102, 128–29, 131, 149, 186, 204nn.5, 6, 205n.7; objections raised, 58, 86–88, 101–02, 113–14; praise of injustice, 64–65. *See also* Glaucon

Aeschylus, 23, 193n. 19, 202n.18, 209n.33, 210n.2

Annas, Julia, 220nn.11, 16; on being, 135, 212n.12, 213n.16, 220nn.13, 14; on Book I of *Republic*, 201nn.3, 5; on dialectic, 217n.29; on divided line and cave, 119, 214nn.21, 22, 215nn.24–26; on *Republic*'s philosophic education, 217nn.29, 30; on virtue in *Republic*, 208nn.31, 32, 209n.35; on women in *Republic*, 211n.5

Apollo, 210n.2

Arendt, Hannah, 191n.10, 213n.15

Aristophanes: Aristotle's response to, 4–5, 150–51, 153–56, 158, 180; and modern philosophy, 183–86; Plato's response to, 3–4, 28–32, 78, 95–96, 100–01, 109, 122–23, 126, 129,

147–50, 221nn.18, 20; *Clouds*, 1–31, 40, 47, 55, 76, 95, 100, 106, 118, 126, 185–86, 193–99nn.2–36, 199n.2; *Assembly of Women*, 210n.4. *See also* Clouds, Phidippides, and Strepsiades.

Aristotle: *Nicomachean Ethics*, 41, 93, 110, 153, 154, 163, 167, 174, 175–76, 179, 180, 189n.2, 190n.3, 191n.8, 194n.12, 198n.29, 224n.15, 228n.35, 229n.1; *Politics*, 1, 2, 4, 5, 75, 83, 151–83 and notes, 189n.2, 190n.3, 191n.8, 208n.30; *Rhetoric*, 167; *Metaphysics*, 203n.33, 222n.7. *See also* Aristophanes

Arrowsmith, William, 193n.5, 194n.13

Asclepius, 81

Athens, 13, 17, 21, 30, 37–39, 131, 135, 140, 165, 172, 189n.2, 201n.12

Athenian Stranger, 221n.19, 227n.30

Barker, Ernest, 67, 204n.1, 206n.16, 207nn.23, 24, 208nn.29, 31, 32, 209n.36, 213n.15, 219n.9, 223n.10, 224n.14

Benardete, Seth, 206n.12

Bergson, Henri, 193n.1

Bloom, Allan, 189n.1, 191n.7, 202n.10, 209n.35, 219n.5; on Adeimantus, 204nn.5–6, 218n.3; on Aristotle, 228n.35; on Cephalus, 42–

justice, 48–53, 207n.22; and perfection, 37, 48, 50–51, 54–55
Thucydides, 201n.12, 217n.30
Toynbee, Arnold, 201n.9
tragedy: and Achilles, 71; attacked by
city, 75–76, 78; attacked by Socrates, 139–40, 142; association of
learning with suffering, 40; as
attempt to escape necessity, 8, 10,
19, 25, 148; Glaucon's dislike of,
111; parodied in comedy, 8, 25–26,
193n.4; and politics, 126, 129, 186.
See also comedy

West, Thomas G., 190n.6
Whitman, Cedric H., 193n.2,
196nn.22, 24, 198n.30
Wolin, Sheldon, 191n.10, 212n.14,
213n.16, 216n.26
women: in Aristotle's political science,
157, 223n.13, 224n.16; and democracy, 219n.7; female nature, 103–06,
210nn.1, 3–5; feminine noun endings, 18, 197n.28; matings in *Republic*'s city, 106–09, 111; and
philosophy, 210n.5, 217n.32
Woozly, A.D., 220n.14

Xenophon, 190n.6, 201n.12, 209n.33,
217n.30

Zaleucus, 173, 174
Zeus: attack on in *Clouds*, 13, 14, 23;
as inventor of sex, 27, 96, 186; in
oaths, 46, 209n.37